A Morally Complex World
Engaging Contemporary Moral Theology

James T. Bretzke, S.J.

A Michael Glazier Book

LITURGICAL PRESS
Collegeville, Minnesota

www.litpress.org

A Michael Glazier Book published by the Liturgical Press

Cover design by David Manahan, O.S.B. Illustration by Rob Colvin, CSA Images (Veer).

	2	3	4	5	6	7	8

Library of Congress Cataloging-in-Publication Data

Bretzke, James T., 1952–
    A morally complex world : engaging contemporary moral theology / James T. Bretzke.
      p. cm.
    "A Michael Glazier book."
    Includes bibliographical references (p.) and index.
    ISBN 0-8146-5158-5
    1. Christian ethics—Catholic authors. I. Title.

BJ1249.B63 2004
241'.042—dc22   2003060219

For Ann and Julia

Contents

Introduction

Framing the Topic

The weekend I was rushing to put the final touches on this manuscript before sending it off to the publisher two things happened to me that helped me get a better perspective on this book. The first was an e-mail I received from one of my former students at the Loyola School of Theology in Manila where I teach in alternating summers. This young man in turn was forwarding an e-mail he had received from a friend working on a project for a college theology course. The project asked for responses to the following four questions: (1) How can people celebrate the gospel of life in their daily lives? (2) Morally speaking, what do you say about cloning? (3) Is euthanasia morally acceptable in certain cases, such as terminal illness? and 4) In case of health reasons, mental illness, pregnancy due to rape, etc., is abortion morally acceptable? In connection with this, are you personally in favor of the use contraceptives, both natural and artificial?

Despite having successfully completed my course in bioethics, my former student lamented that since he "was not a moral theologian" he felt that he could not or should not answer these questions adequately. So he passed them off to me since I was a moral theologian and would be able to handle them better. Flattery often gets you somewhere, and so I did attempt at least a short answer to these queries, but really these are complex questions that go beyond the scope of even a long e-mail. While this book will not answer these questions in exhaustive detail, it is my hope that at least a framework might be suggested for trying to grapple better with both the first question of how we should lead our moral lives in general, as well as some of the concrete ethical issues that the other three queries raised.

1

Many cultures have a proverb similar to our "Well begun, half done." At most this book represents only half a beginning, but it is my hope that the foundations outlined will help people continue to build on these insights so they will not feel that since they are not professional moral theologians they are not qualified to address real-life questions like those my student posed. Let me say a word about each of these questions and indicate how I think I have tried to address them at least implicitly in the chapters that follow. The first question, on how we celebrate the gospel of life, obviously involves in its concrete answer a comprehensive, global task that will probably occupy most of the rest of our personal and corporate history.

Recognition of this fact may be the first point to bear in mind: the moral life is not a simple task for which precise step-by-step directions can be given. Learning to live the gospel is not analogous to learning how to format a computer diskette, drive a car, or master wind-surfing. Celebrating the gospel in our daily lives is probably more akin to learning to live with another person in a committed, life-long, monogamous relationship. While we can solemnize and celebrate a marriage in the space of an hour, both the march up the aisle and back is a journey that takes years and years and years before we can say it has been successfully completed. So too with the moral acumen needed to master our life decisions and values. So my brief answer to question #1 is that morality is not like mathematics: the answers are not in the back of the book or in the teacher's manual, and ultimately only God alone can score correctly how we have performed in our lives.

However, even though the task is both complex and life-long, we can get a start in developing a certain methodological approach to guide us along the path. Chapter 1 tries to outline just such a methodology, and then it is further developed in chapter 2 on the natural law and moral norms, and chapter 3 on the place of Scripture and Tradition in our moral reflection. A key part of the Church's Tradition of moral teaching is the affirmation that if we honestly try to seek God and respond to God in our lives, then we shall grow in goodness. Here is where the whole notion of the primacy of conscience comes into play, and while this theme will run throughout the book, chapter 4 in particular is devoted to it. My student's particular questions about cloning, euthanasia, abortion, and contraception are all excellent examples of contemporary moral hot-button issues which are much debated, sometimes so fiercely that there is more heat than light cast on the contested problem. Methodologically I argue in chapter 5 that we need to step back first and consider how we are going to approach discussion of concrete ethical issues such as these. In this chapter I outline six criteria for gauging how well we engage in moral discourse, as well as noting how the different varieties or genres of moral discourse may actually help shape and even pre-determine to some extent our moral responses.

How about the next three questions then? Morally speaking what do we say about complex ethical issues such as cloning? I posed this question on the first day of the semester to my senior honors moral theology class at the University of San Francisco, and the brave students who ventured a reply began with a question of their own: had the Pope written an encyclical on cloning? Their question to me I think showed two things, which can at the same time be both a help and a hindrance. In asking if the Pope had pronounced on this matter, my students showed a definite willingness to learn what the Church has to offer on moral matters and an openness to take that input seriously in forming their own moral responses. This is definitely laudable, but there are other aspects to their question which can be troubling. I told them that as of that moment there was no papal encyclical on cloning, though there were a number of magisterial statements that opposed cloning of humans. I also said that in many cases we cannot wait for a papal pronouncement before coming to a moral decision of our own. So often concrete moral issues are messily complex and ambiguous, and we cannot cede our responsibility to try and wade through this complexity on our own. To sit back and wait for a clear-cut response from any outside moral authority, even if it be the Pope, would result in a sort of moral infantilism. We all need to grow into moral adulthood, and this means taking the effort to inform ourselves as best we can on moral issues and to come to a timely decision which is put into action when necessary.

Luckily though, none of us had to make a decision about cloning that day, and so we were able to discuss the matter in greater depth. At first glance, in probing the cloning issue with my students, it seemed to them to be a rather clear-cut, black-and-white ethical question: either it's "right" or it's "wrong." However, I asked some further questions to uncover some of the gray areas. For example, can we speak of "cloning" as a monolithic issue? If we answer "yes," then the cloning of Dolly the sheep would be morally equivalent with an attempt to auto-reproduce our own human heirs. Could we consider cloning animal or plant species that are in risk of extinction? Would it be moral to clone pandas so that more people could visit them in different zoos? Clearly these cases are related, yet are also quite different. Most of us, myself included, would be very opposed to the cloning of humans, but the whole question involves so many other issues that really need to be explored in greater depth. For example, why would people contemplate cloning in the first place? What are some of the scientifically related research areas, and could some of these be legitimately further explored?

As an example of this last question, I asked my students about the related issue of stem-cell research: is it right or wrong? By this time some of the wiser students (or those who had more experience with tricky Jesuits!) began to see the pitfalls in a quick decision based on inadequate information. They asked: What kind of stem-cell research are we talking about? What are the related moral issues with each? Research on adult stem cells involves a far different range of issues than would be the case in using left-over embryos from invitro fertilization. Could we possibly do stem-cell research on ova that had been chemically "fertilized" to stimulate development, but which had not actually been fertilized by human sperm? Three very different issues, and so a one-size-fits-all answer will be neat and clear, but probably wrong in at least one of the cases.

Moreover, the history of moral theology has shown us that sometimes a rush to judgment results in arrival at a misjudgment. There was a time in the not too distant past which held as absolutely immoral organ donation, such as giving a healthy kidney to someone in renal failure. The reason advanced for this negative judgment was the interpretation of the principle of totality, or what is sometimes referred to by its Latin formulation *pars propter totum* (see the glossary for definitions of some of the technical vocabulary). This principle held that while it was legitimate to sacrifice a diseased organ to save a person's life (such as amputation of a gangrenous foot to save a diabetic's life), it would *never* be moral to sacrifice a healthy organ, even for an otherwise good purpose like aiding another person. Donation of a healthy organ was considered to be self-mutilation, and self-mutilation was considered to be intrinsically evil, always and everywhere morally wrong, regardless of good intention or mitigating circumstances. Nowadays virtually all moral theologians as well as the magisterium of the Church would condone as a very positive act of charity a person who would freely donate one of his or her kidneys to help another human being. Such donation would not be morally required, but it would be an example of what we might call genuine love and heroic virtue. What has changed in the intervening years? Have we decided that "moral evil" is now "moral good"? Have we thrown all moral norms and ethical principles out the window and turned to a stance of total subjectivism or relativism? Clearly not. What has changed and improved is our ability to frame the moral questions involved in these sorts of concrete issues and to see more of the morally relevant features that go into discerning proper answers and responses to these complex problems.

As I said to my students, getting the question posed correctly also is absolutely critical to this process. For example, let us return to my Philippine student's question about whether euthanasia is ever morally acceptable in certain cases, such as terminal illness. I believe the short answer is no, since by definition euthanasia is deliberately ending a human life that has not otherwise reached its end. However, questions like this need to be opened up so that we can investigate whether the contemplated treatment in certain cases is what qualifies as euthanasia. In my last bioethics course in Manila, I was challenged by two of my students who maintained that one could *never* administer pain medication (what is called palliative care) that would have the foreseen effect of shortening the patient's life, even if the goal of such medication was the relief of pain and *not* trying to cause the individual's death. They told me that any other approach would be tantamount to euthanasia and that the Church had always held this position, and, moreover, it had been prophetically confirmed by Pope John Paul II in his encyclical on the Gospel of Life, *Evangelium vitae.*

I suppose this is why we have courses like bioethics so we can properly distinguish between vitalism, a prolonging of life no matter what, and euthanasia, an immoral ending of human life. It was no easy task for me to elucidate these two terms to my students, nor to convince them that their understanding of what the Church and Pope John Paul II actually had taught was factually wrong. Even when I had them read the relevant paragraphs (e.g., #65) from *Evangelium vitae* that state clearly that pain medication *can* be administered, even if it is foreseen that this will hasten death, my students remained at best uneasily convinced.

I suspect the reason for this was that rather than merely showing them that they were in factual error on the Church's teaching, I had somehow upset a grounding paradigm of theirs which established clear parameters of right and wrong, good and bad. As we shall see in chapter 1 and throughout the book, while everyone needs and uses paradigms to approach complex realities, overly simplistic paradigms often do more harm than good in helping us analyze these realities. Moral clarity is not always identical with moral correctness, as we shall see over and over again in the pages to come. Getting the question correctly formulated will often be half the task in finding the right moral answer.

My e-mail student interlocutor's last question points to several of the most difficult facets of contemporary moral theology in our morally complex world. The question asked whether it would ever be morally acceptable to countenance either abortion or the use of contraceptives. Once again, we need to get clear on the particular aspects of a concrete case if we hope even to begin to address this sort of question adequately. What is meant by "abortion"? Is terminating an ectopic pregnancy the same as ending an unplanned, but otherwise viable fetal life? If one were to call both of these procedures an "abortion," then we have indeed muddied our moral waters. Here is where some of the principles we outline in chapter 2 and their application in moral discourse in chapter 5 will come to the fore.

But let us say for the purposes of argument that a couple is actually planning to terminate an unwanted, but viable pregnancy, or that they are considering the use of some method or another to regulate the number of children in their family. While these sorts of moral questions can be addressed just in terms of abstract moral principles, if we were to stop our discussion there, we will have probably stopped too soon to really help the individuals in question as much as we might in grappling with these issues as they appear in the concrete. If morality is more than mathematics, then it will rarely be enough simply to outline the "right" or "wrong" decision from an abstract perspective. We have to engage people where they are, not where we are, and here is where some pastoral application has to come into play. I have entitled my chapter 6 "Navigating in the Morally Complex World: Casuistry with a Human Face" because I believe that is how we ought to move from moral theory to moral practice, namely, by trying to take in *all* of the morally relevant features and to consider these carefully along with our own presuppositions and the moral principles we believe are appropriate to the situation. If we can do this in a Christian manner, namely, following Jesus' own model of how to respond to people in difficulty, then we will have come a long ways towards developing a moral theology that is sound in theory and helpful in practice.

The second event of the weekend in which I completed this manuscript occurred at Our Lady of Lourdes, the parish in Oakland, California, where I have worked on weekends for the past decade. The parish is culturally extremely rich and diverse, with congregants coming from nearby Chinatown as well as from the outer reaches of the San Francisco Bay area. We have so many ethnicities and cultures represented that no one group, not even all the Caucasians taken together would create a majority. Over the years I have come to know many of these people quite well, and others of them more casually. This particular Sunday as I looked out over the filled church I was humbled by how many edifying moral stories I had been privileged to come to know. Some of these stories are the stuff for modern day sainthood, while others probably would strike us as more prosaic. However, one thread that certainly ran through the whole parish is that I could honestly say that all the people who come together week after week do so in a very honest desire to find God and respond as best they can in their lives to what they believe is the best thing they can do in the particular circumstances of their lives. Since I have had the humbling experience of celebrating the sacrament of reconciliation with many of these people, I know that their individual stories are often marked by pain, suffering, failure, and sin. That is a very definite reality in our world, and to try and run from it, or say it doesn't really exist would be not only unsuccessful, it would be seriously harmful as well. However, as I have tried to argue in the last chapter of this book, we are all ultimately called in faith to believe that the last word in our lives is not sin and judgment, but mercy, forgiveness, and reconciliation. If our theology can somehow get this simple message across in our morally complex world, then we shall indeed have done what God asks of the Church.

Some Admissions and Thanks

It now comes to the point to make some final admissions. No book is really authored by one person alone, and this book is no exception. Its genesis owes a great deal to my own teachers, my colleagues, and above all to my students whom I have taught on three continents in a variety of institutions and venues. I began my teaching career at Sogang University in Seoul, Korea, and currently I am on the theology faculty of the University of San Francisco in California. In between those two assignments I have been privileged to teach at the Pontifical

Gregorian University in Rome, where I also completed my doctoral studies, the Jesuit School of Theology at Berkeley, which belongs to the ecumenical consortium of the Graduate Theological Union and where I taught for the decade between Rome and San Francisco. I have been particularly enriched by my association with the Loyola School of Theology in Manila where I have been a regular visiting professor for the last several years. An additional important stimulus to my own thinking and teaching has been the regular workshops and mini-courses in moral theology that I have given over the last decade in the dioceses of northern California, as well as my weekend parish work with Fr. Seamus Genovese and the people of Our Lady of Lourdes in Oakland. Working in and with all of these various cultural, ecumenical, and pedagogical contexts has convinced me that our world indeed is morally complex and any moral theology or Christian ethics that fails to engage this complexity seriously will be sorely skewed.

This book is hardly the last word on this subject, but hopefully it is a credible first word. I am very grateful to Linda Maloney and the staff at the Liturgical Press for their support and efforts to bring this text into print. A number of my colleagues have graciously read sections of the manuscript and offered me very valuable input. In this regard I am particularly grateful to John Donahue, s.j., Anne Grycz, Richard Gula, s.s., Daniel Kendall, s.j., William Spohn, and Martha Ellen Stortz. The deficiencies that remain are my own alone. Finally, I would like to acknowledge a special debt of gratitude to my sister Ann Alvarez and her daughter, and my niece Julia for their love and support. It is to them that this book is fondly dedicated.

James T. Bretzke, s.j.
Feast of the Presentation, 2 February 2003
San Francisco, California

1

Mapping a Moral Methodology

What Is Moral Theology All About?

By occupation I am a moral theologian. When people come to know that fact about me I usually get one or another typical response. One such response is somewhat like what it must be like for an IRS agent invited to his spouse's office Christmas party: I'm greeted with a bit of nervous laughter and sometimes a half-joking caution that the assembled group should be on its best behavior, as if my particular training or job description somehow enables me to see into the moral equivalent of their personal income tax return, such that I'm likely to discover their unreported income or creative accounting practices in itemizing deductions. Another response is perhaps a bit like a doctor at a similar informal gathering: I am given a certain set of symptoms and asked to diagnose the illness and/or prescribe the correct treatment—usually not for themselves, but for another. Still another response, often from priests older than I, is to take advantage of a free expert consultation and I'm asked if this or that particular activity "is still a sin."

I'm afraid that my reaction to these responses is not especially positive. First, while my training hopefully has given me some insights into the nature of morality and how one might live an authentic Christian life, neither I nor most of my professional colleagues have any advanced degree in spiritual x-ray vision, and so we lack the special ability to read the deepest secrets of another's past or how that person might stand before God. In short, we moral theologians tend to be just like most everyone else in seeing into another person's soul; while certainly we can discern the difference between the actions and personality of a Mother Teresa and an Adolf Hitler, we are on far shakier ground if we attempt to pronounce on the moral standing before God of most every other sort of person!

As to the second type of response, just as I imagine most doctors probably would be uncomfortable with attempting medical diagnosis and treatment of a third party without actually seeing them face to face, so, too, there is no way I can usually give much good concrete advice about an individual case without really knowing the particulars. As I will have occasion to repeat more than once in this book, morality is not like mathematics. While in base ten arithmetic, two plus two always equals four, and to the best of my recollection from Fr. Kelly's sophomore (Euclidian) geometry class, a sum of the squares of the sides of a right-triangle equals the square of the hypotenuse, we rarely find such helpful axioms and proofs in the real world. Morality is usually both much more complex, ambiguous, and unsettled than that. While we can certainly articulate general principles, these rarely can be applied with such scientific precision that at the end we simply write "Q.E.D." (the Latin abbreviation of *quod erat demonstrandum,* usually appended to mathematical or logical proofs to indicate the successful conclusion of the proof of the initial hypothesis).[1] We simply cannot manufacture moral truth in that manner. While some may regret that morality is not neat and orderly like mathematical propositions, I do not.

This brings me to my last typical response, namely, those who have had a certain level of training in the field of moral theology some time ago and want a quick refresher course on this or that particular item. "Is masturbation or artificial contraception still a sin?" they ask, sometimes adding a further question on the Catholic Church's current teaching on the matter. I must confess I am usually less patient with this line of questioning than I might be with the others, since I feel that the priest by now should know a bit better the nature of moral theology, and especially what goes into calling anything a sin. The Church does not have the power to make of something a sin that God does not consider to be sinful, and vice versa. If God were to consider something a sin and the Church did not, the matter would still be sinful from an objective moral point of view.

When we use the term "objective" to refer to morality and the moral order, what we mean is how this or that action appears in God's own eyes. The difficulty for us though is that what we see is not always just exactly what God sees, so we need to discern carefully and reflect

---

[1] For a discussion of this and other Latin terms see my *Consecrated Phrases: A Latin Dictionary of Theological Terms,* 2nd rev. ed. (Collegeville: The Liturgical Press, 1998, 2003).

on what we consider objective morality to be. The Church stands in service to this project, but objective morality is *not* made up by church rules and regulations, like the particular prescriptions for the Lenten fast and abstinence or which Holy Days of Obligation are to be observed in a particular country. While individuals might not be personally culpable for an action committed under the mis-guidance of mistaken church teaching on a particular moral issue, such as was the case for centuries on the moral acceptability of slavery or the torture and capital punishment of heretics, we would still say that if such actions are morally reprehensible (as most of us would now agree), then they were always morally wrong in God's eyes. God is the ground of all morality and hence of our moral truth and knowledge. Sometimes we can see this truth fairly clearly, sometimes more opaquely, and sometimes, as was the case with slavery and torture, only with very great difficulty for far too much of our shared human history.

I have a hunch that Jesus must have been known less as a carpenter and more as a moral theologian, since it seems that he got far more questions of the sort I have just outlined than he ever did about woodworking or construction projects. Therefore, it might be a very good place to start our own reflections on the nature of morality by looking at how Jesus handled one such encounter.

> Then someone came to him and said, "Teacher, what good deed must I do to have eternal life?" And he said to him, "Why do you ask me about what is good? There is only one who is good. If you wish to enter into life, keep the commandments." He said to him, "Which ones?" And Jesus said, "You shall not murder; You shall not commit adultery; You shall not steal; You shall not bear false witness; Honor your father and mother; also, You shall love your neighbor as yourself." The young man said to him, "I have kept all these; what do I still lack?" Jesus said to him, "If you wish to be perfect, go, sell your possessions, and give the money to the poor, and you will have treasure in heaven; then come, follow me." When the young man heard this word, he went away grieving, for he had many possessions (Matt 19: 16-22).[2]

I believe that the above passage, which was also used by Pope John Paul II in *Veritatis Splendor*, his 1993 encyclical on Fundamental Moral Theology, sets out nicely many of the main aspects of what moral theology is all about. This gospel passage introduces not only a number of key terms which concern the discipline of moral theology, but more

[2] Unless otherwise stated, all scriptural quotations are taken from the *New Revised Standard Version* (NRSV).

importantly outlines the larger aim of attempting to live out the life of Christian discipleship. Let us begin our study by looking at a few of these key words.

The first word to consider is just what in fact is meant by the term "good." At first glance it seems that everyone is pretty clear on what this term means, but as we shall see throughout this book, upon deeper reflection just exactly what counts as good or bad, right or wrong, is not always absolutely crystal clear in complex situations. In this gospel passage the young man initially asks about "doing" a "good deed." However, Jesus at first sidesteps this question and responds with one of his own. Jesus' question points us to a more important moral concern, namely, the source, ground, and ultimate reference for our understanding of "goodness." This ultimate source is God, who is both Jesus and our Father. Therefore, a key aspect of lived morality is not just "doing" the right things and avoiding the wrong things, but more fundamentally living in right relationships—first with God and then with the rest of God's children, and finally with the whole of God's creation.

The second key word is "commandments." I remember once seeing a cartoon of Moses coming down the mountain wearing a frown and carrying the two stone tablets, while saying, "It's just a first draft, but it looks like we're not going to get away with anything!" I think this catches well how we often do look at commandments, whether biblical or human, as burdens or obligations that constrain our freedom and possibly limit our pleasure, if not our happiness. However, for the Jewish people the Ten Commandments were not seen primarily as negative boundaries that limited their activities. Rather, for the Israelite nation the Ten Commandments were the Decalogue, the Ten Holy Words, which were a *gift* from God to God's Chosen People. The Decalogue was a "code" in both senses of the word, i.e., a collection of laws, but more importantly a way of deciphering God's own holiness. The context of the gift of the Decalogue is key to understanding how we are to view the Ten Commandments, namely, a gift given to a specially loved community which is "on the way" (a pilgrimage, a holy journey) from slavery to freedom. This gift is certainly God's revelation, but not just of God's rules and regulations, but more as a revelation and concrete sign of God's special relationship (the Covenant) with the Chosen People.

Nevertheless, the concept of commandments does tell us something about what morality is all about. It implies that certain things are to be done and other things are not to be done. The notion of commandments is grounded in a moral rightness and wrongness that stands in some way above us, and which has a claim on us to observe. We will be considering this claim further in the second and third chapters, but for now it is sufficient to acknowledge that commandments presume some sort of normativity to our moral lives. In other words, there are certain moral standards that help guide us in our individual decisions and that also help us grow in our moral character. Commandments also provide us with certain boundaries or parameters of our moral lives and express certain moral duties that we should observe. In moral theology this understanding of morality is often called "deontology." Deontology comes from the Greek word δεον (*deon*) which means "duty." Thus, to be moral means to do one's true duty and to live within the boundaries of human morality. Deontology gives us a very important understanding of part of what morality is all about, but it does not give us the entire picture.

We find another side of this picture of what morality is all about in looking at the next term which comes up in the encounter between Jesus and the young man. This is a pair which at first seems to be polar opposites: "lack/perfect." The young man's question about what he is lacking is answered by the corresponding desire "to be perfect" and this vocabulary needs to be carefully understood. We will look at this vocabulary term again in chapter 3, but for now it will be helpful to note that the word "perfect" comes from the Latin, and in Latin this word usually connotes something that is absolutely complete, without any blemish or deficiency, e.g., a room that is in "perfect" order. However, this notion of "perfection" is rather static and certainly *not* what the original Greek of the New Testament text here primarily means to convey. I will treat this issue in greater depth in chapter 3, but for now it is sufficient to note that the Greek word comes from τελειος (*teleios*) and was probably meant to express the Hebrew concept of *shalom*. Most people know that *shalom* means "peace" but it is a much richer notion that includes the ideas of wholeness, harmony, health, and in that combined sense the word means "complete" and "perfect." As we will see throughout this book, these Greek and Hebrew words are foundational in the moral theory of teleology which stresses the sense of moral striving, becoming, character, and virtue.

This also shows us another important dimension of our moral lives: it is not just a matter of keeping the commandments, but growing and developing ever more into a people of broader and deeper moral character. Much of Roman Catholic moral theology builds on this approach to morality which is called "teleology." Teleology comes from the Greek word τελος *(telos)*, which means a goal, an ideal, and an "end" to which our moral lives should orient themselves. The Latin translation for the Greek τελος *(telos)* is *finis*, and we will see in the next chapter how this notion of a moral *finis* developed as a way of trying to evaluate the moral meaning of an action in itself and the person who performed that action. However, to return to the basic thrust of teleology, perhaps the old expression, "a person's reach should exceed their grasp, or else what's a heaven for," expresses well how teleology works in our lives. We all have ideals which we strive after, yet we know that probably we will never fully realize all of them. Think of a great concert hall musical artist. How did she or he get to be a virtuoso? Certainly they had to have a certain level of native talent, but that alone would not account for success. Lots of practice, supported by a vision or ideal of becoming ever better is what helped them become concert performers. Yet, even after making an appearance at Carnegie Hall, a true artist doesn't stop practicing or striving. The moral life is much the same thing. We really should aim at becoming moral virtuosi. However, as soon as I say this I can hear some people objecting that this then makes morality either optional (since there is no requirement to try to become a concert pianist), or impossible, since very few of us will make it into Carnegie Hall except by buying a ticket.

This though is not a good response. Rather, I mean to suggest through this metaphor that our lived expression of morality bears a relation to the objective moral order of God's will somewhat like a musical score: the notes, time value, key, etc., are standard and are all given, but the level of "perfection" in the execution of the score depends much on the talent, commitment, and passion of the performer. A computer, James Bretzke, and Glenn Gould might all "perform" a Bach variation, with reasonable "accuracy" in terms of sticking to the musical score. However, there is little doubt that most if not all listeners could easily discern whose performance was whose, and probably there would be widespread, if not unanimous, agreement that the noted Bach interpreter Glenn Gould's performance is "best" (Grandma Bretzke being long dead!). While on this side of heaven we can never sit back and say we've finally and fully arrived, yet we should keep on striving. It is this commitment to the ongoing process of moral growth that helps us grow in moral goodness—in short, moral virtuosi.

"Go, sell what you have." At first glance it may seem that Jesus is giving a very difficult commandment, but really he is presenting the rich young man with a mission, not a moral prescription. The Christian moral life should be understood in the sense of being on a God-given mission. "Sell what you have" has two meanings here for the young man. Jesus is inviting him to a new self-understanding that is not predicated on amassing and holding on to material possessions. Jesus shows him and us that in God's eyes our true identity is not grounded in what we have, but who we are. Even without one's "possessions" (whether these be material possessions, honors, accomplishments, etc.) the individual is still worthy in God's eyes. Second, the meaning of divesting oneself of one's possessions is not meant to leave one bereft of all means of livelihood, but is explained in the next phrase, "and give to the poor." Care and concern for the poor is not only a key gospel theme, but should mark our entire Christian moral living. When we pray the Lord's Prayer, with its petition that God's will be done on earth as in heaven, we are expressing a hope that both our desires and our actions correspond more closely to God's own concerns.

We might see this as an example of what later has become termed the "preferential option for the poor," and I think we can also understand this mandate in terms of a key insight in St. Ignatius of Loyola's meditation, the *Contemplation to Obtain the Love of God*, which comes in the Fourth Week of the Spiritual Exercises.[3] Here Ignatius suggests that true love is shown more in deeds than words. The one who "has" shares with those who have not. While Ignatius gives as a concrete example the sharing of knowledge, the whole tradition of moral theology, especially as seen in the sub-area of social ethics, stresses that true moral goodness is always measured not only in individual terms, but more fully in consideration of the flourishing of the whole community, i.e., in social terms related to the common good of all of God's creation, but especially God's prized possessions, our sisters and brothers.

"Treasure in Heaven." In God's economy there is no zero-sum game. The selling and giving of one's possessions always enriches those who give. "Treasure" indicates a solid, lasting, and life-long richness. "Heaven" is used in Matthew's Gospel often in the sense of

[3] For a good contemporary translation and commentary on this text, see Ignatius of Loyola, *The Spiritual Exercises of St. Ignatius: A Literal Translation and a Contemporary Reading*, adapted by David L. Fleming, S.J. (St. Louis: Institute of Jesuit Sources, 1978).

the "Kingdom of Heaven" (βασιλεα τῶν ουρανῶν *[Basilea ton oura-non]*) and thus serves as a short-hand expression not only for the Kingdom itself but also for God whose Kingdom is being brought ever more fully into the world. Treasure in heaven really comes down to accepting that we are treasured by God and trying to live more authentically as God's precious treasures.[4] The Christian moral life is essentially about living in accord with the values and expectation of God's Kingdom to come, and here on earth is lived out best by responding to Jesus' final invitation/command to the rich young man: "Come, Follow Me." The mission given above to "Go, and sell your possessions" finds its completion in Jesus' invitation to return and follow (after) him. The verb "follow" in Greek takes as its object the preposition "after" and so literally means to come and "follow after" Jesus. This is the discipleship stance, following after Jesus. Discipleship, and not just "doing" the "right" action, really is the key to Christian moral living.

Now many people may say, "Well that's all well and good, but how does that apply to *me* in *my* everyday life?! If I go and sell all I have how can I live? What does it mean here and now to 'follow' Jesus anyway? Aren't these really just nice-sounding words addressed to 'professional religious' like nuns and priests?" Bridging the ideal between the gospel vision of the moral life and the concrete realities of our world is in fact what moral theology is ultimately all about. The stakes seem high, not only just what is considered "right" or "wrong" in this world, but entrance into the life that is to follow. Because of this sometimes moral theology has provoked very sharp debates over both methodology and concrete applications, especially in the area of how we judge moral success or failure.

Paradigms for Discerning Morality

A few years back at a theological convention I had been tagged to give a response to two professors who presented papers in a crowded session dealing with contemporary Roman Catholic moral theology. The presenters aggressively criticized a large number of contemporary moral theologians, several of whom were present in the room at the time. The conversation was spirited to say the least, and when it came time for my response I began with the remark that I believed there

---

[4] I am indebted to John Donahue, S.J., for this particular insight.

was an elephant in the room, and the name of the elephant was "moral norms." It seems that most theologians would say they strongly believe in them, but as our introductory section above hopefully has demonstrated, morality and the discipline of moral theology are far broader and richer than even such an important concern such as moral norms, whether in the generic abstract or the concrete particular sense. I have become convinced though that often behind the obvious disagreements in these sorts of debates are real differences in moral methodologies used by the various theologians. If more attention were paid to the framework of our methodologies we would be in a better position, if not to resolve the debates, at least to carry them on in a more dialogical method.

In this spirit of dialogue, the first point I should like to make is that there is no *one* way of looking at moral theology, and how we approach any related or subordinate issue like moral norms depends in large part on the guiding model or paradigm we have for what moral theology involves. A paradigm is not the whole of reality, but rather a good model that helps us get our minds around that reality. Think of the universe. Do we have a map of the whole of the universe with each and every speck of cosmic dust, not to mention whole star systems accounted for? Obviously we do not. We are not even sure just exactly how many planets and asteroids there are in our own solar system. Yet for many centuries our forebears were fairly well convinced that they had a complete map of the heavens and anyone that challenged that dominant paradigm did so at great risk (as Galileo discovered). A paradigm by definition then is a model which seems to work well and which seems to account for all the relevant data and features we are able to observe.

As long as this model continues to work well in explaining the relevant aspect of the world it is likely to go unchallenged. However, once new information comes to light the old paradigm will have to try to fit this new data into the overall picture. If it is able to do so, then the paradigm is refined and still remains serviceable—in fact, it may well be a significant improvement over the older version. However, sometimes certain paradigms have aspects that no longer function adequately in the light of new information and/or new situations or challenges. This was the case with the old Ptolemaic map of space, which eventually had to give way to new models that were better at explaining how the new information that was gained from improved tools and methods of astronomy fit together. We have to honestly admit that sometimes we have held onto certain paradigms long after they have ceased to function adequately. Again, we need to remember that a paradigm does not invent reality; it merely seeks to explain it. The earth did not start to revolve around the sun either when Galileo first put forth his theory of the solar system, or when his condemnation by the Church was finally overturned by Pope John Paul II in 1992. The sun, earth, moon, and stars existed as they have long before either event.

If this is true for the science of astronomy, it is just as true for the science of moral theology, though there will be some differences. In theology a model is an approach towards understanding a complex reality, such as the mystery of the Church, in such a way that we can deepen our theoretical understanding of what is involved in this complex reality. One theologian who has done much in using models for theological reflection is Cardinal Avery Dulles, s.j. He notes that models can be either "explanatory" in that they synthesize what we already know, or "exploratory" or heuristic, lead to new insights, and get beyond limitations of a particular outlook.[5] Models allow for a certain plurality of possibilities, such as various models of the Church which can co-exist, at least theoretically, side by side. Dulles speaks of a number of models of the Church, such as seeing it as an institution, as a herald of the gospel, as Mystical Body, as servant to humanity, as the community of Jesus' disciples, and so on. Each of these various models picks up and emphasizes certain aspects and in this sense they can overlap and complement one another, since no one model can totally exhaust a complex reality such as the Church.

The same can be said for moral theology, especially as we consider complicated issues such as what constitutes goodness, the natural law, moral norms, conscience, sin, and the like. No one paradigm or model exhausts all there is to say about the nature of morality and the moral life. The paradigm we use (whether explicitly or implicitly) often focuses and structures what we believe to constitute the morally relevant features, ethical principles, and the whole understanding of morality itself. If a model is particularly successful in explaining a complex reality such as the solar system, or the Church, it can establish a certain predominance in its field and become established as *the* model, or what is then termed a paradigm. A problem can arise, however, when

---

[5] I am summarizing Cardinal Dulles' treatment in his classic work *Models of the Church* (Garden City: Doubleday, 1974; Image Books, 1978. Dublin: Gill and Macmillan, 1976).

we forget that no one model or paradigm can totally capture all of the abstract *and* concrete dimensions that would go into determining just what is "moral" in every time and place. While models can co-exist, overlap, and complement one another, paradigms tend to become dominant and suppress all other models. Paradigms usually tend to exist one at a time and often take a real revolution (at least in the academic sense) in order to shift. Just as the authorities of the Catholic Church and the world at large did not switch overnight from the view that the sun orbited the earth to the contrary model put forth by Galileo and others, in much the same way our moral paradigms change very slowly, and almost never without a certain amount of tension and conflict.

A Four-Sector Methodology of Moral Sources

How do we evaluate what is a good or bad paradigm in regards to moral theology? One way of answering this question is to outline what should be the principal resources moral theology should use, and how it should use them. The methodology of the pre-Vatican II moral manuals usually listed three "fonts" or sources for moral theology: Scripture, Tradition, and the magisterium. However, in practice these fonts hardly exercised equal force. Scripture was primarily used as a source for proof-texts, i.e., a short biblical verse or reference (often taken out of its own context) and simply marshaled to "confirm" or embellish an argument or moral judgment which had already been established on other grounds. The moral arguments themselves usually developed through a detailed exposition worked out in terms of some version of neo-scholastic theology and/or the position of the magisterium at that particular moment. This manualist methodology was essentially and intentionally "regressive," in the sense that its argumentation began from the magisterial teaching then in place, and worked backward to illustrate how that particular doctrine was originally expressed in Scripture and then how the doctrine was subsequently developed in the patristic and medieval expressions of Catholic faith.[6] Though most

---

[6] Jared Wicks, S.J., notes that in the manualist methodology the theological "sources are read in the light of what is taught and believed in the theologian's own day. The intended result is an account of the harmonious development by stages down to what is explicit in present-day teaching. This method, long dominant in manualist practice, received official sanction from Pope Pius XII in *Humani generis* (1950), who stated that the magisterium is to be the theologian's proximate and universal norm of truth' and that the task of theology is to show how magisterial teachings are found explicitly or implicitly in Scripture and

moral theologians working after Vatican II have moved beyond this three-font methodology, Scripture certainly has not been used as a principal source among too many Roman Catholic theologians for grounding their discussion of moral norms, nor, as my brief list of the various models above shows, can we see that any one model has advanced to the level of becoming a dominant paradigm for the discipline.

The lack of any one model establishing itself as *the* governing paradigm for the discipline of Roman Catholic moral theology or Protestant Christian ethics may actually be quite a blessing. Certainly if one or another paradigm were identified with each tradition, as was largely true before Vatican II, then this very paradigm would inevitably function as an obstacle to ecumenical dialogue and collaboration, not to mention dialogue with those who do not share our faith tradition. The model that I propose for both Roman Catholic moral theology and ecumenical ethics builds on the work of the well-known American Protestant ethician James Gustafson.[7] The key aspect of this model is that it is a hybrid divided into four principal sectors that actually show a good deal of overlap and interaction with each other. I label these four sectors as *Scripture* (the sacred text which has a special sacred claim on the Christian community), *Tradition* (which represents the lived wisdom of the Christian community), *Rational Reflection on the Normatively Human* (e.g., human rights discourse, moral philosophy, and the whole tradition of natural law theory), and *Human Experience*. This *Human Experience* sector involves not just individuals' own experience, but the whole range of scientific and social scientific disciplines that help us to gather, organize, and interpret data drawn from our individual and collective human experience. I also observe that these four sectors are organized along two principal axes: Scripture and Tradition operate principally on what I term the "sacred claim" axis, while Human Experience and the Normatively Human operate on the "rational claim" axis. There is considerable overlap among these four sectors, and the entire grid in turn is held

---

apostolic tradition (DS 3884, 3886)." "Teologia manualistica [Manualist Theology]" in *Dizionario di Teologia Fondamentale*, ed. René Latourelle with Rino Fisichella (Assisi: Cittadella, 1990) 1265–69, and 1267 for the citation quoted here.

[7] Gustafson himself built his model upon the so-called Wesleyan Quadrilateral associated with Methodist ethics (Scripture, Reason, Tradition, and Experience). For Gustafson's exposition of his model see his *Protestant and Roman Catholic Ethics* (Chicago and London: The University of Chicago Press, 1978) cf. 139–44, and his *Ethics and Theology* (Chicago: University of Chicago Press, 1984) cf. 143–44.

together and mediated by our overall worldview (individual, communal, and collective) and therefore involves an essential hermeneutical dimension. Let us look at each sector briefly.

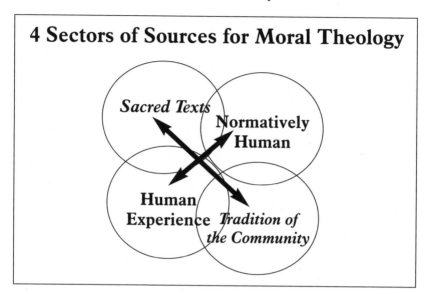

4 Sectors of Sources for Moral Theology

Sacred Texts

Normatively Human

Human Experience

Tradition of the Community

The Scripture Sector

Even though historically Scripture has not played as large a role in Roman Catholic moral theology as it should have, it is important to stress that Scripture is the pre-eminent "sacred text" for Christians and therefore for moral theology as well. This scriptural sacred text bears God's own revelation and divine will in some sense, and therefore Scripture exercises a particular demand on the faith community as what I have termed the "sacred claim." While this claim is "sacred," it is not meant to be simplistic or fundamentalistic. Of the four sectors, Scripture, understood in the canonical sense, is probably the clearest in terms of content and boundaries. Yet, just how Scripture functions in this grid, as well as how it relates to the other sectors in relation to the rest of moral theology, is not so transparent. We will spend more time in this discussion in the third chapter, but here I simply note that it is important to remember that the "language" of Scripture is rather different from the languages used in the other three sectors. This language difference is a crucial point that is often overlooked or oversimplified by moralists in their use, abuse, or non-use of Scripture in moral theology.

I choose the term "language" deliberately, to express this notion of how Scripture works within its own sector, as well as with the other three sectors of Tradition, Human Experience, and Rational Reflection on the Normatively Human. Each sector has its own language system and every individual language has its own vocabulary, syntax, and grammar. Even though we can "translate" from one language to another, anyone who has mastered more than one language knows that often it is difficult to express exactly the same meaning, nuance, feeling, etc., from one to another. This difficulty is compounded when we factor in the difference of genre, style, and so on. Just how could one render the moral teaching from a New Testament parable into a Kantian-style categorical imperative or a Thomistic or Aristotelian logic syllogism?

Therefore, in the area of moral theology we must recognize that it is especially difficult to "translate" Scripture, for example, into the language of deontological (i.e., duty-based) normative moral philosophy. Thus, a moralist who seeks to distill the so-called "normative" content of a particular biblical passage, abstracted from the passage's own context, and to translate it into some expression of a non-biblical philosophical system will be either frustrated or misled (probably both!). If we are really earnest about letting Scripture speak to our moral theology, we must continue to work on a viable moral methodology that will allow the Bible, as well as every other sector in this moral grid, to speak in its own proper "language." At the same time our methodology should facilitate comprehension (rather than "translation") among the various "languages" of all the sectors. It is important to remember that Scripture is not a stand-alone source. It comes out of the tradition of the Christian community, and its normative force or claim will be strongest within the faith community because that community holds the Scripture as revealed and therefore sacred. "Sacred," however, does not mean unquestionably absolute; it is canonical and normative, but its force operates primarily on and within the lived tradition of the faith community, i.e., along what I mean by the "sacred claim axis." To see how this operates more clearly let us turn now to a consideration of what Tradition is.

Tradition Sector

Throughout a good deal of the history of theology the term Tradition referred to the writings of the early Church Fathers, such as Tertullian, Irenaeus, Augustine, et al., as well as the teachings of the Church's magisterium. Tradition was viewed as an important way in which the revelation contained in Scripture could be amplified and applied to successful generations of the Church after the death of the apostles who had followed Jesus. While this is certainly an important part of Tradition, I believe it is very important to widen our lens a bit to take in more of the riches of the Church's whole Tradition. I use the phrase "the wisdom of the Christian community" as a short-hand description of Tradition. In this understanding of Tradition we see that first and foremost, Tradition is *not* primarily just a content-laden set of creedal propositions or extra-biblical revealed truths, but rather speaks of the essential relationship we have as members of a faith community. This living, organic relationship is found in relation not only to the present but also to the past—to the writings of the Church Fathers to be sure, but also to *all* those people who have fostered the growth of the Church through their own lives. Tradition also has a future and in one sense we who live here and now in the present are also an important part of the Church's developing Tradition. While we live in the present, we come out of the past, and are moving into the future. Therefore, we also must look to the future and our roles as faithful transmitters (and transformers) of the deepest meaning of the Christian faith.

Since Tradition is grounded in the historical faith community, it is crucial to bear in mind that it is that faith community then that not only is nourished by that Tradition, but which nourishes the Tradition in turn, augmenting it, refining it, pruning it, etc. We must keep this in mind, lest the Tradition become the "dead faith of the living" (to borrow the well-known dictum from the church historian Jaroslav Pelikan), rather than the ongoing, living faith of the communion of saints whose members include both the living and dead. Scripture helps us in this process, and therefore Tradition, like Scripture, has to be continually re-translated, re-read and re-interpreted, within the context of a faith community that is a believing, worshiping, and acting Community of Disciples. Biblical theologian Sandra Schneiders, I.H.M., expresses this fuller notion of the concept of Tradition as "effective historical consciousness," which she describes as "the actualization in the present, in and through language, of the most valued and critically important aspects of the community's experience, or, more precisely, of the community's experience itself as it has been selectively appropriated and deliberately transmitted."[8] Schneiders goes on to describes three meanings of tradition:

---

[8] Sandra Schneiders, *The Revelatory Text: Interpreting the New Testament as Sacred Scripture* (San Francisco: HarperSanFrancisco, 1991; Collegeville: The Liturgical Press, 1999) 71.

> Tradition, as the *foundational gift* out of which the Church's experience un-
> folds throughout history, is the Holy Spirit who is the presence of the
> risen Jesus making the Church the Body of Christ. Tradition, as *content*, is
> the sum total of appropriated and transmitted Christian experience, out of
> which Christians throughout history select the material for renewed syn-
> theses of the faith. Tradition refers also to the *mode* by which that content
> is made available to successive generations of believers, the way in which
> the traditioning of the faith is carried on throughout history.[9]

In sum, our Tradition sector therefore includes not only theological writings of the early Church Fathers and the development of theological reflection on the meaning of Christian life found in the
magisterium but also the historical collective experience of the entire
Christian community, our liturgical and sacramental life together, as
well as the paradigmatic examples of Christian living given us by the
holy men and women the early Christians referred to as the *haggioi*
(ἅγιοι) or "saints." To be a saint one has to try to live out one's Christian faith in the real world. A saint is made while alive; if one has not
become a true saint while living on earth, one really cannot become a
saint posthumously. Of course, the Church canonizes men and women
as "saints" only after they have died, but this recognition comes first
and foremost for their holy and heroic lives on earth, and not special
miracles performed from heaven!

How the Church lives together is also an important part of our Tradition, even the negative examples from the past of our life together.
Hopefully history can teach us from not only our positive accomplishments, but also our sins, failures, and mistakes. The privileged
location of the Church's life together is found in its communal prayer,
especially the Eucharist. One of the traditional axioms of theology is
lex orandi, lex credendi, which means that *how* the Christian community prays and celebrates its liturgy interacts and helps shape and
strengthen the faith of that same community. This area is one where
we will track a considerable amount of change and development over
the centuries, but some clear examples of how change in our tradition
of both moral life and practices would include not only concrete ethical issues like religious freedom, human rights, and slavery, but how
we deal with our own sins and failures as well as the sins and failures
of others in the community. This will be a topic we will return to in
the final chapter, but it is important to open our eyes wide enough to
take in all aspects, both positive and negative, of our moral striving.

[9] Ibid., 72.

Thus, as with the other sectors, there is a need to avoid a tendency to narrow the range of what "counts" as legitimate content in this Tradition sector. Regrettably, some wish to limit Tradition to simply official texts of the magisterium and/or to identify all of Tradition with only the writings of a few Church Fathers or selected theologians, such as Thomas Aquinas. On the other hand, we need to guard against retroactive or anachronistic readings of the various sources in a reductionistic or dismissive manner that would evaluate authors and texts too harshly in light of contemporary concerns, insights, and sensibilities. For example, if we were to dismiss all of Thomas Aquinas as irrelevant because of his antiquated biology, or the problems in his theological anthropology in reference to women, we would be depriving ourselves of an incredible amount of real moral wisdom which we can still draw on today.

Human Experience Sector

The Human Experience sector is probably the most difficult to describe succinctly and is the aspect that historically has excited the most suspicion and reluctance among theologians. Yet, any reflection on moral theology that ignores or pays insufficient attention to experience will build its system in an unreal world, constructing an abstraction with no correlation to actual human reality. Every human person obviously has both "experience" and "experiences," and these can serve as an important moral source and resource. Experience also highlights more the affective, emotional, intuitive, and imaginative sides of our personhood, and these aspects are crucial for a holistic understanding of, and approach to, the moral life. Often the affective dimension can help us in terms of motivation for our moral living. As one of my own teachers, William C. Spohn, often observed, it's hard to lay down your life for an abstract moral norm, but you may well do it for a friend, or even a cause in which you believe very much.

Experience refers not only to the individual and his or her self-awareness and subjectivity, but also ourselves as members of a number of different human communities. Thus, the locus for the experience sector is the individuals in relationship to themselves, to others, and to a multiple set of human communities (from the local to the global). We have to keep this understanding of the locus of experience in mind in order to avoid the trap of simple subjectivism and/or total relativism. Moreover, we also need to attend to incorporating as many people's experiences as possible into our moral analysis. Often the experiences of any number of marginalized groups have been minimized or completely neglected, and even the experience of lay people in general has not been taken historically into very great consideration in moral theology in the past.

It is difficult to conceive of "raw experience" alone and so our experience must always be interpreted in order to render it intelligible and useful. The interpretation process leads back to a fuller understanding of what it means to be truly human. It is critical, though, before we arrive at a concretization of what is meant by the normatively human (e.g., in regards to human rights, sexual mores, medical care directives, and policies, etc.) that we have the fullest possible picture of what our human nature in this time and place really involves. Any negligence regarding attention to the data from the sciences and human experience often leads to fatal errors of moral judgment. Therefore, in this sector the role of the sciences, including the social sciences, is crucial. In this vein one of the greatest theologians of the twentieth century, Karl Rahner, S.J., observed that "It is at least possible that the very detail of which the theologian is ignorant, or of which he has only a vague notion, might be the decisive factor in his case; it might be the very detail which would alter the whole conclusion," and he offered by way of illustration the following example:

> For a few centuries Catholic moral theology has been convinced that the moment of union of the male and female germ cells is also the moment when an individual human being comes into existence. Will today's moral theologian still have the courage to maintain this presupposition as the basis of many of his moral theological statements, when faced with the knowledge that 50 per cent of all fertilized female cells never succeed in becoming attached to the womb? Will he be able to accept that 50 per cent of all "human beings"—real human beings with "immortal" souls and an eternal destiny—will never get beyond this first stage of human existence? In this particular case he can gain further knowledge and await developments; but what is he to do in other cases, where he merely suspects that neither he nor anyone else knows enough, and yet an answer must be given?[10]

Concurring with Rahner on this point, James Gustafson avers that the "moralist is no longer self-sufficient in knowing the subject matter that is analyzed from a moral point of view, but must rely on knowl-

---

[10] Karl Rahner, "The Problem of Genetic Manipulation," in *Theological Investigations, vol. 9: Writings of 1965–76, I,* trans. Graham Harrison (London: Darton, Longman & Todd, 1972) 225–26.

edge that comes from relevant scientific specialists. Rahner is not naïve about reliance on specialists, but emphasizes the requirement for the moralist to take their conclusions into account. A moral conclusion might well be altered by the inclusion or omission of relevant data."[11] All of the above is simply a call to study the whole of the human situation both carefully and completely. This sort of systematic study may well lead us to revise some of our previous understandings of what it means to be human, and that in turn means that some of our moral judgments will have to change as well. We should underscore here that revision is the dynamic part of the intersection of Tradition with the other sectors, especially with the sector of Human Experience. The ability to recognize the need for revision and the courage to undertake it is a great methodological strength and *not* a weakness. This sort of ongoing, necessary revision is simply part of the complexity of the moral world. If we try to take any shortcuts here, or worse, if we obstinately hold on to older judgments that clearly are inhuman, we shall run the risk of repeating the Galileo affair in our own lifetime.

Rational Reflection on the Normatively Human Sector

From an academic standpoint the last sector, Rational Reflection on the Normatively Human, usually is taken to refer to philosophy and particularly ethics (or moral philosophy), conceived both as independent disciplines, as well as in their ongoing encounter with theology. Yet, more simply stated, this sector refers to our understanding of what it means to be a human person. We cannot find this meaning, however, by mapping the moral equivalent of our genome or doing a CAT scan of our ethical makeup. Building on our starting premise that there is an objective moral order, the conclusions we come to regarding various aspects of that objective moral order, which is grounded in God's providence, should be binding on the whole of humanity. In coming to understand this moral order, we usually start with our own experiences, and then from these try to come to some sort of conclusions on what would constitute true human flourishing. All of the activities which promote such genuine human flourishing would be examples of correct moral behavior. The process by which we come to this sort of conclusion is what I mean by the phrase Rational Reflection on the Normatively Human, since we use our human

---

[11] Gustafson, *Ethics and Theology*, 67.

reason to move to the moral application of our individual and collective human experience to the whole human community.

This process takes time though and often there is a lot of conflict and confusion involved before we come to a general agreement of what constitutes the "normatively human" in a specific instance. Let me give just one example from the history of social ethics. In the early part of the nineteenth century, many people considered it morally acceptable to employ children as long as they were given some sort of "agreed upon" wage. However, as the Industrial Revolution got underway, this practice quickly led to exploitation of these children and conditions that we would now agree prevented genuine human flourishing of those trapped in a harsh factory environment. In our own country these abuses eventually led to significant legislation that strictly controlled what hours a child might work and under what conditions. While this social legislation was resisted by many factory owners at the time, by now most people would express agreement that such child labor is immoral. While it is extremely unfortunate to note that child labor still exists in many parts of the world, at least we have come far enough that many of us can agree that such practices ought not to continue. This agreement came only after a long process of reflection on the actual experiences of children in the factory workplace and thus is an illustration of how rational reflection can move from the data of human experience to the moral judgment of what should be the conditions under which children can be employed.

This conclusion is an example of what I mean by the term "normatively human." If we accept as part of the moral nature of the human community that our children should be protected from exploitation in the workplace, then we have articulated a moral standard or norm that ought to bind us. Our moral conclusion comes out of reflection on our human experience, but then exercises a normative claim on that experience. In other words, we admit that whatever we come to realize is in accord with true human flourishing has a claim on how we ought to behave and how we ought to treat others. This interaction between our human experience and the rational reflection on that experience in light of what we consider to be true human flourishing is what I call the "rational claim axis" of the four-sector grid moral methodology.

In the history of Catholic moral theology the whole natural law tradition comes primarily out of this Rational Reflection sector since a natural law theory exercises its primary claim "rationally" on the human community. We will discuss the natural law at some length in the next chapter, but for the purposes of the discussion of moral methodology I would simply like to stress here that it is crucial to recall that there is no "one" philosophical approach or system which is valid for all times, places, cultures, and so on. This has frankly been a problem in the Roman Catholic tradition since the scholasticism that had been so widely used for centuries appeared to many to be virtually trans-cultural and trans-historical, and therefore valid for all peoples because of its abstract and "universal" rational basis and language employed. Moreover, this philosophical view is often tied to a classicist world-view, and a rather rigid and narrow interpretation of the natural law.

It is important that we remember that any philosophical ethics, including all natural law theories, are not free-floating abstractions or independent realities waiting to be discovered, but rather are grounded in concrete human nature(s) that have to be verified through experience. Our understanding of both human nature and what constitutes the normatively human comes through rational reflection on our individual and collective human experience; it is not imposed on that experience in an external or *a priori* fashion. Rather, there is a reciprocal, dialectical relationship between human experience and our understanding of what is and should be normative human behavior.

Using the Four Sources

As we have already noted above, our four-sector methodology highlights the fact that the discipline of moral theology is essentially a hybrid. Indeed, moral philosophers often accuse their theological colleagues of following a methodology that produces a rather strange fruit, and while that critique is not necessarily fatal, recognition of the hybrid nature of our discipline should attune us to another methodological concern that may have considerable effect on how the individual sources of the quadrilateral interact with one another. Building and expanding a bit on the work of James Gustafson, I would posit five basic questions we always bring to our moral sources when we draw on them for doing moral theology.[12] The first four questions point more to the process involved in drawing content from one or more of the four sectors.

---

[12] Gustafson himself outlines four basic judgments: "(a) which sources are relevant, and why; (b) which sources are decisive when they conflict, and why; (c) what specific 'content' is to be used from these sources, and what is to be ignored or rejected, and why; and (d) how this content is to be interpreted, and why." Ibid., 143–44.

The first question is rather straightforward: what do we *use* from this or that sector, and why? In other words, if we draw upon the Scripture sector, what aspects, themes, passages, and so on do we use in constructing our theological approach to morality or a particular ethical issue? The second question is also content related, but in a somewhat different way: what do we *ignore* from the content of a given sector, and why? We all have heard the old adage that even the devil can quote Scripture to his own advantage. This suggests that even within the single sector of the Scripture quadrant there will be a multiplicity of messages, and therefore some will be listened to, while others will be ignored. The third question is a further refinement of the second, and asks: what is *rejected* from a particular sector and why? Rejection is obviously stronger than neglect or ignoring a certain source. Rejection indicates that there is something contained within this source which we judge to be simply unacceptable for developing our moral theological understanding of a particular theme or concrete issue. As with the first three questions, the sub-question of "why" is methodologically very important to lift up. A sound moral methodology should never shirk from asking and answering this sort of "why" question, since in both the asking and the answering we may discover flaws and prejudices in the way we are doing our moral theology.

A fourth question which is often, though not always, applicable points to how content from a particular source is being adapted. This fourth question asks: what is *reinterpreted* from a given source, and why? The process of appropriation and reinterpretation often points to how our understanding of morality and its concrete application to a particular issue or situation both change and develop over time. The reinterpretation question also points to a very important aspect of our theological understanding of our world and ourselves. We are essentially historical beings, and this means that not only ourselves but all the human aspects of the world we live in will change over time. While change is often discomfiting to many, it is an inescapable part of our very nature. Therefore our use of the various moral sources will at different times lead us to use one particular source, and at some time we ignore or even find it necessary to reject this same source. Reinterpretation can offer a helpful alternative in some cases to simply ignoring or outright rejecting some aspect of a moral source that no longer seems to fit as well as it might have in the past.

The "why" attached to each of the first four questions itself suggests our last and most crucial methodological source question, namely, what do we judge to be *decisive* when one or more sources conflict (or seem to conflict)? We also ask a final "why" here as well: after we have looked at all of our moral sources, what do we use, what do we ignore, what do we reject, what do we interpret, and what is it that ultimately helps us reach a particular judgment when we find conflicting data or contrasting views from one or another sector, or from within a particular sector itself. All of these questions in turn are organized along the lines of our two axes, the sacred claim and the rational claim. What is decisive along the sacred claim axis of Scripture and Tradition will answer the question of what is normative in the understanding of the individual believer and the faith community about what constitutes a proper articulation of the moral life of those who call themselves sons and daughters of God and disciples of Jesus Christ. Similarly, what is decisive in the broader realm of the entire human community will operate primarily along the axis of reflection on human experience and the claim of what constitutes a true picture of normative humanity.

To illustrate how these source content questions might work methodologically along just one of these axes let's take an example from Scripture on the proper role of women in the Church. Obviously this is an area that has undergone both significant development in the last half-century as well as ongoing sharp debate and not inconsiderable neuralgia. Some who would argue for a full and equal leadership role for women in all areas of church authority and ministry might point to a passage in John's Gospel for scriptural affirmation of this stance by citing that the very first recorded resurrection appearance of Jesus to anyone was made to Mary Magdalene and Jesus' subsequent commission of Mary to proclaim his ascension to the rest of the disciples (cf. John 20:11-18). Since Mary was favored not only with the first personal appearance of the Risen Lord but also was entrusted with the initial post-Resurrection mission to proclaim this good news, those who use this passage might argue it would be unscriptural, illogical, if not outright immoral to conclude that Jesus willed as a perpetual norm that women be excluded from positions of leadership and authority in the Church.

However, as we know well, Scripture often seems to give mixed, if not downright conflicting, messages, and others who would argue for the subservience of women in the Church might point to a different biblical injunction, such as 1 Timothy 2:11-15, which states that a woman should keep silent, be modest and submissive, bear children, and above all remain subordinate to men. A passage such as this one gives a good example of source content that might be either ignored or even rejected by those who would favor a fuller role for women, while for those in the opposing camp these verses would be "decisive" in closing off further discussion. While I would hardly join this view I would argue that it is problematic simply to "ignore" or "reject" any key moral source, especially Scripture. Therefore, I argue that often what we must do is "reinterpret" a source that may have functioned one way in the past. Often this can be done by looking at the larger context and values the particular passage sought to guard or foster.

We will look at a fuller consideration of biblical hermeneutics and their relation to moral norms in the third chapter, but here we should note that clearly this passage of 1 Timothy betrays a cultural framework with certain gender relationships and unquestioned roles of husbands and wives which have since changed considerably in the passing centuries. Therefore, the "normative" force of this biblical injunction does not necessarily bind concrete behavior in the twenty-first century in the United States as it might have done in the first-century Mediterranean world. However, this does not necessarily mean that the biblical material always needs to be rejected outright or totally ignored. Reinterpretation is possible if we look at the core values that both undergird the biblical injunction and are expressly mentioned as the goals of the behavior code, namely, reverence for God, respect for one another, lack of ostentation, modesty, faith, love, and holiness. What would it mean to embody these values and convictions in our contemporary culture? The answer to this question would perforce result in a reinterpretation of the biblical text.

Like most concrete moral issues the judgment about the proper leadership role of women in the Church cannot be decided within the scriptural sector alone, or even just along the sacred claim axis of Scripture and Tradition. If our moral theology is going to be true to itself it cannot be sectarian and parochial but must open itself to the larger world. This means that we *must* bring into our methodological use of moral sources the rational claim axis with its sectors of Human Experience and Rational Reflection on the Normatively Human as well. To ignore or reject any sector as a whole would skew our methodology terribly and deprive us not only of much additional wisdom and insight but a good set of checks and balances on how we use the five source content questions outlined above. For example, moving along the rational claim axis might lead us to a normative judgment that no person should be deprived of a proper role of leadership in the human community because of an accident of birth, such as race, ethnicity, or gender. To do so would constitute immoral discrimination. If we were then to turn around and say that this same normative judgment is suspended or significantly altered in the Church because we believe that the sources of either Tradition or Scripture somehow suggest that people should be deprived of proper access to leadership because of these accidents of birth, then we have a serious set of problems. Obviously we have a credibility problem: in short, the wider human community will likely find this volte face to be incredible, literally not believable. But the problem is not simply one of outward appearance or public relations. The deeper problem is internal, as this sort of conclusion would suggest that we are not really serious in our methodology of using all four sectors of moral sources. Or it may be that this sort of conflicted conclusion shows us that we need to go back and revisit the five questions addressed to our moral sources and see if we might be overlooking some important moral insights or that certain other prejudices and biases may be blinding us to the moral truth that is in fact present, but which we have up to now failed to discern.

The Stance and Organizing Concept

Judgments about the use, non-use, rejection, or reinterpretation of the different contents of the four sources for moral theology depend in turn on the overall stance one takes towards the understanding of reality, as well as "morality" and the concomitant methodology of moral theology. In terms of the moral methodology I am elaborating, all these judgments involve not just an appraisal of a particular source, but also an *interpretation* of theological ethics as a whole, and we must grapple with how we understand the "whole" before we can move to a consideration of one part, such as moral norms, or a concrete application to a particular ethical theme or issue. James Gustafson notes there exists in any comprehensive system of theological ethics some "organizing concept, idea, principle, analogy, metaphor, or symbol around which the base points are organized."[13] In other words, our basic stance or organizing concept usually plays the vital interpretative role of how we approach and answer our five source content questions of what is used, ignored, rejected, reinterpreted, and decisive.

---

[13] Ibid., 143.

In theological language these notions of basic stance and organizing concept point to the traditional notion of the *norma normans non normata*, i.e., the "norming norm not normed by something else." This norming norm refers to a principle or concept that grounds a discussion and does not depend on anything else for its basic legitimacy or authority, and therefore is decisive. For Christians I would argue that our only legitimate *norma normans non normata* can be the definitive revelation of God. That definitive revelation of God for us is Jesus Christ. If our ethics and moral theology are to be truly Christian then every other norm, judgment, and conclusion has to be subordinated to our understanding of Jesus Christ and his gospel message.

While I fully accept that we do need some sort of over-arching principle by which we can organize and interrelate the various sectors I have outlined above, however, careful attention must be paid to how this organizing concept functions, as well as to the ways in which it might "dysfunction." Paradoxically perhaps, a particularly strong organizing concept can bring with it several potential weaknesses. The concept may be too restrictive or narrow, and thus may not adequately reflect the whole range of diversity of human moral experience, or it may fail to allow each and every voice of the various sectors to have its say in its proper "language." At its worst, the organizing concept moves along the spectrum from being a dominant concept to becoming a domineering one. In this last case, the organizing concept may actually distort or skew the information offered by one or another of the sectors of moral sources.

I remember a former colleague (who shall remain nameless to protect the guilty) observed that Scripture simply could not really be used in a discussion of moral norms since Scripture was not properly philosophical and the whole discourse of moral norms was essentially a philosophically grounded discussion. I'm afraid that I continue to disagree with my eminent colleague on this key point. This observation is an important challenge not only for approaching the discussion of moral norms but for all of Christian ethics (to use the term preferred from an ecumenical perspective). Each respective ethical tradition, school, or approach tends to have its own "organizing concept," whether it be the language of "natural law" or "biblical warrants." Overly strong organizing concepts may hinder dialogue with, and understanding of other approaches that are organized around different concepts. Therefore, a good moral methodology is one that can accommodate a certain degree of pluralism and even ambiguity. Our morally complex world cannot be grasped totally and entirely by any one person's, tradition's, or school's rendition of what Christian ethics or moral theology has to say either on a particular moral issue or even what constitutes morality, goodness, rightness, virtue, and so on. Pluralism and ambiguity tend to be complex and at times messy. Simplicity and moral dogmatism are neater and clearer. The problem is that the former set is more closely allied to the reality in which we live and the latter set usually gives us false and misleading answers to our moral dilemmas.

A related problem to our domineering organizing concept is the risk of over-emphasizing any one of the four sectors to the point where its voice becomes so amplified that the others fail to make themselves heard. As an example of this problematic let me briefly name some "non- models" for our moral methodology. By "non-model" I mean one which essentially denies or totally eclipses the function of one or more of the four sectors. Thus, any sort of "magisterial positivism" which merely used the latest pronouncements of the magisterium as the practical *exitus et reditus* (starting and ending point) principle for all of moral theology would be non-viable. Another "non-model" would be one which moves out of a basically fundamentalist interpretation of the Bible. By "fundamentalist" I do *not* mean to launch a wholesale attack on the *sola scriptura* tradition in Protestant ethics, but rather to call into serious question the approach which views Scripture as a revelation of strict moral norms and behavior and which moreover considers this normative material to be self-evident and therefore not in need of any exegesis and/or further interpretation. We probably all can give some painful examples of this sort of approach, and therefore we must recognize fundamentalism as a definite practical challenge to our contemporary ethics. Certainly a narrow reading of the passage of 1 Timothy treated above in order to legislate a contemporary marital or gender ethics would be a negative example of fundamentalistic moral dogmatism.

Contrasting Paradigms and Moral Discernment

In the beginning of this chapter, we spent some time discussing the notion of models and paradigms and how these different approaches might influence how we view our moral world. As we stated above, a paradigm is essentially a model that has stood the test of time, and which organizes the various data well, fits it in with larger moral theories (such as deontology and teleology), and helps to move to a comprehensible view of morality and the moral life. In the last thirty-plus

years of moral theology, we have witnessed something of a struggle between two paradigms that are usually called physicalism and personalism. Since these two paradigms and the tension between them have
played such an important role in contemporary moral theology, I
think it will be helpful to conclude this chapter on our overview of
moral theology and moral methodology by taking a quick look at the
two paradigms and then consider how these two different paradigms
might suggest sharply divergent moral evaluations of a concrete case.

The first paradigm, the physicalist paradigm, has dominated moral
theology for several centuries and comes out of the background of
neo-scholasticism. It looks at human nature and moral action primarily through a lens which portrays the moral world and human nature
as a "given essence," that is fundamentally non-changing, static, with
rather clearly drawn lines of what constitutes right and wrong in a
given situation.[14] The physicalist paradigm fits in nicely with what
Bernard Lonergan describes as the "classicist worldview," which
looks on the world as essentially static and unchanging. In this view
of the world, the particulars of the moral order could be outlined in a
fairly detailed way such that they would always be true in virtually the
same way for all peoples, in all times, and in all situations. Physicalism is one way of "reading" these moral norms, and this physicalist
paradigm puts the accent on the abstract nature of the human person
and states that the person should always follow his or her nature,
which will be basically the same for all. Any moral action that would
be contrary to the proper end of this abstract human nature or some
aspect of that nature would be *contra naturam* (against nature) and
therefore always immoral, regardless of intention or circumstances.
Much of the Church's magisterial teaching on sexual ethics, such as
Paul VI's encyclical on the Regulation of Births (*Humanae vitae*, 1968)
and the Congregation for the Doctrine of the Faith's Instruction of
Reproductive Technologies (*Donum vitae*, 1987), utilizes primarily
this mode of reasoning and argumentation.

---

[14] This distinction of Lonergan appears in a number of places, but for one of the earliest
formulations see his article, "The Transition from a Classicist World-View to Historical-
Mindedness," in *Law for Liberty: The Role of Law in the Church Today*, ed., James E. Biechler
(Baltimore: Helicon Press, 1967) 126–33. Richard Gula, s.s., is a moral theologian who has
given a helpful elaboration of Lonergan's notion of the classicist worldview. See Gula's
What Are They Saying About Moral Norms? (New York: Paulist Press, 1982) 20–21 for the
Classicist and Historicist worldviews (Gula terms the latter the "Modern Worldview").

In the physicalist paradigm the morality and the moral norms for human behavior are grounded in what is perceived as the structure of nature, and these in turn are often expressed in terms of both "faculties" of the human person (like speech, or reproduction) as well as individual acts that should conform both to these faculties and the overall nature of the human person. How might these faculties be "read" in terms of concrete moral judgment in this physicalist paradigm? One such physicalist reading is contained in the following condemnation of contraception by scientist-turned-theologian, Paul M. Quay, s.j., who stressed that

> each single act of coition is a natural sign of the full, mutual procreative love of two partners, and that contraception substitutes a sign of "monstrous selfishness." The woman who uses a diaphragm has closed herself to her husband. She has accepted his affection but not his substance. She permits him entrance but does not suffer him to be "master." The sign and symbol of wifely submission, of patriarchal authority, is made over covertly to serve the purposes of a weakly uxorious male and a domineeringly feminist wife. . . . Sometimes the man will use a condom for the same reasons; sometimes for more characteristically masculine reasons of selfishness. In either even if he no longer dominates his wife as person, he does not permit his activity to penetrate her; he takes no responsibility for her. Her helplessness is deceptive—if she is not armored, he is without efficacy. He worships her with his body—but not enough to share with her his substance.[15]

Though there are a number of metaphors used in the above analysis, they all center around a rather narrow physicalist, sexist, and/or androcentric view of what is going on, and that in turn supplies a number of selfish and immoral motives into the couple's choice to practice contraception. In Quay's view it would seem impossible to "read" the moral situation in any other way. While not all who use the physicalist paradigm would necessarily be as bleak in their judgments as Quay, the physicalist paradigm itself does not easily suggest any other possible moral evaluation for a couple that might be considering artificial contraception as a way of deciding how many children they can responsibly bring into the world and care for. The means of artificial contraception themselves would be considered to be always wrong,

---

[15] Paul Quay, s.j., "Contraception and Conjugal Love," *Theological Studies* 22 (1961) 35. I am indebted to Lisa Sowle Cahill for the initial reference to Quay's quote, which she provided in her "Catholic Sexual Ethics and the Dignity of the Person: A Double Message," *Theological Studies* 50 (1989) 128–29.

and therefore any motive whatsoever that would consider using artificial contraception would be strongly suspect.

However, another moral paradigm might take the same basic "facts" of the issue, but analyze and interpret them differently. One such alternative paradigm, called "personalism," was initially popularized by Louis Janssens, though it is used by many others, including some of the writings of Pope John Paul II. Building on the traditional moral principle of totality, Janssens highlights eight key aspects which he claims are fundamental dimensions for the human person, namely (1) subject, (2) embodied subject, (3) part of the material world, (4) inter-relational with other persons, (5) an interdependent social being, (6) historical, (7) equal but unique, and (8) called to know and worship God.[16] If these aspects are indeed absolutely foundational to the human person, then they must be factored in before we can move to any articulation of what is morally normative for human persons. In short, we cannot look for the moral meaning of the human person in a classicist, abstract, ahistorical consideration of "human nature," but rather we have to look at this or that concrete human person, in his or her matrix of relations, with his or her talents, concrete circumstances, personal history, and so on. To ignore any of these fundamental aspects of the human person would lead to a mistaken and misleading view of human nature. In other words, according to the personalist paradigm, we can never speak of true human nature in terms of a timeless abstraction, but always and only in reference to a concrete, historical, individual, and unique person.

So how might the same issue of contraception discussed above be viewed according to the personalist and physicalist paradigms? Let us briefly consider two hypothetical, but realistic (i.e., possible), married couples, Bob and Carol Greene and Teodoro and Alicia Marrone. Bob and Carol are professionals in their early 30s, each with a good job, enjoy excellent health, and have been married for two years. They desire to avoid having any children since they fear that having youngsters of their own would be inconvenient and might cramp their comfortable lifestyle. Therefore the Greene's choose to utilize the chemical contraceptive implant *Norplant* since it is both effective and quite easy to use.

---

[16] These are found in Janssens' classic article for the expression of the principle of totality in the personalist model, "Artificial Insemination: Ethical Considerations," *Louvain Studies* 5 (1980) 3–29, and also more recently in Janssens' "Personalism in Moral Theology," in *Moral Theology: Challenges for the Future. Essays in Honor of Richard A. McCormick, S.J.*, ed. Charles E. Curran (New York: Paulist Press, 1990) 94–107.

Our second couple, Teodoro and Alicia Marrone, are Filipino immigrants in their mid-40s. They have been married for twenty years and have five children. Ted, Jr., the eldest, is a freshman in college, John and Mary are in high school, Susan is in the fifth grade, and Andy, who is five, is a Downs Syndrome child. Teodoro just managed to graduate from high school and has struggled to make ends meet over the years as a sales representative of various companies. He must be on the road a considerable amount of time. The last two pregnancies were especially hard on Alicia, and her doctor has strongly advised her to avoid another pregnancy, since it might actually put her life at risk. Teodoro and Alicia are aware of the Church's teaching on artificial contraception, and sincerely want to follow it, yet they are also grappling with the belief that they simply cannot have any more children. They have tried various natural family planning methods ever since Ted, Jr. was born, but their success has been limited. Ted's travel schedule and Alice's irregular cycle seem to have conspired to render this method rather ineffective, and so they have reluctantly decided that Alicia should take the pill.

Despite the pronounced obvious differences between the two couples discernable at first glance, viewed through the lens of the physicalist paradigm the moral aspects of the cases of Bob and Carol Greene and Teodoro and Alicia Marrone are actually quite similar: each couple has a constant moral obligation to allow each and every marital act to remain open to procreation. As *Humanae vitae* stresses, any usage of artificial contraception, not to mention more permanent measures such as sterilization, would be against the nature of the sexual faculty and therefore intrinsically evil. All of the other information regarding the Greenes and the Marrones might be helpful in discussing the degree of subjective culpability regarding their respective decisions to utilize artificial contraception, but from the point of view of objective normative morality both couples are morally wrong in their decision to use these forms of birth control.

However, if we change our moral glasses and look at this case through the lens of the personalist paradigm some might come to see a different sort of evaluation of the respective decisions of the two couples. In this personalist paradigm perspective there are fundamental and essential differences between the Greene's and the Marrone's decision not to have children. The Greenes might be basically self-centered and selfish, and the personalist paradigm probably would not evaluate such an action as good or moral. Yet, perhaps Bob and Carol are just not

ready yet in their married life to be parents. If they judge themselves incapable of being good parents at this point in their lives, then a decision
to not take precautions and an unwanted pregnancy occurs might seem
to be immoral. Who should make this decision? The personalist paradigm might seem to offer Bob and Carol a justification (or perhaps just
a rationalization) for any choice they might make, as long as it is made
by them personally. This seeming moral ambivalence points to one of
the weaknesses in the personalist paradigm.

However, Teodoro and Alicia Marrone clearly seem to be in a quite
different situation—one that differs from Bob and Carol Greene's in
several essential aspects. Teodoro and Alicia already have demonstrated
their openness to children. They are seeking to be good and responsible parents within the confines of the limited means at their disposal.
They tried other methods of birth control and came to the decision to
utilize artificial contraception as an anguished last resort. The physicalist paradigm, though, does not seem to give much moral weight to these
considerations. This one-size-fits-all morality is a weakness of the physicalist paradigm. However, in the personalist paradigm some might see
Teodoro's and Alicia's situation in a different perspective and conclude
that this couple not only has a "dispensation" to use artificial contraception, but possibly even a moral obligation to use such means in order
to foster their love for each other as husband and wife and as parents of
their children.

Can both paradigms be right? What would this and similar cases
look like if viewed more through the lenses of biblical normative
morality? Would cultural differences play a substantive role in analyzing this situation? Are there other factors and features that one or
the other paradigms is obscuring and/or misreading? The case we
have just given is actually rather simple, and yet there are so many
other more complicated cases in the general area of regulation of
births. What does one do in situations of absolute dire poverty, where
the large number of children virtually condemns entire families and
communities to a life of subsistence living at best?[17] What do we do in

---

[17] Bishop Teodoro Bacani has tackled just this issue in his *The Church and Birth Control*,
2nd rev. ed. (1991, 1993). Bishop Bacani, then an auxiliary bishop of the Archdiocese of
Manila, looks at the issue of birth control in the context of the population crisis in the
Philippines and also considers the possibility that a wife might legitimately use artificial
contraception if her husband refused to cooperate with her in the practice of natural family
planning. Bacani was installed in January 2003 as the first bishop of the new diocese of No-
valiches in Metro Manila.

cases in which one of the couple knows that she or he is a carrier for a terrible genetic disease for which there is no cure at present? All of these questions only begin to scratch the surface of our morally complex world. Certainly none of these issues has simple and easy answers. However, these are precisely the sorts of issues and cases that more explicit attention to our moral methodology, sources used (or ignored or rejected), and subsequent judgments made will bring into sharper focus. Now let us continue our discussion by looking more closely at the whole issue of doing moral theology as it moves from methodology into concrete applications to critical life issues.

Before we can complete this journey we need to do a little more map-work, especially outlining our understanding of the "objective" moral order, as found in moral norms and the natural law (chapter 2); considering how the Bible fits into moral theology (chapter 3); what we mean by conscience as the basic modality of our moral lives (chapter 4); articulating our approach to moral discourse on concrete ethical issues (chapter 5); looking at how we might respond pastorally to individuals faced with difficult decisions in a morally complex world (chapter 6); and finally, considering the reality of sin and failure (chapter 7).

2

The Natural Law and Moral Norms:
Moving Along the Rational Claim Axis

> All who have sinned apart from the law will also perish apart from the law, and all who have sinned under the law will be judged by the law. For it is not the hearers of the law who are righteous in God's sight, but the doers of the law who will be justified. When the Gentiles, who do not possess the law, do instinctively what the law requires, these, though not having the law, are a law to themselves. They show that what the law requires is written on their hearts, to which their own conscience also bears witness; and their conflicting thoughts will accuse or perhaps excuse them on the day when, according to my gospel, God, through Jesus Christ will judge the secret thoughts of all (Rom 2: 12-17).

It may seem odd to begin a chapter on the natural law by quoting Scripture, yet we must keep in mind that for Christian ethics even our natural law theory must in some sense be subject to the *norma normans* ("norming norm") of God's revelation. These five verses in St. Paul's Letter to the Romans are the *locus classicus* for a sort of biblical proof-text of the validity of the whole natural law tradition in moral theology. While it is dangerous to ground any moral argument on just a few verses from Scripture, the above passage has been referenced so often by Christian ethicians working in the natural law that the verses have virtually become part of the tradition itself. Furthermore, the passage contains several of the central elements of natural law theory as it has been used by theologians since the early days of the Church, as well as a number of points that continue to be debated between Protestant and Roman Catholic moralists. Since the use of the natural law tradition is oftentimes a key methodological tension between Roman Catholics and Protestants, citing this biblical reference plays an important ecumenical role as well.

This last-mentioned debate revolves around the disputed issue regarding any use of a natural law theory in Christian ethics. Protestant theologians have usually grounded their ethics firmly in the Scripture quadrant of our four-sector grid. *Sola scriptura* became, if not a battle cry, at least a distinctive hallmark of Protestant ethics, while Roman Catholic moral theology often cut the other way, basing much of its concrete applications as well as undergirding principles and theory along the rational claim axis. While we cannot resolve this ancient debate here, it is important to identify some of the principal arguments.

Why have Protestant theologians traditionally tended to resist using the natural law to ground their discussion of moral norms? It is not that most of them believe that any Christian ethics must be based only (and completely) on what is found in the Bible, but rather that a heavy reliance on "reason" is fraught with both practical and theological peril. The practical difficulty seen by many since the Protestant Reformation is that, due to original sin of humanity, recounted biblically in the story of the fall of Adam and Eve, our very human nature has been corrupted. While our capacity of human reason has not been destroyed, it has been so seriously compromised that we should not trust the moral conclusions we might arrive at based on reason alone. It would be a bit like continuing to use a computer file or program that had been infected with a virus; the program might seem to be functioning adequately, but over time we would realize (if we were lucky!) that something had gone terribly awry. The traditional Catholic response has been that while human reason was certainly affected by the fall, it was not totally destroyed, and for biblical evidence to support this claim the above passage from Romans is often cited.

However, this is not the only point concerning the legitimacy of a natural law based on Christian ethics that has been traditionally contested between Protestants and Roman Catholics, and more recently even among theologians of the same confessional background. Broadly speaking, the second point of contention concerns whether, or to what degree, a Christian ethics is a revealed morality. Some theologians would maintain that God has communicated the divine plan for human morality primarily through the biblical witness. Christian morality, therefore, should be basically a response to God's commands, and neither the individual Christian nor the faith community should look to secular human ethical standards to discover how to live in an authentic moral manner. Though this position would have counted more adherents in past centuries than at present, certainly the great twentieth-century Swiss theologian Karl Barth did much to popularize a renaissance of this approach, and many aspects of his position have found a certain resonance in the writings of other contemporary Protestant ethicians such as the late Mennonite John Howard Yoder and the Methodist Stanley Hauerwas.

Other theologians would take a more modulated position and argue that for the most part what constitutes a "Christian" morality is largely identical with an authentic human morality, which could be known apart from revelation. Nevertheless, there are certain themes, values, or precepts that are only discernable to the believer through revelation received, read, interpreted, and lived within a faith community. Much of the work of Latin American liberation theologians, such as Gustavo Gutiérrez, represents this view. The commitment to adopting what is often termed the "preferential option for the poor" is grounded primarily not in a natural law theory of justice and the common good, but finds its persuasiveness or ethical warrant in a theological interpretation of God's will. We should be committed to act in solidarity with, and on behalf of the poor because this is the way God acts. In other words, we are to make God's preferences our own, and God has chosen in a special way the poor. We come to know this preferential choice through the biblical stories of liberation and redemption, and therefore the validating warrant for this claim is grounded primarily in Scripture and not human reason.

There is yet another school of thought which could be located between these two positions whose adherents primarily are Roman Catholic and which is often called the Faith Ethic school (or sometimes is denoted simply by the German term *Glaubensethik*). Like the other positions touched on above, this school of thought also holds that the Bible is an important source of moral teaching that is absolutely necessary to aid human reason. This necessity is due to the fact that human reason may be clouded by sin, or unconsciously influenced by other pressures and factors in contemporary secular society. So even though hypothetically we humans might be able to come to the basic moral truths and norms without the aid of the Bible, according to the proponents of this group, we would be unlikely to get a full and accurate picture of these moral norms through our natural reason alone. Human reason must be illumined by faith, and the Bible is obviously indispensable to a complete understanding of our Christian faith.

Catholic theologians identified with this position would include one of the greatest moralists of the twentieth century, the German

Redemptorist Bernard Häring, as well as the late Swiss theologian Hans Urs von Balthasar, the German exegete Heinz Schürmann, and the person who has been head of the Congregation for the Doctrine of the Faith for most of the pontificate of John Paul II, the German theologian Joseph Cardinal Ratzinger. Ratzinger's own writing on this issue raises another point, namely, the relationship of the hierarchical teaching office of the Roman Catholic Church, the magisterium, and the exposition of moral norms contained in both the Bible and in the natural law. Briefly stated, Cardinal Ratzinger's position is that part of the task of the magisterium is to preserve the apostolic teaching contained in the deposit of faith found in biblical revelation and that this process is aided by God's continuing grace that in turn aids human reason. However, Ratzinger warns, any "flight into pure orthopraxis and the withdrawal of objective morality from the field of faith (and the magisterium belonging to the faith) are equivalent, despite first appearances, to an accusation of heresy against reason."[1] Thus, while the magisterium has a key role to play in ensuring an authentic interpretation of both Scripture and natural law, it cannot do this in isolation from the rest of the Church as Ratzinger notes in the very next breath:

> In the process of assimilating what is really rational and rejecting what only seems to be rational, the whole Church has to play a part. This process cannot be carried out in every detail by an isolated Magisterium, with oracular infallibility. The life and suffering of Christians who profess their faith in the midst of their times has just as important a part to play as the thinking and questioning of the learned, which would have a very hollow ring without the backing of Christian existence, which learns to discern spirits in the travail of everyday life.[2]

Ratzinger's nuance here echoes the methodology we outlined in chapter 1, especially in holding the necessity for sufficient attention to the Human Experience quadrant of our four sources for doing moral theology.

Though the influence of the Faith Ethics school in contemporary discussion on moral norms is clearly important, probably the majority of contemporary Roman Catholic theologians, as well as a great

---

[1] Joseph Cardinal Ratzinger, "Magisterium of the Church, Faith, Morality," in *Readings in Moral Theology, No. 2*, ed. Charles E. Curran and Richard A. McCormick, S.J. (New York: Paulist Press, 1980) 185. This article first appeared in Ratzinger's *Prinzipien Christlicher Moral* (Einsiedeln, 1975).

[2] Ibid., 186.

deal of the actual tradition of how moral norms were presented in the tradition of moral theology would be more closely identified with another school of thought, often called the Moral Autonomy school. This view holds that Scripture itself adds nothing *distinctive* to Christian ethics and that in terms of the *content* of morality, Christians have no special commands nor special revelation. Therefore, the Christian demands of the moral life would be identical with those for non-Christians. Some of the major theologians associated with this school are Josef Fuchs, Richard McCormick, Alfons Auer, Bruno Schüller, and Klaus Demmer.

Yet even though there remain definite debates and differences in how one should use the natural law tradition in Christian ethics, we need to pay attention in our survey of the landscape that there are large numbers of people who strongly resist any integration of the so-called natural law into their own personal moral framework. While this tendency can be found more easily in certain post-modern secular philosophical ethical theories, I discovered first hand in one of my classes on sexual ethics that even the mere words "natural law" often set off all sorts of explosive reactions. In this particular class I had asked my students to divide into small discussion groups and to come up with what they considered to be the key criteria for developing and evaluating a positive theology of sexuality. One group surprised me more than just a little when they came back and said, "We don't want to use the natural law in our Roman Catholic sexual ethics!" Now it was clear to me that these people were hardly relativists or hedonists or anything else of a similar nature. But they had recognized that often various *theories* of the Roman Catholic natural law tradition had been employed in ways that unfortunately led in their opinion to conclusions that did not promote true human flourishing, but which had rather the opposite effect.

My basic point here is the necessity to distinguish between the assertion on the one hand of the natural law itself (which is grounded in a certain basic human nature that calls us to live ethically in relation to some sort of an objective moral order) and on the other hand, of particular articulations and understandings of the ramifications of these two foundational assertions that go into a specific theory of the natural law. Building on the methodological insights of chapter 1, I would argue that the natural law itself is more complex than can be grasped in its totality by humans at any point in history. Therefore, the best we can do is elaborate various theories of the natural law which will be paradigm based, and like all paradigms will be somewhat incomplete and probably partially incorrect. Therefore, any specific natural law theory should be open to examination, revision, and perhaps even rejection if it can be shown to be at variance with a coherent understanding of our common human nature and shared moral order. A natural law theory is somewhat analogous to a construction blueprint, but any realistic blueprint has to take into sufficient consideration the topography of the landscape on which the edifice is to be built. So let us look at some of the key features of our particular landscape before we lay our cornerstone of any moral norms we might draw from our natural law theory.

Drafting a Blueprint for a Theory of the Natural Law

As we outlined above the treatment of the natural law found among both Roman Catholic and Protestant ethicians shows both a certain fundamental convergence, as well as important differences in emphases as well as disagreements about certain aspects and/or ramifications of natural law theory. In order to track more easily the various positions, their points of agreement, convergence, divergence, and outright disagreement, it will be helpful to step back a bit and outline the basic claims and criteria of most, if not all, natural law theories. First, we need to emphasize here that we are talking about *theories* of natural law, and not the natural law itself. As we have noted, no one human person or group of human persons can grasp the entirety of the natural law whole and complete, in all of its fullness and without any distortion. The natural law involves us in an ever deepening process of discovery and refinement. It has taken us centuries to get as far as we have, and we have centuries more to go. We can never say at any point in history that we have now finally discovered all that the natural law holds in regards to what we are called to embody in our cooperation with God in the task of promoting true human flourishing. Nevertheless, a methodological theory of the natural law can help us realize better the moral progress we have already made, as well as sharpen our focus for questions yet to be refined.

With that caveat in place, I would observe first that most natural law theories are grounded in two fundamental premises or claims: namely, the ontological (reality-based) and the epistemological (knowledge-based). In turn, each foundational claim elaborates two further claims, each related to normativity and universality, producing what we will call a draft blueprint of six basic aspects. In architecture, a draft blueprint is a bit like a preliminary building plan that gives an overall outline of the structure, indicating key elements that must be incorporated into the building. However, this schema does not specify in precise detail all the possible architectural and design choices that will be made by the various artisans and workers employed before the edifice is complete and ready for habitation. If we conceive of a theory of the natural law analogously in this way, we should be able to mark out certain aspects that are indispensable conditions, but which at the same time will allow for differences of approach and opinion as to just how these elements are best incorporated in the final structure existing in a particular time and place. Thus, looking at how our ethicians implicitly treat one or more of these six aspects should prove helpful in seeing more clearly how the different theories operate when it comes to the particular discussion of the application of moral norms in relation to the overall understanding of human morality.

Natural Law Draft Blueprint

ONTOLOGICAL CLAIM: The Objective Moral Order Exists	EPISTEMOLOGICAL CLAIM: We Can Know It In Some Real Sense
Normative Claim: *We must follow the moral norms of this objective moral order*	*Normable Claim:* *This moral order can be expressed as moral norms*
Universalist Claim: *Some of these moral norms bind all peoples in all times in some way*	*Universalizable Claim:* *Some of these moral norms can be formulated to apply to all peoples*

The First Claim: Ontological

Stated in its simplest terms the first foundational claim of the natural law holds that in some real sense there is an objective moral order, i.e., that there is a certain basic rightness and wrongness of moral standards in our world and that our human moral actions also can be judged as being right or wrong. Moreover, the ontological claim asserts that these moral standards are not simply the social construction of a given age or culture, but are grounded in our human nature that in some sense transcends any given time or point. In other words, there is a common human nature that we share with all men and women who have lived, are living now, and will come to live in the future. We term this the "ontological" claim since it does come from a well-established philosophical-theological metaphysical tradition that deals with the nature of being and its interrelations (*ontos* οντως comes from the Greek for "to be"). An ontological claim is that certain things really are, and that they really are in a certain way; they are not merely myths, legends, metaphors, or figments of our imagination. We might call this ontological claim the "how-ness" of moral life, i.e., how we are meant to live morally. Thus, the foundational assertion of the natural law is that there is a moral universe in which we live, act, and interact, which we certainly influence, but ultimately is not essentially of our own making. The reality of this moral nature demands that we conform ourselves to it, and not vice versa.

Of course, we should admit that many of our contemporaries would not share this fundamental premise and would argue instead that there is no common human nature that can provide a cross-cultural or trans-historical grounding for ethical judgments. Instead, there are a number of other ethical theories that are put forward, such as consequentialism or utilitarianism that gauges the morality of an action based on its consequences or whether it produces the greatest happiness for the greatest number of people. Enjoying a certain popularity are varieties of other theories such as emotivism or intuitionism, which hold that morality is really just a construction of human feelings or emotions, so that when I say "this action is immoral" what it really comes down to is my communicating that "I don't like this action, and I don't want you to like it either." While various versions of these ethical theories continue to hold sway in secular philosophical ethics, I would argue that virtually all Christian ethicians accept the ontological claim of a common human nature that in some sense furnishes the grounding for our standards of morality. So for the time being we shall leave aside these other theories that would deny this fundamental claim and continue on to our next premise of a natural law theory.

The Second Claim: Epistemological

The second foundational claim is grounded in the first claim and takes it an important step further. There is in some sense an objective moral order, a rightness and wrongness that is neither individually, collectively, nor culturally determined, and that human beings can in some real sense know the nature of this moral order. If the ontological claim points us toward the "how-ness" of our moral living, the epistemological claim points us to the "what-ness" of the moral life, i.e., in what manner do we come to know, and with what amount of certitude just "what" the moral order actually calls us to do and to be. The remaining four aspects of our natural law draft blueprint are actually just further elaborations and specifications of either the ontological or epistemological claim.

However, before we move on to these we should note that the epistemological claim has been the aspect that traditionally has caused the most difficulty with Protestant ethicians. It is not that Protestants do not believe that there is an objective moral order which expresses God's creative will for humankind. Rather, they have traditionally held that due to the fall of humankind and the sinfulness that still resides in the world at large as well as in all of us individually, the combined effect has been to cloud both our individual and communal use of human reason, with the result that we cannot adequately trust that reasoning power as we seek to discern through the natural law just what is morally required of us. Instead of relying on the natural law many Protestants have turned instead to Scripture and explicit faith in God and trust in God's grace.

These positions have been modified over the centuries and even some Protestant theologians are suggesting that the natural law might be a helpful resource in Christian ethics. For example, the Lutheran theologian Carl Braaten suggests that in light of secularism, pluralism, and the general breakdown of moral standards in the contemporary world, a reformulated natural law theory can be of crucial importance.[3] Meanwhile, the Anglican John Macquarrie argues for a reformulated natural law theory that could help solve the problems of linking Christian and non-Christian morals, as well as help in shaping a contemporary Christian ethic, and also describing the relation between faith and morals. Macquarrie considers the *proprium* or "distinctive element" of Christian ethics to be the Christian context in

---

[3] Carl E. Braaten, "Protestants and the Natural Law," *First Things* (January 1992) 20–26.

which the moral life is perceived.[4] However, many others continue to resist these approaches. In a somewhat belated rejoinder to Braaten's article, the Evangelical theologian Carl Henry critiques all natural law traditions, including Braaten's modest proposal to recover what might be a legitimate "Protestant" understanding of the natural law. For Henry all such efforts are wrong-headed as they divert the proper understanding of Christian ethics from its necessary dependence on biblical revelation.[5] Probably the most notable contemporary Protestant opponent of any rapprochement with a natural law tradition is Stanley Hauerwas whose whole understanding of the Church is that it must conform itself only to the Scriptures and can never seek any peace with an ethics that is non-biblically grounded.[6] Even though this discussion could easily merit a book of its own, we now must leave that topic aside for the time being and continue with the other features of our blueprint of natural law theory.

The Third Claim: Normable

The normable claim builds on the epistemological premise (the what-ness of the objective moral order) by showing us that the nature of the moral life can be fashioned into ethical norms that ought to help form our moral character and guide our ethical choices and actions. In short, we are saying that not only do we have a certain sort of knowledge about the moral order that exists (the ontological claim), but that we can discern the relation this moral order has to our own selves. Therefore we can use this moral knowledge to help guide our

[4] John Macquarrie, "Rethinking Natural Law," in his *Three Issues in Ethics* (New York: Harper and Row, 1970) 82–110. This same article is more easily found in *Readings in Moral Theology, no. 2*, eds., Charles E. Curran and Richard A. McCormick, s.j. (New York: Paulist Press, 1980) 121–45; as well as in Curran and McCormick's *Readings in Moral Theology, no. 7: Natural Law and Theology* (Mahwah, N.J.: Paulist Press, 1991) 221–46.

[5] Carl F. H. Henry, "Natural Law and a Nihilistic Culture," *First Things* 49 (January 1995) 54–60.

[6] Hauerwas' polemics in this general area surface markedly in most of his writings since the publication (with William H. Willimon) of *Resident Aliens: Life in the Christian Colony: a Provocative Christian Assessment of Culture and Ministry for People Who Know that Something is Wrong* (Nashville: Abingdon Press, 1989). For some writings more narrowly focused on the natural law polemic, see Stanley Hauerwas, "Natural Law, Tragedy and Theological Ethics," *American Journal of Jurisprudence* 20 (1975); "Nature, Reason, and the Task of Theological Ethics," in Curran and McCormick, *Readings in Moral Theology, no. 7: Natural Law and Theology*, 43–71. This last item originally appeared as ch. 4 in Hauerwas' *The Peaceable Kingdom: A Primer in Christian Ethics* (Notre Dame and London: University of Notre Dame Press, 1983) 50–71.

actions and promote our human flourishing through the development of moral norms. So we are saying that the kind of knowledge we have allows us to move from perception to reflection and on to action. The perception and reflection phase leads us to formulate this knowledge in a certain way, i.e., into moral norms that will help guide our concrete lives in our actions as well as indicate to us the sorts of persons we should try to grow into.

Perhaps an example from the history of moral theology might illustrate this point. Building on a specification of the ontological claim about human nature moralists noted that humans are endowed with the faculty of purposeful speech or communication, and they further concluded that the exercise of this ability to speak ought to be for the communication of truth. Therefore, the manulists constructed a moral norm that an individual ought always to tell what she or he believed to be true, and that if someone knowingly were to tell a lie then this would be a *locutio contra mentem*, literally "speech against (what is held in) the mind." To speak against what one held to be true seemed to violate the very nature of speech (i.e., it was labeled *contra naturam* ["against the nature of the faculty"] and therefore was judged to be *ipso facto* immoral).

The corresponding moral norm that was formulated to safeguard this perceived aspect of the natural law was that no one could ever say something they knew to be untrue, regardless of other reasons and circumstances, and still have "untrue speech" considered morally correct. Now as we shall see shortly, this particular moral norm became the locus of considerable debate amongst theologians and ethicians, but we can all agree that the formulation itself is expressed as a norm. Thus, a key aspect of our draft blueprint of the natural law is that the moral prescriptions and proscriptions, the ethical do's and don'ts of our lives, can be fashioned into these sorts of moral norms. While most of the ethicians we treat acknowledge at least implicitly this claim, there will be significant disagreements raised at just how these moral claims can and ought to be normed, as we shall soon see when we pursue the history of the casuistry about the norms connected with truth-telling. This debate will move us from a consideration of what can be formulated as a norm to a judgment over whether this norm in fact should be binding on us.

The Fourth Claim: Normative

If we accept the third claim that we can come to know the true nature of the moral order by forming its demands in terms of moral norms, then the next step is to apply these norms to ourselves. In other words, not only can we fashion our knowledge of the moral order in a normable manner, but then this knowledge exerts a claim on us, i.e., the norms become binding on us, irrespective of our own particular inclinations and desires. As with the previous claim, we will note substantial agreement on this principle in theory (i.e., few Christian ethicians would argue for complete moral relativism), but again we will find important disagreements as to just how we can understand the claim that this or that specific moral norm has in a particular instance. This debate is carried on more pointedly in terms of one or both of the last two claims of our draft blueprint.

There is, however, an important observation we should draw from the connection between the foundational ontological claim that an objective moral order exists and the epistemological claim that we can know it. There are several types of knowledge that may deepen our understanding of the universe, such as those treated in the physical and social sciences. That kind of knowledge certainly intersects with moral knowledge but it is very hard to make a "norm" out of facts we come to realize through biology, for example. The simple fact that mammals procreate through sexual relations and nurse their young does not of itself lead to the conclusion that this must be the only morally valid way we have to reproduce offspring and nurture them as well. Such a way of thinking would involve what philosophers and theologians generally term the naturalistic fallacy, i.e., moving from an observation that something exists or "is" in a certain way in the physical universe to the conclusion that one therefore "ought" to conform one's moral behavior to that fact. If this were so then virtually everything artificial would be *ipso facto* immoral: electric power, machines, clothing, as well as bottle-feeding and so on.

While most of the ethicians we treat acknowledge at least the difficulties involved in establishing this sort of moral normativity, there will be significant disagreements raised at just how these moral claims can and ought to be binding, as well as another debate as to the types of moral norms that exist and their relative authority. We will see this debate most sharply as we move to the last two features in our blueprint, namely, the universalizable and universalist claims, as well as when we move from blueprint to construction of actual moral norms that evaluate certain ways of being and action. In short, can we really say that any moral norm, such as our "no telling of falsehoods ever," is truly universal in the sense of always binding on us regardless of further reasons or circumstances? Before we return to this question directly let us briefly consider these last two foundational aspects of moral norms in the natural law, namely, universalizable and universal moral norms.

The Fifth Claim: Universalizable

If there is a moral order and we can both know it and norm it, then this penultimate claim raises the stakes one step higher by asserting that our moral norms can be constructed in a certain way so as to apply to all peoples at all times and in all places. In short, the epistemological nature of the natural law allows us to construct our moral norms in such a way that they are universalizable, i.e., formulated so to apply to all peoples in all times and all places. There is little disagreement on the theoretical level that moral norms can be fashioned into universals; clearly such formulations exist in most philosophical and theological traditions. A good historical example of a universalizable claim is contained in this well-known sentence from the United States *Declaration of Independence:* "We hold these truths to be self-evident, that all men are created equal, that they are endowed by their Creator with certain unalienable Rights, that among these are Life, Liberty and the pursuit of Happiness." This is not a mere statement of fact, but is rather a universalizable moral claim. Because all people are created by God as having an equal human dignity, certain moral norms can be derived from this moral fact, namely, that all people should enjoy the human rights of life, liberty, and the freedom to pursue a life which will lead to true human flourishing. That we can "speak" in this way is not so much a matter of debate, as we've just proven that we can do so. Rather the debate intensifies more on the final claim, namely, whether such universalizable moral norms in fact exist, and if so just what is their degree of moral obligation.

But before we move to this last facet, perhaps we should take a moment and summarize the two principal claims or facets of our natural law draft blueprint outlined so far, namely, the ontological claim, upon which is built the normative claim, and the epistemological claim, which in turn provides the foundation for the normable claim.

First, to torture the architectural metaphor just a bit further, the ontological claim asserts that we are trying to build a structure on a real landscape and not just to create a castle in the air. Thus, the ontological claim says that there is a moral order that exists in some definite sense and, like an actual plot of land upon which a building is to be erected, this ontological moral order is real and not just a figment of our imagination. Second, the epistemological claim argues that we can in fact fashion a natural law blueprint that, just like an actual construction blueprint, will contain key features that must go into a building if it is to hold together and work well for its stated purposes.

There is an old story in American Jesuit lore which might illustrate this point. Plans for the construction of a residence that had been sent for approval to the Jesuit headquarters in Rome were returned with just one cryptic notation, *Suntne angeli?* ("Are they angels?"). After carefully re-examining the blueprint for some time the American superiors suddenly realized that a certain key feature was in fact missing: the building had no lavatories! Obviously one can "construct" a blueprint for a large building without making provision for such amenities, but the resulting edifice will not function well for very long! Thus, it is very important to make as certain as possible that the ethical precepts formulated as universalizable norms are in fact truly universal and therefore normative, or in other words, genuinely binding on all peoples.

The Sixth Claim: Universal

This brings us now to the last core facet of our draft blueprint of the natural law. Building on the epistemological universalizable claim that we can indeed formulate moral norms in such a way that they apply to everyone and at all times, this last claim of our blueprint returns to the foundational ontological claim and states there *are* such norms that are binding on all of us. Certainly not every moral norm is universal in this sense, but the sixth claim states that there *are* moral absolutes, norms that are not merely "counsels" or ideals to strive towards, but are actual demands that in some fashion compel us to do certain things and not to do others. Such universal norms apply not only to us as Christians (or whatever subset of humanity we wish to speak of), but they apply to all peoples, regardless of any other factors such as historical context, individual or collective circumstances, and the like. This last claim is the most sweeping, and not surprisingly it is the assertion that will attract the most discussion, debate, and downright disagreement.

To show some of the potential problems in the precise formulation of universal moral norms, let us return to our discussion about speech and the communication of truth. The ontological claim would suggest that there is a moral rightness to truth-telling and a moral wrongness to lying that does not depend for its justification on human consensus or cultural convention. In other words, we tell the truth not merely because it is useful for the smooth functioning of human societies, but because it is right in and of itself. This is the ontological claim of the objective moral order. Similarly, we know that such truth-telling is required of us, and this comes from the epistemological claim of the natural law. Building on these two claims we then move to the construction of an appropriate moral norm, namely, that we should tell the truth. This is the normable claim and when we render ourselves answerable to this norm we recognize that it is in fact binding on us; it is normative. So far so good.

But is the norm "tell the truth" in fact universal? Clearly we can fashion the norm in a universalizable way: "always tell the truth, regardless of other reasons and/or circumstances." That would be a universalizable formulation since no provision is made for any exceptions for any reason whatsoever. For a good number of years many moral theologians believed that this formulation of the moral norm was truly universal. Everything seemed to hold together logically. Anything that violated the true nature of a human faculty was *contra naturam* and therefore immoral. In a logical syllogism this would be the major premise of the syllogism, while the claim that the nature of speech was always the communication of truth of what one believed in his or her mind to be true would be a minor premise of the syllogism. Therefore any form of speech which knowingly was to contravene what one believed to be true in his or her mind would be an attack on the moral nature of speech and *ipso facto* immoral and the conclusion of the syllogism. As a logical syllogism this construction seemed to work—until unforeseen circumstances intruded into the moral calculus. If this norm as formulated were truly universal, then there would be no possible set of circumstances that would justify its violation. But if there is a legitimate exception to truth-telling, then the norm as formulated is not in fact universal. So can we find some such set of circumstances?

The year is 1943 and the place is Nazi-occupied Amsterdam. You have an office building with a converted hidden attic in which you are harboring an extended Jewish family. A knock comes at the door and you are horrified to discover the Gestapo on your front steps. They ask you a straightforward simple question: Are there any Jews in this building? How do you respond? You know that the Jewish family is secreted away in your attic, but if you answer "truthfully" to the question these innocent people will certainly be sent to a concentration camp and will likely lose their lives. This sort of dilemma has provoked a number of responses amongst theologians in the past. Some have actually argued that you must tell the Gestapo the truth, holding that you have an obligation to the tell the truth, but the Gestapo have an obligation to respect the legitimate human rights of these innocent people. This approach would be in accord with more of the physicalist paradigm analysis of truth-telling: any physical telling of a falsehood would be *contra naturam* and therefore always immoral.

Others have argued differently, looking for what amounts to an exception to the general norm to always tell the truth. This exception involves what is often called either the "mental reservation" clause or a "legitimate right to know" clause. In the former the individual makes a mental reservation in his or her mind, admitting interiorly the truth but externally lying to the Gestapo. It is sort of like crossing your fingers behind your back while telling the lie. This mental reservation is meant to safeguard one's respect for the general norm of truth-telling, while at the same time trying to protect the innocent people who would be harmed by the Gestapo. The "legitimate right to know" approach recognizes the validity of the general moral norm that requires truth-telling, but argues that the right to the truth is not enjoyed by all people. Thus, if someone tells me something in legitimate confidentiality, just any other person in the world does not have a right to know that secret. In our current case we would argue that the Gestapo do not have a legitimate right to know if innocent Jews are hiding in the attic, so the person at the door is justified in trying to put the Nazis off the track.

Both of these approaches operate less from a physicalist paradigm which morally evaluates the factual accuracy of the words said. Instead, this approach corresponds more to what we have called the personalist paradigm in discerning how the norm of truth-telling ought to apply in this scenario. Here we look at the bigger picture, taking into greater consideration the circumstances and the impact our speech will have on the persons involved, giving special weight to the relationship we have with the hidden Jews in our care. This case also shows us that we can still have a moral norm that generally holds true in most cases and still have legitimate exceptions in other situations. Here one might then ask the logical question: if such norms can be said to be only "generally true," but not "always" true in the concrete, can we really speak of universal moral norms? This is precisely a much disputed question among moral theologians, and an attempt to answer this conundrum brings us to the next part of our discussion, namely, how we are to understand the various types of moral norms, since by now most of us would probably agree that one size of moral norm does not fit very well all possible concrete life situations.

Constructing the Edifice: Levels of Moral Norms

Once while teaching my standard course in fundamental moral theology, I began my introductory lecture, noting that through the centuries some of the Church's teachings on moral norms have undergone significant change. The examples I used are well-known and, I thought, largely non-controversial. I began with slavery by noting that both theologians and the magisterium supported this practice as being moral under certain theoretical conditions, and moreover a large number of Catholics, including my own religious order, bought, sold, held, and used slaves. It took literally centuries before the human community, including the whole Church, came to realize that slavery could never be justified under any circumstances and that it violated basic human dignity and was therefore always opposed to the natural law—what the Catholic moral tradition terms "intrinsically evil." Thus, with slavery we have an instance of a moral norm that has shifted from proscribing absolutely something that had been previously permitted. To illustrate the opposite shift, namely, permitting something that had formerly been prohibited on the grounds of being intrinsically evil, I turned to usury, which had been defined by the moral manuals as *any* taking of interest on loans (and not merely at exorbitant rates) since this was viewed as fundamentally inimical to a just economic order.[7] However,

---

[7] Though these examples are widely used, I am particularly indebted to the work of legal historian John T. Noonan both for the formulation and treatment of these basic issues. For a short sketch, see his, "On the Development of Doctrine," *America* 180 (3 April 1999) 6–8, which outlines how the Church has developed its moral doctrine in five key areas: adultery, the death penalty, religious liberty, slavery, and usury. Noonan has also written extensively on the tradition of church teaching regarding abortion, marriage, and contraception.

For a fuller treatment of these topics see his *Contraception: A History of Its Treatment by the Catholic Theologians and Canonists*, enlarged ed. (Cambridge, Mass.: Harvard University Press, 1965, 1986), *Power to Dissolve: Lawyers and Marriages in the Courts of the Roman Curia* (Cambridge, Belknap Press of Harvard University Press, 1972), *The Scholastic Analysis of Usury*, (Cambridge, Mass.: Harvard University Press, 1957), and his edited volume, *The Morality of Abortion: Legal and Historical Perspectives* (Cambridge, Mass.: Harvard University Press, 1970).

with the shift from agrarian-based economies to capitalist economies, this teaching fell into desuetude. While never formally abrogated, the traditional prohibition was largely ignored in both theory and practice. After all, I noted, even the Vatican Bank engages in the practice of interest-bearing savings and loans!

I used these examples to illustrate the point that any theory of the natural law and moral norms does not exist in timeless and static abstraction, but grows, develops, and of necessity, changes according to different situations, insights, and issues which arise in the real, historically grounded lives of men and women. However, after I had finished with what I thought to be a rather modest set of operating premises, one of my students approached me privately after class. He had clearly understood the various historical examples I had used, as well as the basic point I had endeavored to make, but was nevertheless genuinely disturbed by a prospect that such an approach to moral norms might entail. He asked if it weren't true that if we took this historically conditioned approach to the natural law wouldn't we run the risk of leading people to believe that there were no fixed absolutes at all, and therefore people could (and should) do just as they pleased. His question was honest and genuine and I thought to myself, yes, this can be a real danger, and certainly it is a legitimate concern, and perhaps for this very reason the whole area of the natural law and moral norms continues to be so hotly debated, not only among professional theologians and the magisterium, but by just about everyone else as well.

The great thirteenth-century theologian Thomas Aquinas also faced a similar set of questions in his own treatment of the natural law (cf. *ST I-II*, q. 94). He noted that there are two types of human reason that people use in trying to discern what is the best moral response to a given situation. Thomas calls the first type of reason "speculative," and by this term he does not mean trying to guess where the stock market might be headed in a month's time, but rather what we might term the reason that deals with evaluation of abstract truths. For example, if we hold that in Euclidian geometry a triangle is defined as a polygon having three sides and the sum of whose angles equals 180 degrees, then each and every object that has these characteristics will be a triangle. This proposition would be universally or "necessarily" true by its very definition. If someone were to call a four-sided polygon a "triangle" this would be demonstrably false since we have posited that the definition of a triangle contains three and only three sides. Universal moral precepts tend to be on this level as they express general truths about the objective moral order. Thomas Aquinas expressed the foundational moral precept as *bonum est faciendum et prosequendum et malum vitandum* (*ST I-II*, q. 94, art. 2) that I think I translate faithfully (if not literalistically) as "the nature and meaning of what we term the 'good' is that we are to be engaged in doing, fostering, and supporting it, while the nature and meaning of what we term 'evil' we ought to be seeking to minimize or avoid as much as possible." Thomas says that all the other principles of the natural law depend on this first principle. He offers no further proof for this principle since he believes it to be self-evident, that is, true in the abstract, and that any rational person would affirm these definitions of "good" and "evil" even though we might have different words for these concepts such as *bonum, die Güte, il bene, la bonté,* and so on through the world's languages.

Important as this and related universal precepts of the natural law are, Thomas notes that these principles are insufficient for giving us concrete guidance in a vast number of our ethical decisions. There is another type of reason he calls practical reason, by which we apply the universal precepts of the natural law in our everyday lives. For Thomas practical reason does not mean "efficient," "effective," or "pragmatic," but simply is right reason *(recta ratio)* that is put into concrete practice. Thomas sums up the differences between speculative and practical reason in this way:

> The speculative reason, however, is differently situated in this matter, from the practical reason. For, since the speculative reason is busied chiefly with the necessary things, which cannot be otherwise than they are, its proper conclusions, like the universal principles, contain the truth without fail. The practical reason, on the other hand, is busied with contingent matters, about which human actions are concerned: and consequently, although there is necessity in the general principles, the more we descend to matters of detail, the more frequently we encounter defects (*ST I-II*, q. 94, art. 4).[8]

Some of the vocabulary Thomas uses here needs to be clarified. First, the term "contingent" does not refer to some sort of future conditional status such as "if it rains on Saturday the parade will be canceled," but simply means that our concrete situations in which we find ourselves are "changeable" or "able to be changed," and thus we

---

[8] Unless otherwise indicated, all references to the *Summa Theologiae* of Thomas Aquinas are taken from the translation of the Fathers of the English Dominican Province (1947 Benzinger Brothers Inc., Hypertext Version 1995, 1996 New Advent Inc.) and available electronically through the New Advent web-site at http://www.newadvent.org/summa/.

cannot come to specific moral conclusions in the concrete that will be universal in the sense of absolutely the same in every time and place. Thomas notes that the general principles may hold true, but as we get down to the nitty gritty of our actual situation ("the more we descend to matters of detail"), he notes that here we will encounter what he calls "defects." The word "defects" does not mean moral lapses or failures but probably would be better translated as "legitimate differences or deviations" from the general principle. Thus, the more concrete we become the more of "necessity" our moral conclusions about what is objectively right will be open to error, fallible, incomplete, and/or open to change or modification in the future. Thomas expresses this important distinction in this way:

> But as to the proper conclusions of the practical reason, neither is the truth or rectitude the same for all, nor, where it is the same, is it equally known by all. Thus it is right and true for all to act according to reason: and from this principle it follows as a proper conclusion, that goods entrusted to another should be restored to their owner. Now this is true for the majority of cases *[ut in pluribus]*: but it may happen in a particular case that it would be injurious, and therefore unreasonable, to restore goods held in trust; for instance, if they are claimed for the purpose of fighting against one's country. And this principle will be found to fail the more, according as we descend further into detail, e.g. if one were to say that goods held in trust should be restored with such and such a guarantee, or in such and such a way; because the greater the number of conditions added, the greater the number of ways in which the principle may fail, so that it be not right to restore or not to restore (*ST I-II*, q. 94, art. 4).

What Thomas Aquinas shows us here is that there are not only two types of moral reasoning going on, but also there are important differences in the types of moral norms we use in the exercise of both speculative and practical reason. Building on Thomas' basic insights, I offer three general levels of moral norms. The first level is what Thomas himself has called "universal precepts" and refers to those moral concepts that are universally true by relation to the foundational precept about the nature of good and evil, in that the former is to be done and fostered and the latter avoided or minimized. For example, we might say that the maxim "Drive safely" is just such a universal principle. While all people might agree that this is a valid moral principle, it really does not help us much in the orderly regulation of vehicular traffic. Therefore we need additional moral norms to guide us.

Thomas calls this next level "general principles," and thus these moral norms are good standards that help us to come to a better understanding of what it means to drive safely. I term this second level "middle axioms," since these are located between universal precepts and the more concrete material norms that further build on both the universal precepts and the middle axioms. In the section from the *Summa Theologiae* quoted above, Aquinas used as an example of a general principle (or middle axiom) the notion that "goods entrusted to another should be restored to their owner." However, Thomas went on to add immediately that while this principle was generally true, it was not absolutely true: "This is true for the majority of cases *[ut in pluribus]*: but it may happen in a particular case that it would be injurious, and therefore unreasonable, to restore goods held in trust." Here we find Thomas' exposition of the principle that certain moral norms or "laws" hold *ut in pluribus,* that is, in most, but not all, cases. This *ut in pluribus* principle does not mean that the moral norm is rendered useless by the legitimate exception. Rather, this principle shows us that while the principle enunciated is important, its application is somewhat incomplete and still needs to be guided by our practical reason and discernment process before we can conclude that it truly binds us in this or that particular instance.

To return to our traffic discussion, we might call this sort of middle axiom that binds *ut in pluribus* the moral norm that we obey the posted speeding limit. Now as soon as we suggest that there are certain moral norms that do not apply in each and every case, some people will become very uncomfortable and begin to wonder if we are not lapsing into a sort of moral relativism where anything goes. This is simply not true, whether in the thirteenth century of Thomas Aquinas who articulated this position, or anytime before or after. Morality is not mathematics and so there will necessarily be a certain amount of ambiguity and changeability (what Thomas Aquinas called "contingency") in our morally complex world. We could construct an abstract set of moral norms which would never admit exceptions; the problem is that this set would not be grounded in reality.

To return to our ongoing example of speed limits, we know that generally speaking if we obey the posted limits we will be driving safely and responsibly. However, are there any legitimate instances in which it might be morally possible and even obligatory to ignore the posted speed limit of fifty-five m.p.h.? I suspect that even traffic officers might join most of the rest of us in answering in the affirmative. For example, let us consider the following scenario: it is three o'clock in the morning and you are living on a sheep ranch in Montana about forty miles outside of Billings, the nearest town. Suddenly you are awakened by your spouse who is suffering from severe chest pains. To summon an ambulance to make the eighty-mile round trip would take a significant amount of time, and you know that immediate medical care is crucial in the successful treatment of heart attack patients. So what do you do? The civil law, i.e., the posted night-time speed limit of fifty-five m.p.h., is crystal clear, and yet if a highway patrol officer were to intercept you driving at eighty-five m.p.h., s/he would probably not issue a ticket, but rather give you a high-speed escort into town.

This reasonable dispensation from the law in force is an example of the principle of *epikeia,* and in turn this well-established principle of moral theology shows us again how moral norms are of various kinds, and that very often they need to be interpreted and refined in order to fit adequately the concrete situation at hand. The term comes from the Greek and means "fitting," "suitable," or "reasonable." It was used by Aristotle in his *Nichomachean Ethics* (5.10) to correct a defective law in terms of universal legal justice. Such correction was envisioned in terms of interpreting the intent or mind of the law-giver as it would be applied to this anomalous situation that was either not foreseen and/or covered by the actual law. Thus, it is applied to human law traditionally as a dispensation from the law in a particular instance, since if the legitimate law-givers could have foreseen this particular set of circumstances then they certainly would have approved of the dispensation from observing the speed limit in this case. Thomas Aquinas also treats *epikeia* (see his *Summa Contra Gentiles,* 1.3, c. 125 and c. 122). However, Thomas does not really see *epikeia* so much as "dispensing" one from the observance of the law, as an exercise of human right reason to improve and make the concrete law more perfect. For Thomas *epikeia* was a virtue, and like all virtues it should be practiced in order to become stronger and more helpful to the human community.

To return to our discussion of moral norms and the natural law, we might chart the relevant traffic norms in this way. "Drive safely" would be a universal precept; even if my spouse needs to get to the hospital quickly, this does not suggest that I drive at such a high rate of speed that would put both of our lives at serious risk. While the norm "drive safely" might be universally true in the abstract realm, it still lacks concrete specificity to aid us in trying to determine what we should do in this or that situation on the road. Thus, the second-level moral norm (a middle axiom) in this case would be "obey the posted speed limit." This is the kind of norm that will be true in most cases, but as we have seen from the above example, not in each and every case. This kind of middle axiom is what Thomas Aquinas means by his expression that this law would bind *ut in pluribus,* literally in most, but not every, instance.

While middle axioms move towards greater specificity and concreteness, they too need further detail. The middle axiom of "obey the posted speed limit" would make no sense if there were no posted speed limits. The various posted speed limits are the concrete material norms for different circumstances, such as drive fifteen m.p.h. in a school zone and on the expressway drive sixty-five m.p.h. by day and fifty-five m.p.h. by night. Obviously one concrete material norm of a single speed limit would not fit the variety of different cases. There are so many different driving contexts, such as the interstate expressway, a state highway, a country road, a city arterial, and a residential boulevard. Obviously these different types of roads imply different driving conditions and require different speed limits. Similarly, even on the same road there can be different contexts which in turn require different speed limits. A school zone might have a posted limit of fifteen m.p.h. when children are present, but at other times of the day or night the limit might be twenty-five m.p.h.

These differing speed limits take into account what Thomas Aquinas terms contingency, namely, the changeable aspects of our concrete lives. This contingency will change our moral norms. Finally, as we have demonstrated with our nocturnal Montana heart-attack scenario, even the best devised traffic laws cannot foresee *every* possible set of circumstances that might confront us at one time or another. This is where our practical reason needs to be helped by the virtue of *epikeia* so that we can apply the relevant moral norm to our concrete situation in a prudent manner. The exercise of this virtue requires a certain amount of freedom, and this necessary moral freedom often makes us leery of falling into some sort of moral laxism or relativism, in which we seem either not to care if there are moral norms or not, or we pretend to make them up as we go along to suit our own needs and desires. While this is certainly a real danger, it is a danger we will have to face. A one-size-fits-all set of concrete moral norms would probably cause more harm than good. If this conclusion is true for speed limits, then it will be true for a considerably wider range of moral situations, and here is where the moral debates have become particularly sharp and even acrimonious.

Levels of Moral Norms Summary

- Universal Precepts
- Middle Axioms
- Concrete Material Norms

- *Always* binding, expressed as abstract truths, such as "drive safely"
- *Generally* true, in most cases (*ut in pluribus*) but exceptions exist
- Apply to a specific situation but are more open to both *change* and *fallibility*

Moving In: From Norms to Moral Action

We have now seen that moral norms do not exist in just one variety nor that they are all equal in authority. Even if we attend carefully to the level and variety of moral norms, that still does not give us the whole picture of the meaning of moral actions either in themselves or as they relate to the person who performs them. Evaluation of moral acts in the tradition of Roman Catholic moral theology always has turned to a consideration of the so-called *fontes moralitatis* or sources (fonts) of morality. These three aspects of a moral act are: (1) the action in itself as seen by its goal or purpose (what was called the *finis operis* or "end" or goal of the action), (2) the intention the person had in doing this action (called the *finis operantis* or "end" or goal of the agent), and (3) the circumstances, or in other words, the real-life context out of which the person is performing the act. Only by considering all three of these fonts together can we come to a moral evaluation of any moral action.

Even though the manualist tradition held that one had to take into account all three aspects of a moral action, it was difficult to talk about intentions and circumstances since these would necessarily differ according not just to each person but with each and every action. Since one could not possibly anticipate every conceivable set of circumstances and intentions, the manualists tended to focus just on the so-called "objective" nature of the acts in themselves. These were treated in an abstract manner, that is, removed from a consideration of the moral agents themselves, their intentions in performing these actions, and their concrete situations and circumstances in which the intentions were formed and the actions done. Thus, over time in the minds of many Catholics the impression grew that one could identify with virtual certainty the moral meaning of an entire action just by looking at the so-called objective nature of the act itself, without considering either the intention of the persons in doing the action or the situation in which they found themselves as well as the other factors that led them to do this or that (i.e., the circumstances of the moral action). To a large extent the over-reliance on the physicalist paradigm for moral analysis reinforced this tendency.

In the Middle Ages there was a sharp debate among theologians as to what ultimately determined the moral meaning of an act. Was it primarily the action in itself, the so-called *finis operis* that was the key criterion in determining whether an action was morally right or wrong, or was it rather the intention of the agent in performing the action, the *finis operantis*, that was paramount in evaluating a moral action? Peter Lombard, Bernard of Clairvaux, and others held that it was the *finis operis*, the action itself which determined the moral rightness or wrongness, and therefore the moral goodness or badness of the moral agent. In their view it was the end of the action itself and *not* the intention (and presumably the circumstances) of the person performing the action which was morally determinative. This position was contradicted by Thomas Aquinas who judged that the ultimate moral meaning of an action had to be found within the intention of the moral agent who performed the action. The reasoning Thomas employed noted that a true moral action had to be what the tradition called an *actus humanus*, a human act. For an act to be genuinely human meant that it had to be willed, or voluntary in Thomas' vocabulary. The voluntary action arises from the will of the agent and expresses the agent's intention (*finis operantis*) in performing the act.

Thomas recognized that while this intention was the key to any genuine moral act, the intention by itself did not fully describe the moral action in its totality. Thomas said there was another aspect of the act which is found in the end of the act in itself, the *finis operis*. It may be helpful to quote Thomas himself on these points, and I include in brackets Thomas' reference to the key moral concepts:

> Certain actions are called human [*actus humanus*], inasmuch as they are voluntary. . . Now, in a voluntary action, there is a twofold action, viz. the interior action of the will, and the external action: and each of these actions has its object. The end is properly the object of the interior act of the will [*finis operantis*]: while the object of the external action, is that on which the action is brought to bear [*finis operis*]. Therefore just as the external action takes its species from the object on which it bears [*finis operis*]; so the interior act of the will [*finis operantis*] takes its species from the end, as from its own proper object (*ST II-I*, q. 18, art. 6).

Here we should note that Thomas asserts the end of the human act "is properly the object of the interior act of the will [*finis operantis*]." Thus, the true *moral* meaning of the act cannot be considered apart from that which the individual intends or wills in his or her action. Nevertheless, there is a way in which we can consider, from an observer's perspective, the morality of an act by looking at the impact of the action on the world, i.e., the *finis operis*. However, Thomas notes that this consideration will give us only the "material" meaning of the act in question, and *not* the "formal" meaning. It is the formal meaning which constitutes the moral meaning of the act for the agent him/herself, i.e., it "forms" the person's own intention, which in turn guides the action undertaken. For example, to return to our encounter with the Gestapo, the intention behind our speech is not to tell a lie, but to safeguard the lives of the innocent Jews we have hidden in the attic. Thus the *finis operis* of our speech is not a lie, but safeguarding innocent life. How do we know this? By looking at the factual accuracy of the words? No! By looking at the *finis operantis* or the moral intention behind those words. It may be helpful to quote Thomas Aquinas directly on this point:

> Now that which is on the part of the will is formal in regard to that which is on the part of the external action: because the will uses the limbs to act as instruments; nor have external actions any measure of morality, save in so far as they are voluntary. Consequently the species of a human act is considered formally with regard to the end, but materially with regard to the object of the external action (*ST II-I*, q. 18, art. 6).

The above discussion admittedly is a bit complex, and requires that we enter into the philosophical and linguistic world of scholastic theology in order to follow it clearly. Yet, it is crucial that we do understand these terms, their inter-relations, and the ensuing distinctions clearly if we are to be able to follow some of the current debates within contemporary moral theology, which of course does not invent itself anew *ab ovo* in every age, but always works out of its own tradition. Thomas Aquinas and scholastic theology is a critical part of that tradition.

That tradition, however, needs to be recast into a language that contemporary men and women can understand clearly and completely. I suspect that one reason for some of our tensions and debates in moral theology today is that not everyone really understands just what is being said. To try to summarize the neo-scholastic tradition of Thomas Aquinas and those who followed him is certainly no easy task.[9] What Thomas has shown us though is that we cannot discover the true meaning of any moral action without looking carefully at the action itself, the circumstances in which the action was performed, and the intention that the person had for performing the action. In the real world we have to admit that often these three component parts are themselves multi-layered and many-faceted. Why did the benefactor give a large donation to a school? What was his or her *finis operantis* or intention? To aid the school certainly, but probably also to gain a bit of positive press as well. The human heart has many, many compartments and it is difficult at times, if not impossible, to separate out our magnanimity from our vanity. Similarly, the impact of our actions is rarely clear-cut and neat as well. While the school may be helped by this benefactor's donation, this means that the money will not be used for some other legitimate need. We could go on and on, but by now it is clear that morality is rarely divided into two neat categories labeled right and wrong that all can agree upon. Our moral world is complex indeed.

Debate over Intrinsically Evil Acts

While the major points of our general discussion of the natural law and moral norms to this point probably would garner support from most moral theologians, there is still one area connected with this area which remains one of the sharpest debates in contemporary moral theology, namely, the precise meaning of the term "intrinsically evil" acts. However, unlike other debates that center on a real difference of opinion about either "truth" or "practicality" of a certain position, I believe that the debate over intrinsically evil acts could be amerliorated if not

[9] The bibliography on Thomas Aquinas is vast, but some particularly helpful works which would help in understanding his ethics include the following: Paul Waddell, *The Primacy of Love: An Introduction to the Ethics of Thomas Aquinas* (New York: Paulist Press, 1992); Pamela M. Hall, *Narrative and the Natural Law: An Interpretation of Thomistic Ethics* (Notre Dame, Ind.: University of Notre Dame Press, 1994); and Jean Porter, *Natural and Divine Law: Reclaiming the Tradition for Christian Ethics* (Grand Rapids, Mich.: Eerdmans, 1999).

actually resolved by a more careful investigation into the precise meanings of terms that stand behind the claim or counter-claim that there
are actions that are always and everywhere wrong regardless of the
moral agents' own intentions and the circumstances in which they find
themselves. Discussion of this debate will also serve as a way of bringing together some of the loose threads in a previous treatment of the
natural law and lay some further groundwork for our discussion of
conscience and culture in chapter 4.

To begin our discussion of the contemporary debate, let us consider
carefully the exposition of the claim for intrinsically evil acts that
Pope John Paul II put forth in *Veritatis splendor,* his 1993 encyclical on
Fundamental Moral Theology. In order to understand the points contained in this encyclical, we have to consider the larger context out of
which the Pope was writing and some of the aims he hoped to achieve
in this treatise. Much of the encyclical is concerned with the perception that contemporary morality has become excessively relativistic
and denies both the existence of an objective moral order as well as the
possibility that we can know and act in accord with this order, or in
other words, the ontological and epistemological claim we discussed
earlier in this chapter. It is important to keep in mind these concerns
so that we can properly interpret what Pope John Paul II actually said
in this document. Here is the beginning of the paragraph that treats
most explicitly the notion of intrinsically evil acts:

> Reason attests that there are objects of the human act which are by their
> nature "incapable of being ordered" to God, because they radically
> contradict the good of the person made in his image. These are the acts
> which, in the Church's moral tradition, have been termed "intrinsically
> evil" *(intrinsece malum)*: they are such *always and per se,* in other words,
> on account of their very object, and quite apart from the ulterior inten-
> tions of the one acting and the circumstances (*VS* #80, emphases in the
> original).

In order to understand this text fully we need to do a little exegesis
of some of the terms employed. When the Pope says that "there are ob-
jects of the human act which are by their nature 'incapable of being ordered' to God," he is referring primarily to the *finis operis* of a moral act,
that is, its goal as an action. Moreover, the formulation here is in the abstract: no particular moral act has been named; the Pope is simply saying that we can conceive of certain sorts of actions that would contradict
the moral dignity of the human individual who is made in God's image
and therefore ought to be treated with the respect that dignity implies,

as well as to reflect that same dignity in his or her own moral life. In other words, there are real actions and attitudes that would embody our human dignity, as well as counter actions and stances that would conflict with and/or attack our human dignity. This position is the grounding premise of moral theology that there is an "objective" moral order that is our first ontological claim of the natural law. It then follows that certain moral actions would be in accord with this moral order and others would be at odds, or contradict this moral order.

There really is no disagreement over this fundamental assertion among contemporary moral theologians, though many of them would choose not to use the vocabulary of "intrinsic evil" since it can be easily misunderstood or confused. But virtually all Roman Catholic theologians would be in substantial agreement with the basic premises of the claims involved since ultimately they do support the notion of an objective moral order. The alternative would be to deny this objectivity to morality and if that were the case, whatever one would consider "moral" would have to be grounded in some other way. If there were no objective moral order, "morality" would refer to whatever a culture, individual, or group considered to be good or bad, right or wrong. Of course such moral theories exist, and they are all varieties of some form of relativism, such as emotivism, intuitionism, utilitarianism, or consequentialism.[10]

Returning to *Veritatis splendor*, the Pope goes on to provide some concrete examples of such intrinsically evil acts, quoting a list that is given in Vatican II's Pastoral Constitution on the Church in the Modern World, *Gaudium et spes:*

> Whatever is hostile to life itself, such as any kind of homicide, genocide, abortion, euthanasia and voluntary suicide; whatever violates the integrity of the human person, such as mutilation, physical and mental torture and attempts to coerce the spirit; whatever is offensive to human dignity, such as subhuman living conditions, arbitrary imprisonment, deportation, slavery, prostitution and trafficking in women and children. . . (*VS* #80, quoting *GS* #27).

[10] Though sometimes those of one school of moral theologians may accuse others of another school as espousing one or another version of these relativism theories, I know of no Catholic moral theologian him/herself who accepts the label of being a moral relativist. Since no moral theologian self-identifies as being a relativist, I believe we should be very circumspect in attaching this label to another. It is more likely that we have simply failed to understand the other theologian's position clearly. In that case our efforts would be better spent at seeking clarification rather than vilification.

The Pope's initial description of intrinsically evil acts as "whatever is hostile to life itself" echoes the definition of sin employed by Thomas Aquinas: "God is only offended by us because we act against our own well-being" (*Summa contra gentiles*, III, 122: *Non enim Deus a nobis offenditur nisi ex eo quod contra nostrum bonum agimus*). Again, on the level of abstraction the Pope and most moral theologians would stand in perfect agreement. But once we consider just exactly what kind of concrete action genuinely is "hostile to life itself," we begin to see some difficulties. Let us take just a couple of examples to illustrate this point. The official Vatican English translation of the encyclical changes the quotation from *Gaudium et spes* in one key word, by replacing "murder" with "homicide." Thus, while the official Vatican English translation of *Gaudium et spes* still reads that "any kind of murder" is wrong, the translation of *Veritatis Splendor* does seem to say that "any kind of homicide" would be intrinsically evil. Here we can see the importance of linguistic as well as moral distinctions, as evidenced in these choices of one term or translation for another.[11] If one uses the simple definition of "homicide" as the "killing of a human person" then either this encyclical seems to be reversing centuries of Roman Catholic moral teaching in this regard, or its position needs to be translated and nuanced more carefully in order to be correctly understood and applied. St. Thomas Aquinas, for example, argues that one *can* engage in "homicide" in the case of killing an unjust aggressor (cf. *ST II-II*, q. 64, n. 7).

This position of Thomas is foundational not only to the principle of the double effect, but to a whole range of other actions including the just war theory, as well as the moral justification of capital punishment. Likewise our legal traditions recognize a whole range of moral meanings for homicide, ranging from self-defense (justifiable homicide) through manslaughter (involuntary and voluntary) to various levels of pre-meditation involved in murder (e.g., first degree, second degree, and so on). What both Thomas Aquinas and our legal tradition point to in reference to the killing of a person is that we cannot have any complete moral analysis of the act *in the concrete* without attending both to intention and circumstances. Thus, we can say that while murder is intrinsically evil, not each and every act that results

---

[11] In both instances I am relying on the English translation provided on the official website of the Holy See, found at www.vatican.va in July 2002. The Latin text for both terms is the same, but unfortunately most people reading and using *Veritatis splendor* would not be consulting the Latin *editio typica* (i.e., the official version of a Vatican document).

in a person's death is murder. What would be the key differences? Intention and circumstances!

In summary, we can accept the notion of intrinsically evil acts as long as we recognize that this expression is more helpful in detailing the sorts of acts that should never be done because they fundamentally contradict human flourishing and God's goodness. But whether this or that particular concrete act qualifies as being intrinsically evil depends at least in part on a presumptive analysis of intention and circumstances along with the action in itself. The simple physical performance of a set of activities that together comprise the action cannot be moral or immoral unless the intention and freedom of the moral agent is actualized in the concrete. Otherwise we would have described what traditionally was termed an *actus hominis*, an activity of a human person, but one without the necessary freedom and intention to make it a truly moral act (i.e., an *actus humanus*).

Perhaps an admittedly ridiculous example may illustrate this point. An actor who plays a role which involves him firing a pistol in the course of the murder scene in Act II obviously is not trying to murder in reality his fellow actor. But what if by accident the prop master inadvertently replaced the stage pistol with a real loaded gun? The critical moment in the play arrives, the actor draws his pistol and bang! . . . but this time his fellow thespian falls truly dead. Has the actor who pulled the trigger committed the intrinsically evil act of murder? Clearly not. What then was missing? We have a dead body killed by the firing of the gun—what might *seem* from a photographer's perspective to be the "objective nature of the act." Certainly this is a homicide, objectively speaking. But this homicide, tragic though it is, is not a morally evil act on the part of the unfortunate actor who fired the fatal shot. What is missing from a moral point of view is the intent to commit murder. Furthermore, the circumstances of the homicide (e.g., the actor is justly playing out the murder scene and has no idea that he is wielding a loaded gun) further excuse this unfortunate fellow from moral culpability.

So we have to concede that we cannot have a genuine intrinsically evil act unless to a sufficient extent the requisite moral intention and concrete circumstances have already been adequately factored into our moral analysis of the act. Hopefully both the Pope and all those moral theologians who still prefer to employ the terminology of intrinsically evil acts in fact would be in general agreement with the above analysis. Certainly none of them would suggest that the actor who unwittingly fired the gun had in fact committed murder. So if, when *Veritatis splendor* asserts that there are the acts which are termed "'intrinsically evil' *(intrinsece malum)*: they are such *always and per se,* in other words, on account of their very object, and quite apart from the ulterior intentions of the one acting and the circumstances" *(VS* #80), this statement can make logical sense then the encyclical must mean something more than just what we might call the photographic account of what transpired.[12] The photographic account may seem to show us clearly that one man has pulled a gun and fired it at another. Yet this photographic account does *not* show us the indispensable element for any *human moral* action, namely, the moral agent's intention *(finis operantis).* Only by looking carefully at the intention and circumstances can we see that the object of this act, the *finis operis,* was not murder by effective drama. What then shows us the true object or *finis operis* of the act in question? Not the photographic account, but rather the combination of the intention of the agent operating in this particular set of circumstances, in other words his *finis operantis.* In short, this echoes Thomas Aquinas' observation that the moral analysis of the *finis operis* ultimately is found in a careful consideration of the *finis operantis.*

It might be possible to interpret *Veritatis splendor* in this way since Pope John Paul II does include a gloss on the culpability or moral responsibility of the person who might commit such an action, and here he explicitly references what otherwise seem to have been the two missing fonts of morality in his earlier formulation, namely, the intention of the moral agent and the given circumstances out of which she or he was performing the evil act: "If acts are intrinsically evil, a good intention or particular circumstances can diminish their evil, but they cannot remove it. They remain 'irremediably' evil acts; *per se* and in themselves they are not capable of being ordered to God and to the good of the person" *(VS* #80). In the case of the actor mistakenly

---

[12] *Veritatis splendor* has been justifiably critiqued on precisely this point, namely, that the encyclical's presentation of both the moral tradition and contemporary versions of moral action are incomplete and seriously misleading at times. See the essays in Joseph Selling and Jan Jans Kok, eds. *The Splendour of Accuracy: An Examination of the Assertions Made by Veritatis Splendor* (Grand Rapids, Mich.: William B. Eerdmans; Campen, The Netherlands: Pharos Publishing Co., 1994); and Michael E. Allsopp and John J. O'Keefe, eds., *Veritatis Splendor: American Responses* (Kansas City: Sheed & Ward, 1995); and John Wilkins, et al., ed., *Understanding "Veritatis splendor." The Encyclical Letter of Pope John Paul II and the Church's Moral Teaching* (London: SPCK, 1994). This last book is also published as *Considering Veritatis Splendor* (Cleveland: Pilgrim Press, 1994).

shot dead, we are all agreed that an evil has taken place, though not a moral evil on the part of the actor who fired the gun. A man is dead; this is evil, but just as in any other accident or natural tragedy, we would not term this a moral evil. If we look at the intention in the performance of the dramatic act of firing the pistol, we see it to be good or right, i.e., to provide dramatic entertainment. The particular circumstances (the gun mistakenly having been switched by the prop master) would seem to do more than merely diminish any moral evil in this case; they remove it entirely. Yet we can agree that an evil remains in the fact that an innocent person has died before his time, though we cannot call this either an intrinsic or a moral evil. In this sort of circumstance moralists often employ another term such as ontic or pre-moral evil. The evil is a real evil; a man has been killed, but we judge this to be a tragic accident and not a culpable moral act.

If in fact the Pope and most theologians would be in agreement on this preceding analysis (as I believe they would), then what is the reason for the continued emphasis of this expression regarding intrinsically evil acts? Some theologians would argue that the term creates more confusion than it resolves, but clearly the Pope and others do not agree. So what is their point? I think a clue is found in the final part of this paragraph when even though the Pope does acknowledge that intention and circumstances must play a role in the moral evaluation of the act, he still desires to underscore that the intention and circumstances cannot of themselves change a morally evil act into a morally good act: "Consequently, circumstances or intentions can never transform an act intrinsically evil by virtue of its object into an act 'subjectively' good or defensible as a choice" (*VS* #80). In short, he believes that one of the critical dangers we are facing in our contemporary situation is that many people are losing a sense of morality and that they feel that virtually *any* "good" intention and/or virtually *any* combination of mitigating circumstances would justify doing that which from a truly moral perspective we would agree is morally evil.

While this may be a real danger, there are other dangers if we fail to make the careful distinctions involved in a full understanding of the term intrinsically evil act. I have encountered many instances in which people have insisted that this or that action is always wrong because the Church says that it is intrinsically evil, when in fact the particular act they believe is condemned is in fact allowed. For example, one of my theology students in a bioethics class told me that under no circumstances could the progesterone pill ever be taken, regardless of intention and/or circumstances, since the pill was contraceptive and that both Paul VI's *Humanae vitae* and John Paul II's *Veritatis splendor* stated emphatically that artificial contraception was intrinsically evil. Therefore, my student erroneously concluded, any usage of this medication for any reason whatsoever would be morally wrong. One simply could not take into any moral evaluation of the act other possible circumstances in which the use of the pill would be medically indicated. For my student this would be tantamount to bringing intention and circumstances into consideration, and he felt this was explicitly forbidden by calling the pill intrinsically evil. I asked him to read to me paragraph 15 of *Humanae vitae,* which states that "the Church, on the contrary, does not at all consider illicit the use of those therapeutic means truly necessary to cure diseases of the organism, even if an impediment to procreation, which may be foreseen, should result there from, provided such impediment is not, for whatever motive, directly willed." When I asked my student if this paragraph allowed for the use of the progesterone pill to help regulate a woman's menstrual cycle (as is common), even though the contraceptive effect could be foreseen he replied in the negative: if there was any possibility of a contraceptive effect then the pill could not be used, since contraception was intrinsically evil, and the notion of intrinsic evil meant that we could never take into account any other intentions or circumstances. While I would give high marks for tenacity to this student, I would have to give him considerably lower marks on the correct reading of both the tradition and the current teaching of the magisterium on this issue.

I recount this anecdote to point out both that an unnuanced bandying about of the term "intrinsic evil" from an overly narrow physicalist paradigm may lead to false moral analysis. We need to indicate once again that in the concrete the evaluation of any and every moral act *must* take into sufficient account the intention and circumstances involved. The use of the term intrinsic evil simply means that supposedly this consideration of intention and circumstances has already been done, such as when we maintain that while each and every killing of a human person is not intrinsically evil, murder most certainly is. What is the difference between killing and murder? Intention and circumstances! In order to look more carefully at just how intention and circumstances enter the moral arena we must now shift our focus from the abstract theory of the natural law and look at how individual men and women seek to foster the good and avoid the evil in their everyday lives. This is where conscience and culture come into the picture, and where the rational claim and the sacred claim axes intersect. Yet before we turn to this intersection, we need to look more carefully at the sacred claim axis, and this will be the focus of our next chapter.

3

Scripture and Ethics:
Moving Along the Sacred Claim Axis

> Jesus went on with his disciples to the villages of Caesarea Philippi; and on the way he asked his disciples, "Who do people say that I am?" And they answered him, "John the Baptist; and others, Elijah; and still others, one of the prophets." He asked them, "But who do you say that I am?" Peter answered him, "You are the Messiah." And he sternly ordered them not to tell anyone about him. Then he began to teach them that the Son of Man must undergo great suffering, and be rejected by the elders, the chief priests, and the scribes, and be killed, and after three days rise again. He said all this quite openly. And Peter took him aside and began to rebuke him. But turning and looking at his disciples, he rebuked Peter and said, "Get behind me, Satan! For you are setting your mind not on divine things but on human things" (Mark 8: 27-33).

Though this particular biblical passage did not find a prominent place in the architectural adornment of St. Peter's Basilica in Rome (Peter's confession in Matthew 16, "You are Peter and upon this rock . . . ." was used instead), it does contain several important elements that all Christians ought to bear in mind as they seek to live out their lives in a distinctively Christian manner. First, in Mark's version Peter is given a stark choice in this encounter: either he changes a key facet of his value system and theological world view, or he can no longer be a disciple of Jesus. Jesus does not articulate a logical, reasonable, or ethical argument in natural law terms—rather he shows us that if we have faith that he indeed is the Messiah then this belief lays a sacred claim on our entire lives. This sacred claim calls on us not only to revise how we think and look on ourselves and our world, it also calls us to concrete action as Jesus makes clear in the very next verses:

> He called the crowd with his disciples, and said to them, "If any want to become my followers, let them deny themselves and take up their cross and follow me. For those who want to save their life will lose it, and those who lose their life for my sake, and for the sake of the gospel, will save it. For what will it profit them to gain the whole world and forfeit their life?" (Mark 8: 34-36)

Jesus lays out a vision which demands a choice and a response that ultimately comes down to life or death. However, he does not call us in the language of abstract moral norms of a natural law as much as he challenges to find our formative identity in a close discipleship relation to himself.[1] But this discipleship call is not in the last analysis only Jesus-centered—it is gospel directed as well. Thus, the Christian moral life has to be oriented to both Jesus the Christ (Messiah) and to the gospel that Jesus preaches at God's command, and which mission is handed on to the whole Church. Discipleship therefore involves every follower in a group that is more than a collection of individuals gathered for a common purpose; it is a real community that likewise has to find and continually test the truth of its formative identity in fidelity both to Jesus and to the gospel message. This is the deepest meaning of the genuine Tradition of the Church, namely, how it is authentically lived both in its identity as disciples of Jesus Christ and as co-proclaimers of the Lord's Gospel. It is this reciprocal interrelation between Christ and the discipleship community that comprises what I term the sacred claim axis.

As we discussed in chapter 1, the sacred claim moves back and forth from God's revelation contained in Scripture to the living out of that sacred claim in the ongoing life of the community. What is it that makes this claim sacred? The quick and obvious answer is that it comes from God; in other words, we believe the Bible is not just a book of wisdom but God's own special revelation to us. However, when we apply the Bible to our moral discernment and actions we need to take special care that we have a proper understanding of just what is meant by referring to the Bible as the revealed word of God.

---

[1] On this point see David Rhoads, "Losing Life for Others: Mark's Standards of Judgement," *Interpretation* 47 (1993) 358–69. Rhoads shows that Mark contrasts the ways of the world and the self-centeredness of people's desires for what they want for themselves (e.g., saving one's own life, acquiring the world, lording it over others, etc.) with the vision of what God wants for people, namely, to have faith, loyalty to God's word, the courage to live for others, to give up one's possessions, to be the least and the servant of all. Living out God's vision gains the disciples a new family and life eternal.

First, we should be clear that what makes the Bible truly revelatory is not so much found in the nature of its composition process. We do not count the Bible as revelation because we believe that somehow God dictated its contents word for word to the various authors. Rather as Christians we hold the Bible as sacred because of what it reveals to us about who God is. Who is God exactly? Theologically this question is answered in any number of ways such as "God is love" (cf. 1 John 4:16), but one traditional answer always drove the question deeper: *Deus semper maior*—God is always more—more than we can ever imagine, more than we can nail down here and now, and more than we can ever know. This description of God is important for the sub-discipline of theology we call moral theology, since it means that in our attempts to live out our lives in ethical conformity to the image of God and God's will for us. All of us will have to practice ongoing discernment of God's Spirit to make sure that we are responding as best as we can to the one and true God, and not worshiping some false image of God.

As Christians we believe that God's highest and definitive revelation is *not* found in the Bible as a sacred text, but rather in the *person* of Jesus Christ. Thus it will have to be Jesus Christ and not a given biblical text that has final authority as the ultimate norming norm, the *norma normans non normata,* of our lives. This basic point will be crucial when we turn to how we are to consider Scripture as a moral resource for our lives, especially when various scriptural texts and themes point in different directions. The term "morality" does not occur as such in the Bible, and therefore we have to look more to the Bible more for an overall moral vision than to a set of ethical proscriptions for which to guide and conform our lives.

Similarly, it is not a particular set of scriptural verses that in itself exercises a sacred claim on us, but only insofar as that biblical claim corresponds to an overall sound vision of God and God's definitive revelation of God's self in Jesus Christ. Perhaps a biblical example may clarify this point. "If your right eye causes you to sin, tear it out and throw it away; it is better for you to lose one of your members than for your whole body to be thrown into hell. And if your right hand causes you to sin, cut it off and throw it away; it is better for you to lose one of your members than for your whole body to go into hell" (Matt 5:29-30). These verses taken from the second of the Six Antitheses in Matthew's version of the Sermon on the Mount may well be part of the *ipsissima verba,* the very words of Jesus, and so we might think that either his followers would be virtually sinless or that self-mutilation would be widely practiced. History tells us though that neither is the case. Even if Jesus did utter these words, a literal interpretation and application would not seem to correspond to his larger gospel message of compassion and mercy, forgiveness and reconciliation. This example shows us that what is sacred, what has a claim on us, is Jesus and the gospel, and not a particular passage or verse.

But how are we to approach the Bible if we mean to take it seriously as a moral source and resource for our lives? What would be a methodology that might help guide us in this task? Returning to the model proposed in chapter 1, while Scripture is a very important source for our moral lives, it is neither the only source nor does it stand apart from the others. The scriptural quadrant overlaps and integrates with the other three sectors of Tradition, Human Experience, and especially our understanding of the Normatively Human. This integration is another reason why we should not take the gospel verses from Matthew 5 in a literal fashion: mutilation for any sort of sin would be cruel and inhuman punishment, and the overall biblical vision cannot be at odds with what we understand to be true human flourishing, for as Jesus tells us he has come not to judge the world, but so that all might have life and have it to the full (cf. John 12:47 and 10:10). Thus, the intersection with both the Human Experience and Normatively Human sectors would help interpret the true moral message of the Scripture sector in this instance. I believe though that we can outline some steps which allow Scripture to speak in its own authentic voice and which also bring the Scripture sector into a balanced integration with the other three sectors in our moral methodology.

As a way of elaborating on this moral methodology, let us read a more extended passage of Scripture and interpret it to see what sorts of concerns will surface that we have to deal with in bringing Scripture into our moral reflection:

> "You have heard that it was said, 'An eye for an eye and a tooth for a tooth.' But I say to you, Do not resist an evildoer. But if anyone strikes you on the right cheek, turn the other also; and if anyone wants to sue you and take your coat, give your cloak as well; and if anyone forces you to go one mile, go also the second mile. Give to everyone who begs from you, and do not refuse anyone who wants to borrow from you. You have heard that it was said, 'You shall love your neighbor and hate your enemy.' But I say to you, Love your enemies and pray for those who persecute you, so that you may be children of your Father in heaven

[υἱοί τοῦ πατρὸς ὑμῶν][2]; for he makes his sun rise on the evil and on the good, and sends rain on the righteous and on the unrighteous. For if you love those who love you, what reward do you have? Do not even the tax collectors do the same? And if you greet only your brothers and sisters, what more are you doing than others? Do not even the Gentiles do the same? Be perfect [τέλειοι], therefore, as your heavenly Father is perfect [τέλειός]" (Matt 5: 38-48).

Context is important for interpreting any particular biblical text and in this instance the passage comes from the Sermon on the Mount and the sermon as a whole has long enjoyed a special authority as setting out Jesus' moral vision. The part quoted above contains the last two of the Six Antitheses in the sermon. What sense can we make out of these commands? Like the preceding four Antitheses these last two also call on the disciples to reconsider and re-orient their traditional values, and with a particular community dimension. These are hard sayings indeed and the disciples might well have wondered what Jesus really meant, since the commands went smack against the seemingly prudent values of this world. The disciples must reorder their values and actions, even to the extent of actually loving their enemies. But what is involved in this reordering of the love command? Jesus' reference to the Torah command to love one's neighbor is found in Leviticus (cf. 19:17-18), and the Torah commandment centers on the relationship within the Israelite community, grounded in the common ancestry the Israelites share, as well as the holiness demanded of them by YHWH. There is no injunction as such to "hate" either one's enemies or even non-Israelites, though elsewhere in the Old Testament hatred of God's enemies seems to be legitimated (e.g., cf. Ps 139:19-22).

Jesus begins the Sixth Antithesis[3] by recalling for his listeners their popularly held interpretation that the obligation to love fellow-Israelites included at least tacit permission to hate those enemies who were not

---

[2] The Greek text here reads υἱοί τοῦ πατρὸς ὑμῶν (*uioi tou patros humon*), which the NRSV renders as "children of your Father." *Uioi* (υἱοί) is the plural of *uios*, which means son, but in its plural form *uioi* has two other basic meanings that go beyond "sons." It can mean simply "descendants," or also those of similar character. Matthew uses this latter meaning to emphasize that the disciples must pattern their attitudes on the attitude of their heavenly Father. *Uioi* can be employed negatively as well: at Matt 23:31 the Pharisees are condemned as "sons of those who murdered the prophets," that is, they are called "sons" precisely because their attitudes were the same as those who had murdered the prophets. In any case, it would be highly improper to the meaning of the Greek text to translate *uioi* as referring only to males and therefore excluding females; the meaning here is clearly inclusive.

[3] Though the term "Antitheses" is a staple of biblical scholarship for this section of the Sermon on the Mount, more recently some biblical scholars prefer the term "hypotheses"

part of the cultic community. Jesus then goes on to reject any such lax interpretation. Logically speaking, to "love" an enemy if one is strong might be possible, but to love a powerful enemy when one is weak can be very dangerous for both the individual and the community. Jesus grounds this radical extension of the precept to love in the identity of the discipleship community, and on the part of the disciples Jesus' injunction will involve a total trust and reliance on God, as well as the necessity to conform their attitudes to those of the Father who sheds his light even on the evil, and sends his rain even on the unjust. This will transform them from mere followers into something more, namely, sons and daughters of the Father, the υἱοί τοῦ πατρὸς ὑμῶν (*uioi tou patros humon*), not in terms of biological ancestry, but more importantly in the spiritual sense.

Taken as a whole, the Six Antitheses treat the basic principles of the moral community of those who wish to be Jesus' disciples. The identity of this community is grounded in the gospel message that they are called to be the sons and daughters of the Father in heaven, and to enter into his Kingdom. Living out that identity means that they must behave as children of God and brothers and sisters to each other. This relationship commands them to live in love and harmony (Matt 5:22-24), to examine one's heart in a radical manner, to purge it of any evil inclinations (Matt 5:27-30), as well as to maintain a continual guard against the wily machinations of the evil one (Matt 5:33-37). Each antithesis is a paradigm of the righteous living proclaimed in the Beatitudes, which begin the Sermon on the Mount, and which are demanded as a prerequisite for entrance into the Kingdom. The first three antitheses focus more on concrete aspects of intra-community relations, while the last three center on a radical re-orientation of values, possible only if the moral community accepts their identity as God's children and adopts the attitude of the Father's righteousness.

The last line of our passage can be especially troubling for our sacred claim, both morally and methodologically, since it seems to set up an impossible ethical ideal as we hear Jesus' command: "Be perfect, therefore, as your heavenly Father is perfect" (Matt 5:48). Several things should be observed here. First, this verse is not meant to stand alone as a timeless ethical ideal, but to be read in its particular context: "For if you love those who love you, what reward do you have? Do not

---

since it seems that Jesus is trying more to bring out the deeper implications of the Mosaic Law rather than trying to replace it outright.

even the tax collectors do the same? And if you greet only your brothers and sisters, what more are you doing than others? Do not even the Gentiles do the same? Be perfect, therefore, as your heavenly Father is perfect." In these verses Jesus is commanding the disciples to extend the boundaries of their community by modeling themselves on the Father. Once again Jesus is bringing the Old Testament Scriptures to fulfillment, this time by recalling a command from Deuteronomy 18:13, which is often translated as "You shall be blameless before the Lord your God" [RSV], but which the NSRV gives as "You must remain completely loyal to the Lord your God." In the Septuagint the Greek word translated as "blameless" or "completely loyal" is τέλειός (*teleios*),[4] the same word which is translated as "perfect" in Matthew 5:48. Thus, the relationship which the disciples are meant to have with the Father fulfills the covenant relationship Israel was to have had with YHWH. In both Deuteronomy and Matthew, the notion of perfection connotes fidelity and love, and not some sort of stainless, static aloofness from the world. We also see that just one biblical vocabulary word, τέλειός (*teleios*), has been rendered as "blameless," "completely loyal," and "perfect." While these three words have a certain similarity probably few of us would equate being "completely loyal" as exactly the same as being "perfect" or even "blameless."

To return to the larger context and message of the passage in the Sermon on the Mount Jesus is not trying to call the disciples to be "perfect" in the sense of without any blemish or defect. Rather, like the Father who cares so much for all people that he sends his rain and sun on the just and the unjust, so too the "perfection" as a moral trait of the disciples must flow from a whole-hearted love for all in the world. Through manifesting this perfect love, which comes from the Father and is revealed in Jesus, the disciples fulfill their commission to be the light for the world. This is the light which makes the love of God visible to all. This same light reveals the disciples to be the sons and daughters of God the Father, and inheritors of the Kingdom of heaven.

What can we learn about constructing a viable methodology for integrating Scripture and ethics from the preceding brief exegesis of this short passage from Matthew's Sermon on the Mount? Several points

---

[4] In Deut 18:13 τέλειός (*teleios*) translates the Hebrew *tamím* (תמים). *Tamím* carries a notion of something that is whole, complete, sound, undivided, and without blemish. This same word is used to describe Noah as being blameless in Gen 6:9, and is also used to speak of the sacrificial animals which are to be without blemish. The first syllable of *tamím* (תמים), *tam*, connotes innocence, simplicity, and even naivete.

come forward. First, in recognizing Scripture as the text which has a sacred claim on the Christian community we realize that like all written texts the Bible is hardly self-interpreting. It has to be read and interpreted both in its textual context as well as in relation to the ongoing tradition of the Christian community. However, as we have seen from the comments above, before it can be read by most of the community it must first be translated, and translation is at best an inexact and somewhat open-ended process. As we saw with just a couple of words and phrases, it is virtually impossible to translate completely and unambiguously the whole range of meaning from one language into another. Just which English word completely and accurately renders the word τέλε ιός *(teleios)* or the phrase υἱοί τοῦ πατρὸς ὑμῶν *(uioi tou patros humon)*? There is no perfect equivalent for either!

Yet, we cannot let these translation difficulties short-circuit our attempts to let Scripture engage us. The Bible remains the sacred text of our community, and we keep in mind that it did not drop down out of heaven but arose out of the lived tradition of the earlier Judeo-Christian community, and we share not only the Bible as text, but also the history of the efforts of those earlier communities as they grappled with how to understand the Bible's normativity in their own lives. In short, since the Bible is sacred to our community it must also become ever more formative of the community's self-understanding, or in other words, it must become increasingly normative for both the community's history as well as its own self-understanding of what it should be in the world.

Models of Scripture and Ethics

While most Christian ethicians and moral theologians would probably agree with what I have outlined up to this point, there is a considerable range of opinions and approaches to just how this sacred claim axis intersects with the rational claim axis. While we cannot give an in-depth answer to this question, it will be helpful for our ongoing reflections to touch on some of the major approaches and issues that enjoy a certain amount of favor.[5] In the last chapter we outlined some

---

[5] The amount of material on this theme is vast and growing. For a good introduction to the material available see James T., Bretzke, s.j., *Bibliography on Scripture and Christian Ethics*. Studies in Religion and Society, 39 (Lewiston N.Y.: Edwin Mellen Press, 1997). Still the best single book which gives an excellent overview of the principal approaches used by leading Protestant and Roman Catholic ethicists is William C. Spohn's *What Are They Saying About Scripture and Ethics?*, rev. ed. (New York: Paulist Press, 1984, 1995).

of the traditional differences between Catholics and Protestants regarding natural law or Scripture as the key authority for Christian ethics, as well as some of the differences found within the Roman Catholic community of moral theologians (i.e., the so-called "Faith Ethics" school and the "Moral Autonomy" school). Not surprisingly some of these same differences carry over into the discussion of how Scripture itself should be used.

We could line up the different models along a spectrum, going from an approach that gives the least amount of methodological weight to Scripture in moral discourse to those which give it the most. On the low end of the spectrum would be someone like the Roman Catholic moralist Bruno Schüller who holds that the Bible adds no new ethical content to morality and that what is contained in the Bible is just moral exhortation. For Schüller, ethics is grounded primarily along the rational claim axis, and while the Bible may be a help to some people in seeing this ethical truth, they really should try to grow into greater moral awareness so they do not need this biblical crutch:

> There are really only relatively few individual precepts that the NT sets forth explicitly. To the extent that the word of revelation does contain individual precepts of the law of Christ, it probably intends to help people out at those points where they have not yet managed to apprehend moral precepts on their intrinsic grounds. Even if human beings should never manage to dispense with this assistance totally, nonetheless they should strive to require it as little as possible. They should constantly endeavor to match their faith knowledge of moral precepts as far as possible with a knowledge that grasps their intrinsic intelligibility. Finally, only the latter sort of knowledge can undertake to decide, in the interpretation of scripture and tradition, which elements of traditional morality are binding for all time and which have only temporally conditioned binding force.[6]

---

[6] Bruno Schüller, s.j., "A Contribution to the Theological Discussion of Natural Law," in *Readings in Moral Theology, No. 7: Natural Law and Theology*, ed. Charles E. Curran and Richard A. McCormick, s.j. (Mahwah, N.J.: Paulist Press, 1991) 89. Another key article on this same theme is his "Zur Discussion über das Proprium einer christlichen Ethik," *Theologie und Philosophie* 51 (1976): 321–43. In English it is found as "The Debate on the Specific Character of Christian Ethics: Some Remarks," ch. 1 of his *Wholly Human: Essays on the Theory and Language of Morality*, trans. Peter Heinegg (Dublin: Gill and Macmillan; Washington, D.C.: Georgetown University Press, 1986) 15–42. This article first appeared in English in 1980 in *Readings in Moral Theology, no. 2: The Distinctiveness of Christian Ethics*, eds., Charles E. Curran and Richard A. McCormick, s.j. (New York: Paulist Press, 1980.) 207–33. For a good critique of, and response to, Schüller's position, see James Gaffney's "On Paranesis and Fundamental Moral Theology," *The Journal of Religious Ethics* 11 (1983) 24–34, also found as ch. 10 in Gaffney's *Matters of Faith and Morals* (Kansas City: Sheed and

While probably very few moral theologians are quite as extreme in the formulation of their position, in general those who identify themselves with the so-called Moral Autonomy school would resonate with Schüller's basic stance.[7]

Moving along the spectrum we would come to moral theologians such as Bernard Häring, C.SS.R., and Gérard Gillemann, S.J. Both of these men in their moral manuals tried to find some key scriptural theme that would help focus their moral approach. For Gillemann it was "charity" and for Häring it was initially the "law of Christ," but later on he changed his theme to freedom and creative fidelity in Christ. Häring believed that the real thrust of Christian morality was to realize that Jesus Christ had come so that all men and women should be free and that our moral response therefore was to respond in freedom and fidelity to the gospel message in our concrete moral lives.[8] Häring expressed his vision of moral theology in these terms:

> Moral theology, as I understand it, is not concerned first with decision-making or with discrete acts. Its basic task and purpose is to gain the right vision, to assess the main perspectives, and to present those truths and values which should bear upon decisions to be made before God. . . . We can gain the necessary vision of wholeness only by listening to the word of God and, in the light of his word, searching the signs of the times.[9]

The response of Christians in searching the signs of the times in light of God's word is not to try to replicate first-century Palestine, nor to try to be a clone of Christ in the sense of answering every moral ques-

---

Ward, 1987) 134–51. Gaffney's basic critique is that "exhort" is a transitive verb and requires an object, therefore, the Bible does not merely exhort us in the abstract, but it exhorts us to do something, and thus moral content is always involved.

[7] I would include in this group moral theologians such as Josef Fuchs, S.J., Klaus Demmer, M.S.C., Franz Böckle, Richard McCormick, S.J., and Alfons Auer. These issues, as well as the counter position of the "Faith Ethics" (*Glaubensethik*) school are well discussed in Vincent MacNamara's *Faith and Ethics* (Dublin: Gill and Macmillan; and Washington, D.C.: Georgetown University Press, 1985).

[8] Gérard Gillemann, S.J., *Le primat de la charité en théologie morale* (Brussels: Editions Desclée, 1954); the English version is *The Primacy of Charity in Moral Theology*, trans. William F. Ryan, S.J. and André Vachon, S.J. (Westminster Md.: The Newman Press, 1959). Häring's watershed work was his multi-volume *Das Gesetz Christi. Moraltheologie für Priester und Laien* (Freiburg: Erich Wewel Verlag, 1954); in English as *The Law of Christ* (Westminster: Newman Press, 1963). This work was then superseded by Häring's *Free and Faithful in Christ: Moral Theology for Priests and Laity*, 3 vols. (Slough, United Kingdom: St. Paul Publications, 1978, 1979, 1981).

[9] Häring, *Free and Faithful in Christ*, 6.

tion in terms of *WWJD?*: "What would Jesus do?" For Häring a more authentic response would be to see that "Jesus is not only the Word of the Father to us; he is also the perfect response. Thus he is the rallying call, inviting and enabling us, by his Spirit, to listen to him and to join him in his adoring, trusting and loving response to the Father. His call to discipleship is, therefore, a call to creative responsibility in freedom and fidelity."[10] When it comes to using the Bible explicitly, Häring states that

> a moral theology of creative liberty and fidelity finds its distinctively Christian quality in the light of the dynamic dimensions and perspectives which we find in the Bible. Their normative value is quite different from any kind of norms fitting external controls. They are, however, binding—and at the same time liberating—guidelines, norms in a very broad but real sense. They depend thoroughly on faith and thus are distinctively Christian. This does not exclude that generous people not professing Christian faith might, in one way or the other, be guided by the same dynamics.[11]

Both Gilleman and Häring, and many others who have been influenced by their seminal works, were innovative in trying to bring Scripture more directly into moral theology. At Vatican II Häring played an important role as a *peritus,* or theological consultant, in the drafting of *Optatam totius,* the Decree on the Training of Priests, which said that Scripture was to be the soul of all theology and this scriptural soul in particular was to reanimate moral theology:

> Students should receive a most careful training in holy Scripture, which should be the soul, as it were, of all theology. . . . They [seminarians] should learn to seek the solution of human problems in the light of revelation, to apply its eternal truths to the changing conditions of human affairs, and to express them in language which people of the modern world will understand. In like manner the other theological subjects should be renewed through a more vivid contact with the Mystery of Christ and the history of salvation. Special care should be given to the perfecting of moral theology. Its scientific presentation should draw more fully on the teaching of holy Scripture and should throw light upon the exalted vocation of the faithful in Christ and their obligation to bring forth fruit in charity for the life of the world (*Optatam totius,* #16).[12]

[10] Ibid., 20.

[11] Ibid., 23–24.

[12] For a fuller discussion of efforts made since the Vatican Council to integrate Scripture into moral theology see James T. Bretzke, S.J., "Scripture, the *Soul* of Moral Theology: The Second Stage," *Irish Theological Quarterly* 60 (1994) 259–71.

Of the post-Vatican II moral manualists, Häring has probably done the best job in letting Scripture be the animating force for his vision of moral theology. He has gone beyond biblical proof-texting which marked the pre-Vatican II manuals' use of Scripture, in which a biblical verse or two was used as a sort of add-on to clinch a moral argument constructed largely from a combination of natural law theory and/or church Tradition. Häring realized that it was Scripture itself that should furnish many of the key themes and images for theological elaboration and development, and therefore some traditional manualist approaches would have to be either purified or purged if Scripture was to become the true soul of moral theology and its *norma normans*, or ultimate norming principle. Those moral theologians who share these convictions realize that rather than serving as a court of first, last, or intermediate appeal, the authority of Scripture means that as a whole it is constitutive of the community's identity, and therefore is absolutely essential both to the establishment and preservation of that community's self-understanding. This means that Scripture itself has a sacred claim on that community's identity and understanding. Scripture helps not just to "inform" the community's views, but actually to form them into a community of a particular character. In that way Scripture is "authoritative" in the sense of being decisive for both the individual and common life.

While Roman Catholic moral theologians have been playing a certain amount of catch-up in integrating Scripture into Christian ethics, Protestants have traditionally made Scripture central to their theological reflection, and so as we move along our spectrum we will now outline some of the principal approaches they have used. The term *Sola scriptura* "Scripture alone" often is misunderstood as meaning that the Bible somehow is the complete answer book or recipe for moral living. Classic Protestant theology has not one "*Sola*" but four: *Sola scriptura*, *Sola fide* "faith alone", *Sola gratia* "grace alone," and most importantly *Solus Christus* "Christ alone." These four are meant to be integrated and thus we are saved through our faith in the grace of Jesus Christ, which is witnessed in both Scripture and the life of the Church. This Protestant theology therefore corresponds to the Roman Catholic understanding articulated in Vatican II that God's definitive revelation of God's self is found in Jesus Christ and that we are saved in Christ.

Yet, Scripture is indispensable to this whole process and theologians approach the normative character of the Bible in markedly different ways. If Bruno Schüller might represent the minimalist position, theologians such as Karl Barth, Stanley Hauerwas, and John Howard Yoder would argue for a more maximalist position.[13] We do not have the space to go into each of these positions in detail, but we should highlight some of the key characteristics of the different approaches as they will be important as we come to our final considerations of how we should better understand the integration of the Scripture sector with Tradition along the sacred claim axis, as well as how these sectors and axes intersect with the rational claim axis.

Karl Barth's approach to Christian ethics is often called "Divine Command" ethics. For him the fundamental question of Christian ethics would be "What is commanded of us by God?" The answer he finds primarily in Scripture as Word of God which exercises a commanding claim on Christians. Barth would not consider this Word of God as similar to a natural law objective moral truth inscribed on the human person, but rather a direct revelation by God to human persons calling them to obedience. Thus the Christian has just two choices: acknowledge and obey God's command expressed in Jesus Christ, or cut oneself off from God's grace. Stark as it is, Barth's approach does have several positive elements. First, it obviously takes Scripture very seriously for informing our ethical life, and Barth's corresponding notion of faith embraces the totality of one's life, and not just a "religious" sphere. His approach accents the necessary role of discernment in Christian life and underscores the possibility of norms in Christian ethics, and so can be an important corrective to an excessive existentialism or individualism. However, ultimately Barth's approach is inadequate because of what William Spohn aptly calls its "missing element":

> Finally, one must admit that something is missing from this theological ethics. All the characteristics of the moral agent are derived from the event of being addressed by the Word of God. Moral agents have character, a unique history and moral responsibility only because they are constantly addressed by God. The self cannot be considered apart from God's action. This leads to an impoverished view of moral experience

[13] It would be impossible to give a complete bibliography here, but some representative titles for each of these theologians would be the following. For Barth, see his multi-volume *Church Dogmatics* (Edinburgh: T & T Clark, 1955–1961), and/or his shorter *Ethics*, trans. Geoffrey W. Bromiley, ed. Dietrich Braun (New York: Seabury Press, 1981). For Hauerwas, see especially his Gifford Lectures published as *With the Grain of the Universe: The Church's Witness and Natural Theology* (Ada, Mich.: Brazos Press, 2001), and for Yoder, see his classic *The Politics of Jesus*, 2nd ed. (Grand Rapids: Eerdmans, 1972, 1994). These thinkers are treated well in Spohn's *What Are They Saying About Scripture and Ethics?*

because there seems to be no self between moments when God is commanding. Moral life is more than simply discrete moments of decision; it refers to the continuous aspects of the self: virtues and vices, character, identity, memory, commitments and roles. Even if one grants the priority of the faith assent over moral reflection on theological grounds, Barth seems to have maximized the role of obedient faith at the expense of a coherent sense of the moral self.[14]

Spohn's critique of Barth shows us again that while Scripture is crucial in our understanding of Christian ethics, it is a not a stand-alone source. Scripture must be integrated with our other sources and the sacred claim axis must allow for intersection with the rational claim axis if our moral methodology hopes to involve the entire human community in its complexity. To return to our earlier reference to Jesus' admonition about permanently removing offending organs, while Barth certainly never suggested this sort of passage be taken literally, we have tragically seen in our post-September 11th world just how religious fanaticism can lead to actions we would otherwise call objectively immoral. In a morally complex world the sacred claim axis *must* be integrated with the rational claim axis, and vice versa.

Between these two poles of a Schülleresque biblical minimalism and a Barthian maximalism are found most of the rest of the Christian ethicians. Of these, perhaps the work of H. Richard Niebuhr has been most influential in the United States theological community. For most of his academic life, Niebuhr taught at Yale and his principal contribution to Scripture and ethics is found in a series of articles and a seminal book on the theological meaning of revelation written during World War II. In his writings Niebuhr did not begin with the question, "What does the Bible say about the morality of this or that?" but rather with a more fundamental, grounding question, namely, "What does the Bible reveal to us about the reality of our situation?" In outlining an answer to this question Niebuhr maintains that one of the most important things the Scriptures reveal to us is a certain point of view. No one has a neutral standpoint, and as Niebuhr trenchantly observed, "As a rule men are polytheists, referring now to this and now to that valued being as the source of life's meaning. Sometimes they live for Jesus' God, sometimes for the country and sometimes for Yale."[15] Thus, critical to this Christian standpoint would be the central

---

[14] Spohn, *What Are They Saying About Scripture and Ethics?* 35.

[15] H. Richard Niebuhr, *The Meaning of Revelation* (New York: Macmillan, 1941 and 1960) 57. Besides this book, Niebuhr's other foundational insights into Scripture and ethics are

truths of the faith, such the goodness of God's creation, the reality of sin and finitude, the saving power of the Cross, the Resurrection, and eschatology which show us how God sees our reality. All of these core biblical themes help us remember that our lives have both a direction and a terminus that are not found ultimately in this world.

The Christian standpoint then helps us to first decode and then read the signs of the times. Scripture helps us in this discernment process principally by unmasking for us what Niebuhr calls "evil imaginations" and lifting up the truer reasons of the heart which are made intelligible through a faith in Jesus: "Reasoning on the basis of revelation the heart not only understands what it remembers but is enabled and driven to remember what it had forgotten. When we use insufficient and evil images of the personal or social self we drop out of our consciousness or suppress those memories which do not fit in with the picture of the self we cherish."[16] Niebuhr calls this process "progressive revelation," and here he resonates with the role of the Holy Spirit as promised by Jesus in John's Gospel, namely, our Advocate who will help us recall what we've forgotten, and teach us what we could not earlier bear (cf. John 14:16-17; 14:26; and 16: 7-15), or as Niebuhr puts it, "through the cross of Christ we gain a new understanding of the present scene; we note relations previously ignored; find explanations of our actions hitherto undreamed of. Deeds and sufferings begin to compose themselves into a total picture of significant action in which the self no longer occupies the center."[17]

A Multi-Strand Double-Helix Model for Scripture and Ethics

While Niebuhr offers some excellent foundational insights and considerations for how Scripture should inform our Christian ethics, we still are not given all that much in terms of a concrete methodology to guide us in the process. I will outline one such approach. One essential aspect of integrating Scripture with ethics we have not yet explicitly addressed is hermeneutics, that is, a consideration of what the process of biblical interpretation and application involves. Again, this is a topic that is both complex and vast and has an extensive bibliography,

---

contained in his so-called "War Articles," "War as the Judgment of God," *Christian Century* 59 (1942) 630–33; "Is God in the War?" (with Virgil C. Aldrich), *Christian Century* 59 (1942) 953–55; "War as Crucifixion," *Christian Century* 60 (1943) 513–15.

[16] Niebuhr, *Meaning of Revelation*, 83.

[17] Ibid., 90.

and so all I shall attempt here is to provide one simple model that will help illumine what goes on when an individual or community in the twenty-first century tries to engage sacred texts composed two millennia or more ago.[18]

In the language of hermeneutical theory the Bible is a "classic text," which means that it has a wealth of meanings that can never be fully and completely realized by any given audience at any given point in history, nor even by the accumulation of readings and interpretations over the whole of our shared history. Certainly the tradition of biblical scholarship and community interpretation is a key aspect of our Tradition sector and illustrates well how the Bible as sacred text continues to interact in a dynamic way with the living Tradition of the faith community along the sacred claim axis. In theology this inexhaustible depth of Scripture is termed the *sensus plenior*, which literally means the "fuller sense," and suggests that the Bible contains meanings that go beyond the literal sense or meaning explicitly intended by the original human author for the specific cultural-historical audience of the period in which the text was written. Thus, the Scriptures can always yield new and deeper meanings which may come up in new and different situations, or which are realized through ongoing study and/or reflection and meditation. This *sensus plenior* is involved in what both H. Richard Niebuhr and Vatican II's Constitution on Divine Revelation, *Dei verbum*, called "progressive revelation," in which the revelatory moment contained in the Scriptures "makes our past intelligible. Through it we understand what we remember, remember what we have forgotten and appropriate as our own past much that seemed alien to us."[19]

Each of us comes to both Scripture and any given moral issue with a certain set of convictions and predispositions, or perhaps even a governing "analogy" firmly in place. If we look to the Bible simply to validate or confirm these convictions, then while the effort may initially seem rewarding, upon closer examination we recognize that we are not

---

[18] An excellent introduction and treatment of hermeneutics in biblical interpretation is Sandra Schneiders, *The Revelatory Text: Interpreting the New Testament as Sacred Scripture* (San Francisco: HarperSanFrancisco, 1991; Collegeville: The Liturgical Press, 1999) mentioned in ch. 1. Also helpful for a liberation theological treatment of the same theme is J. Severino Croatto's *Biblical Hermeneutics: Toward a Theory of Reading as the Production of Meaning*, trans. Robert R. Barr (Maryknoll, N.Y.: Orbis Books, 1987).

[19] Niebuhr, *Meaning of Revelation*, 81. On this same notion see also *Dei verbum*, and especially paragraphs 8, 12, and 26.

being open to the triple role of the Spirit as Advocate and Spirit of Truth (John 14:16-17), Teacher (John 14:26), and Progressive Revealer (John 16:7-15). As a means of helping create and maintain this openness to the Spirit, analogy may be an appropriate way to engage ourselves with Scripture since it opens us up to seeing and responding to our world in new ways. This is the dynamic of the discernment of the Spirit that William Spohn has developed as looking on Jesus as the "concrete universal" in the construction and application of our analogical imagination. Jesus as concrete universal does not ask the popular question, *WWJD?* (What Would Jesus Do?) but suggests a more reflective and nuanced "going and doing likewise," as Jesus commanded in the parable of the Good Samaritan (Luke 10:31-37).[20] It is in first imagining both what the going and the doing of the "likewise" means for us that the Bible can play a crucial role.

But before we can use our analogical imagination in bringing Scripture to bear on our moral living, we still need to address more explicitly the problematic posed by the process of biblical interpretation called hermeneutics. A number of different models have been advanced to describe how this interactive process of reading, interpretation, and appropriation of the biblical texts by the community of believers works. Probably the most famous of these models is the so-called "hermeneutical circle," which moves between the reader and the text and back to the reader in his or her concrete reality. The problem with this model is that it is somewhat circular in that it is hard to see how the Scriptures change the reader's world. Rather, it seems that the Scriptures are employed to confirm the perceptions and prejudices the reader brought to the text in the first place: in short, the problematic of bringing an agenda to our biblical exegesis which largely predetermines our interpretation. For example, in the ante-bellum South white slave owners used texts from Paul to justify the institution of slavery, while in more modern times the Dutch Reformed Church in South Africa found biblical warrants for ethnic diversity that would be best maintained in the system of institutional apartheid.[21] The other end

---

[20] William Spohn, *Go and Do Likewise: Jesus and Ethics* (New York: Continuum, 1999).

[21] See their statement, *Human Relations and the South African Scene in the Light of Scripture"* which is the official English trans. of *Ras, Volk en Naise en Volkereverhoudinge in die lig van die Skrif*, accepted by the Dutch Reformed Church's General Synod in October, 1974. There is an excellent discussion of this case and the problematic of bringing our agenda to biblical interpretation in Stephen E. Fowl and L. Gregory Jones, *Reading in Communion: Scripture and Ethics in Christian Life* (Grand Rapids, Mich.: William B. Eerdmans, 1991).

of the political and theological spectrum can also be guilty of the same biased approach.[22]

One way to break free of the hermeneutical circle is to posit a different geometric figure to help us visualize the process. The figure I propose is that of a multi-strand double helix, admittedly more complicated to draw, but ultimately more apt. One helix is the texts of the Scriptures and the other helix is the person who encounters those texts. However, each helix is woven together of many other strands. For example, it is misleading to speak of the "biblical text" in the singular. Even the shortest verse is part of a larger text and the Bible as a whole comprises an amazing plurality of strands of its own which is clear if we just skim through the table of contents. We have to keep in mind, too, that the Bible as our sacred text was written at diverse periods of time by a wide variety of individuals, all of which contributed to the revelatory plurality that comprises our canonical collection. Similarly, the human person is much more than a simple biological identity. Each of us has our own personal uniqueness that comes from our individual history, the cultures we grew up in, the experiences we have had, and so on.

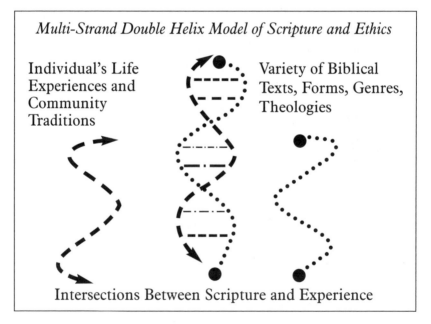

Multi-Strand Double Helix Model of Scripture and Ethics

Individual's Life Experiences and Community Traditions

Variety of Biblical Texts, Forms, Genres, Theologies

Intersections Between Scripture and Experience

---

[22] E.g., see John Howard Yoder's critique of forced uses of Scripture found in some liberation theology in his essay, "Exodus and Exile: The Two Faces of Liberation," in *Readings*

Neither helix is made up of just one simple element and as these two helixes come into contact with one another they develop a history of their own. At some moments the intersection and connection points seem very close, at other times they are more distant. For example, at one point in my life I may encounter a biblical passage that will speak to me especially strongly at that moment, whereas at other moments the very same passage may have little impact at all. On one hand, this is certainly due to the *sensus plenior* of the text itself, whose wealth of meanings can never be fully realized at any given reading, but on the other hand the different impact that the passage may have on me is because I am also a different person today than I was last year or even last week—and this is because of the different strands that are continually woven together to make up my life. These strands are my particular life experiences, my deepening knowledge of human values, my own growth in the realization of the progressive sense of revelation that Niebuhr and *Dei verbum* speak of, and so on. In short, as long as I am alive, not only do I change, as seen in the Human Experience sector of our quadrant, but the other sectors will change as well. Even the sacred text of the Bible itself changes—not in the sense that we are going to add or subtract parts of the canon to the Bible itself, but as our appreciation of what the biblical texts actually mean grows and develops, we can say that in a very real sense the Bible itself is transformed in the way it transforms the community that holds it sacred. For example, we now realize that when Paul said to the slaves of his time that they should be obedient to their masters, he did not mean that slavery was a divinely sanctioned institution. Thus, in this and so many other senses we can say that the Bible itself changes as the various strands that go into the construction of the biblical helix come into contact with the different strands that make up the helix of our personal lives. Just as I am not frozen in time, so that there is a sort of wax museum version of the fifty-year old James Bretzke, neither is the Bible itself fixed in one way for all eternity. While this may seem like a very simple insight, it does have profound implications—especially if we try to let the Bible speak in new ways to life situations that

---

in Moral Theology no. 4: The Use of Scripture in Moral Theology, eds. Charles E. Curran and Richard A. McCormick, s.j. (New York and Ramsey: Paulist Press, 1984) 337–53. See also John P. Meier's critique of the exegesis and interpretation employed by Jon Sobrino and Juan Luis Segundo in their use of Scripture for their liberation theology: "The Bible as a Source for Theology," *Proceedings of the Forty-Third Annual Convention*, Catholic Theological Society of America 43 (1988) 1–14.

challenge us. As one example of how this might play out let me share an anecdote involving a problematic reading of the Bible as a sacred text.

Core, Context, and Coherence as Criteria
for Using Scripture in Ethics

Some time ago I was asked to help facilitate an in-service retreat for the religious studies department of a Catholic high school in which we focused on some of the challenges in presenting and mediating the Church's moral teachings to students in a credible manner. In the course of the discussion, one teacher shared a recent class session that had touched on the area of homosexuality. The students expressed sharply divided opinions over the moral acceptability of gay men and women living out their same-sex orientation in a non-celibate manner. Some argued that these people and their relationships should be judged according to the same standards and criteria of heterosexual unions, and thus if two men or two women were committed to one another in a stable, loving, monogamous relationship this union should be accepted by the community as morally good. In support of this position several students spoke from the Experience sector, sharing their personal knowledge of family members or close friends who were living in just such a relationship, and they argued that these people were obviously good, caring, and conscientious individuals and hardly promiscuous profligates or self-indulgent, lust-driven sexual perverts.

Others, however, took strong exception to the view that any same-sex union could ever be morally justified. While this second group did not deny the reading of the personal experiences offered by the first group, nevertheless they argued that this sort of activity violated the moral order. The teacher noted the reasons advanced by this second group were not those usually employed in the bulk of the contemporary official Church positions on homogenital activity. The high school students did not claim these unions were wrong by using the adolescent semantic equivalents of being intrinsically disordered, nor because they lacked the possibility for physical procreation, nor even that this behavior was wrong because the *Catechism of the Catholic Church* or any other authoritative document or person(s) said so. Rather, the students pointed to one authority that in their view seemed clearly to condemn such activity—namely, the Bible. It was this text, and its concomitant sacred claim, rather than any other authority or argument that closed off debate and resolved any moral doubts they might have on the matter.

The teacher said that the class seemed to have reached an impasse, and she suggested that as a way of more directly engaging the line of arguments put forward by the first group, namely, on how experience should be evaluated, the class might for the time being "put the Bible on the shelf" in carrying on the discussion. While putting the Bible on the shelf might have helped break this particular logjam, or resolved it favorably in terms of the arguments of the first group, ultimately I think that it is a sort of "resolution" that accomplishes at best an uneasy cease-fire, but does not truly resolve the deeper issues of just how Scripture is meant to function as a normative voice in moral issues.

The second group might still not be convinced, seeing that their prime moral authority seemed to be silenced without having its voice ever heard. I believe from the perspective of fundamental moral theology the question becomes one of how we can take the Bible off the shelf and bring it back into ethical discussions in a way which uses Scripture in a constructive and authentic dialogical manner—a way that may not "clinch" moral arguments from the start by closing off any subsequent debate or discussion, but through a process that will allow the voice of Scripture to be heard, engaged, and evaluated in a manner that properly forms and informs both our character and our moral reasoning which flows out of that character. While it would be extremely unrealistic to hope that one short article would resolve to everyone's satisfaction many of the contentious issues regarding the interplay between Scripture and concrete hot-button moral issues, I do believe that it might be helpful to confront the issues of normativity and applicability in a manner in which the Bible need not be "put on the shelf" when such contentious issues emerge. To this end I suggested a tri-partite template of context, core, and coherence in assessing biblical moral normativity and to address the application to concrete moral situations.[23]

"God hates fags! (Lev 18:22)" is a placard we unfortunately still see too often today. There is even a web-site, *www.GodHatesFags.com,* whose opening page informs the viewer of the "danger" that there is "Serious

---

[23] For a more detailed treatment of my methodology, see my, "Scripture and Ethics: Core, Context, and Coherence" in *Moral Theology: Fundamental Issues and New Directions. Festschrift for James Hanigan,* ed. James Keating (Mahwah, N.J.: Paulist Press, 2003).

Gospel Preaching Ahead" and goes on to list a number of biblical texts culled from both the Old and New Testaments to "prove" that gay men and women are beyond the reach of redemption because they persist in their sinful inclination. When I browsed the site in late November 2002, the hit-o-meter indicated that well over three million people had already visited. Browsing further one is taken to a "memorial" which indicates how many days in hell the young man killed in 1998 by gay-bashers in Colorado, Matthew Shepherd, has languished, and other such similar absolutely venomous and vile musings.

While neither my friend's high school students, nor most educated Christians, would countenance such inflammatory, hateful, and perverted uses of Scripture, still we do need guidance to see how the Bible should inform our response to these sorts of ethical challenges. In dealing with these questions, I propose an evaluative template of three key elements. First, we need to look carefully at the *core meaning* of the biblical texts; second, we need to pay sufficient attention to the *context* of these texts themselves; and third, we need to make sure that both our texts and our interpretation of them exhibit *coherence* (or consistency) with the rest of Scripture, the whole of our Christian tradition, and our shared standards of human morality.

"Core meaning" refers not first and foremost to a given biblical text per se, but rather points to God's definitive revelation to humankind of God's own self, namely Jesus Christ, as we discussed earlier in this chapter. This reflects Vatican II's mandate that Scripture animate our theological reflection (cf. *Dei verbum* #4, and *Optatam totius* #16). The core criterion focuses on the gospel message not just as a "canonical" text, but as the standard against which every other individual biblical text is measured, as well as the lived expression in the concrete lives of the Christian community throughout history. Thus, the core of God's revelation in Jesus Christ exercises a sacred claim on all those who share in the Christian tradition (cf. *Dei verbum* #8–10). Since it is the whole of Jesus Christ that stands as the pinnacle of God's revelation, we must be particularly receptive of the presence and role of the abiding gift of his Spirit in the Church. As we have already stressed, it is this progressive revelation by the Spirit, rather than any given logion or biblical verses, that reminds us of what has been taught by Jesus, and teaches us those things we could not bear earlier and thus leads us deeper into the hierarchy of truths that express the central core considerations (cf. *Dei verbum* #5, 8). Does the testimony of the Bible to the definitive revelation of God's love expressed in

Jesus Christ support the core assertion that somehow there is an exception clause, or an outcast group for whom this message is not meant? This is a question which clearly touches on the core meaning of the Scriptures as our revelatory text.

"Context" looks more explicitly at the text in order to illumine more clearly the core. As we have pointed out, Scripture is a text that is neither self-evident, self-translating, self-exegeting, self-interpreting, nor self-applying. Only after Scripture is translated, read, analyzed, understood, and interpreted can it be applied. These six integrated tasks from initial translation to final application require great time and effort, study and reflection, and in particular greater attention to context that can help in each of these tasks individually, as well as furnish an integrative theme to hold them together. While it is true that the several biblical texts do seem to condemn homogenital activity, many biblical scholars caution us against trying to apply these passages directly to contemporary gay men and lesbian women.[24] What is condemned clearly though is any sort of attitude or behavior which puts the individual above God and neighbor, as we see clearly in 1 Corinthians 6:9, one of the texts that is often cited as biblical proof of the immorality of homosexuality: "Do you not know that wrongdoers will not inherit the kingdom of God? Do not be deceived! Fornicators, idolaters, adulterers, male prostitutes (μαλακοι *malakoi*), sodomites (αρσε νοκοῖται *arsenokoitai*) . . ." But it is important to note two things in this proof-texting verse: first, we seem to have a translation issue, since the term "homosexual" is not found in this verse, and second, the verse stops in mid-sentence. Let us treat the translation problem first. The NRSV translates μαλακοι *malakoi* as "male prostitutes," but other possible translations are "soft," "weak," "effeminate," "abusers," "a boy kept for homosexual relations with a man," and so on. This word is used exactly three times in the whole

---

[24] There is a vast amount of scholarly material that discusses these issues. In my *Bibliography on Scripture and Christian Ethics*, see the section on "Homosexuality," 299–312. For the general reader, I would recommend Victor Paul Furnish's *The Moral Teaching of Paul: Selected Issues*, 2nd ed. (Nashville: Abingdon, 1985), which treats sexual questions, such as marriage and divorce, homosexuality, as well as other issues, such as the place of women in the Church, and the relationship between Christians and governing authorities. Also very helpful is the collection of essays in Patricia Beattie Jung, with Joseph Andrew Coray, eds., *Sexual Diversity and Catholicism: Toward the Development of Moral Theology* (Collegeville: The Liturgical Press, 2001). For further specialized study of the biblical interpretation questions, see especially Choon-Leong, Seow, ed., *Homosexuality and Christian Community* (Louisville: Westminister/John Knox Press, 1996).

New Testament and the other two instances refer to soft clothing with absolutely no sexual overtones whatsoever (cf. Matt 11:8 and Luke 7:25). The other term, αρσε νοκοῖται *arsenokoitai*, seems to be more explicit, and while the NRSV renders this as "sodomites," other translators give it as "abusers of themselves," "one who lies with a male as a female," and even "homosexual." Like μαλακοι *malakoi*, αρσε νοκοῖται *arsenokoitai* is hardly a common vocabulary term or moral concern of the New Testament; it only appears one other time, in a similar vice list in 1 Timothy 1:10. Whatever these two Greek terms might have meant in Paul's day, it is clear that neither speaks to the reality of gay men and women in the twenty-first century. Rather, it seems that Paul was using these terms as commonly accepted synonyms for those who do not do good—perhaps like we might use terms such as "liars, cheats, spouse abusers, Mafiosi," and the like. Such "sin lists" are relatively common in Ancient Near Eastern literature and in much of this literature the sin lists are employed as a literary genre to indicate negative models which should not be followed rather than strict legal code of prohibitions as such.

This point is confirmed when we move to our second observation, namely that the proof-text of 1 Corinthians 6: 9 isn't even a complete sentence, much less a complete thought. Let us try to finish both. The sentence which begins with "Do you not know that wrongdoers will not inherit the kingdom of God?" goes on to supply a long list of examples, half of which we find in verse 9 (fornicators, idolaters, adulterers, male prostitutes [μαλακοι *malakoi*], sodomites [αρσε νοκοῖται *arsenokoitai*]), but which is completed in the next verse with "thieves, the greedy, drunkards, revilers, robbers—none of these will inherit the kingdom of God." If we look at the list as a whole it seems that the community of those who could be discomfited would grow indeed. Without making a public confession I think that most of us could admit to being at least greedy on occasion, and if my twenty-plus years' experience as a confessor indicates anything, others on this list also are found in the community of Jesus' disciples.

The point clearly is not that these sorts of people will be excluded from God's kingdom just because they may have failed or are weak in any number of ways. Rather, as Paul makes clear in the next verse, this vice list is meant as a sort of wake-up call to us all: "And this is what some of you used to be. But you were washed, you were sanctified, you were justified in the name of the Lord Jesus Christ and in the Spirit of our God." The key then is to try to live our best as those who find our identity in Christ—even if this means that we fail often and remain weak and imperfect.

Thus, the assertion that "God hates fags" or any more nuanced version of exclusion for gay men and women from God's universal salvific will expressed in Jesus Christ would fail the evaluative criteria of both core and context, as well as the third criterion of our template, "coherence." Coherence flows naturally from a proper consideration of both core and context and works particularly well against proof-texting and/or biblical literalism by looking at how the core gospel message functions in the various contexts to make its central points. As we noted above, while Jesus' admonition to cut off any organ that causes one to sin (cf. Matt 5:29-30) might indeed be the very words of the historical Jesus, we could hardly argue that literal application of this admonition is consistent with his larger preaching and public ministry. Thus, the coherence criterion points us back to the core criterion, which would deny that this kind of injunction could be a legitimate biblical or divine command. The context criterion confirms this analysis by showing this particular logion as an example of hyperbolic discourse used to underscore the importance of the moral life, but not as a sentencing guide for infractions thereof!

The coherence criterion involves more though than simply reconciling the odd hyperbolic verse with the rest of Scripture. In its deepest sense the coherence criterion finds its real meaning in pointing us to the core message of the whole of Scripture as a sacred text that reveals God to us. In short, then, we have to ask whether our biblical interpretation of a particular passage or theme ultimately coheres with a theologically sound image of God as revealed in Jesus Christ. Here we see the manifest importance of a proper Christology for moral theology, and so we may have to jettison some "negative" biblical images, such as the "Crusading Warrior" of the Holy War, which seem essentially inconsistent with the New Testament character portrait of Jesus, or a God who hates fags or sends evils as just desserts for sinners. The coherence criterion also guides us methodologically in our concrete selection and usage of scriptural texts that should be appropriate to the moral situation under reflection, and shed light (rather than heat) upon it.

While I think it is clear by now that the web-meister of *GodHatesFags.com* fails the coherence criterion, the notion that God somehow maintains the objective moral order by visiting wrath on those who forsake God's ways is an idea that is a bit harder to dispel, and which may have been in the back of the minds of those students who were hesitant to accept gay men and women even if they are in committed, stable, monogamous, and seemingly truly loving relationships. All that may be true, they might respond, but if God's will is otherwise, aren't we playing a very dangerous game to risk God's displeasure?

This question seems to take both God and the sacred claim seriously, and I suspect there is no once-and-for-all simple answer that once uttered will bring all sides of the debate into immediate agreement. There are so many arguments and counter-arguments that perhaps we can leave this issue open for further discussion in our morally complex world. But does this mean then that Scripture fails us? I think not, but we have to be careful of what questions we bring to Scripture as our sacred text, and how we seek the answers. If my model of the multi-strand double helix is apt, then it may be that the "answer" of one moment may have to give way to another insight as we continue to grapple with these sorts of issues and honestly seek to keep ourselves open to the Spirit who will not only remind us what Jesus has taught us, but who will also teach us what we could not earlier bear (cf. John 16: 7-15).

Something like this happened for me a number of years ago when I was beginning to teach in Rome. I had spent the summer working in southern Italy in a drug rehabilitation program, and I came to know well a number of young men who had become infected with the HIV virus through sharing of needles. As I returned to the Gregorian University, I was trying to write something about how the Church might respond to the AIDS crisis when I came across an article that at first glance seemed to treat the same topic. In the late 1980s when I was finishing my doctorate, the archbishop of Genoa, Cardinal Siri, sent a shockwave through Italy by proclaiming that AIDS was the *castigo di Dio* (wrath or punishment of God). While much of the official Vatican and Italian hierarchy tried to ignore or downplay the Cardinal's remarks, John Michael McDermott, S.J., one of my colleagues then at the Gregorian, published an article entitled "Is AIDS God's Punishment?" and carefully concluded that "yes"—AIDS *is* God's punishment, and more importantly this affirmative answer requires us to revisit how we consider God and God's actions in the world.[25] Throughout his article he uses Scripture extensively, if selectively.

---

[25] John M. McDermott, S.J., "Is AIDS God's Punishment?" *Homiletic and Pastoral Review* 7 (1991) 32; 50–58.

McDermott begins with Genesis 2:17; 3:19 which he asserts "proclaims that God punishes sin and the punishment of sin is death."[26] The covenant demands that evil be punished so that "God would not be mocked but would ultimately set his justice through (Ps 37; Ezek 26–28)" and ultimately the Jews "came to recognize the existence of a life beyond the present one in which rewards and punishments would be justly apportioned" (Isa 53:10f; Dan 12:2f; Wis 1-5).[27] Passages such as Amos 4 and Hosea 11 show that God brings people "to their senses by chastising them, even to past sins; for men had to be purified from the abiding results of sin."[28] The New Testament, McDermott claims, repeats, fulfills, and deepens the "Old Testament's doctrine on sin and punishment"[29] and though the "simple rule of justice, good rewarded—evil punished, is maintained in its vigor"[30] McDermott allows that "the innocent Christ crucified warns against a direct equation of suffering and sin" (cf. Matt 5:45; John 9: 1-3; Luke 13:1-5).[31] Punishments likewise are inflicted "as warnings 'lest we be condemned along with the world'" (1 Cor 11:25-32; 2 Cor 7:8-12; Matt 26:24; 27:25; Mark 13), and "like the prodigal son, the sinner has to 'come to himself and return to the Father" (Luke 15:18-20; Heb 12:5-7; Rev 3:19).[32] Echoing Cardinal Siri's assertion that AIDS is the *castigo di Dio* McDermott concludes that "[a]pplied to homosexual AIDS patients, the message of God's Word means simply that the disease is a punishment for those refusing his mercy and trying to justify their own perversity" (cf. Rom 1:18-32).[33]

Turning to the larger community McDermott allows that Christians do have some sort of obligation to help those who suffer from AIDS, but cautions that fulfillment of this obligation "does not mean that all the community's financial largess and health care are to be spilled out indiscriminately."[34] More importantly, though, is the "obligation to uphold certain moral principles and limit the further spread of AIDS. . . . When pleasure and not duty becomes the norm

---

[26] McDermott, "AIDS," 50.
[27] Ibid.
[28] Ibid., 50–51.
[29] Ibid.
[30] Ibid., 52–53.
[31] Ibid., 53.
[32] Ibid.
[33] Ibid., 55.
[34] Ibid., 56.

of a society's behavior, disaster inevitably follows."[35] The dangers of a misguided sexual ethics, McDermott contests, are critical:

> Without doubt a society that regards homosexual behavior as normal is doomed to extinction, and it is utopian at best to think that two cultures, heterosexual and homosexual can coexist without conflict, especially if guilt feelings are involved. . . . A society without clear guidelines in sexual morality heightens their confusion, especially when the aggressiveness of some 'liberated' females questions the traditionally accepted sexual roles. . . . A healthy society . . . cannot allow an equal standing to homosexuality nor permit flagrant, public homosexual behavior.[36]

Though at first glance McDermott does appear to use Scripture extensively throughout his article, the citations are brief and often stretch the context at best. His core message seems ultimately to be grounded on a view of both God and the moral order that is little informed by Jesus' gospel kerygma of mercy and conversion, and thus seems inconsistent with many of the central themes of the New Testament which stress caution at quick judgment, and which evidence more care for the individual (even if a "sinner") than we find here. McDermott's God may not exactly "hate fags," but is certainly portrayed as just in punishing them with disease and death. Moreover, McDermott's concluding observations give the impression that certain deep-seated convictions about what constitutes "nature," "morality," and a rightly constituted society govern not only the overall structure of his argument, but the selection, interpretation, and application of the biblical material as well.

Having lived and worked with McDermott for three years, I know him to be a sincere and honest person, but I cannot share either his basic exegesis or many of his conclusions outlined in this article, as I believe they do not measure up adequately to our three evaluative criteria of core, context, and coherence. Alternative readings of the same basic issue indicate a variety of other approaches, and so from an academic perspective I suppose we might have to agree to disagree on this issue.[37]

---

[35] Ibid., 57.

[36] Ibid., 58.

[37] Jeffrey Siker, an ordained Presbyterian minister and professor of New Testament at Loyola Marymount University, has wrestled with some of the same root issues, but comes up with a significantly different set of conclusions. See his "How to Decide? Homosexual Christians, the Bible, and Gentile Inclusion," *Theology Today* 51 (1995) 219–34. This same article is also found as "Homosexual Christians, the Bible, and Gentile Inclusion: Confessions

However, at a deeper level it seems that many of the concerns McDermott raises revolve around to what extent people such as homosexuals can be incorporated as full members into the Christian community of disciples, and I suspect this issue is similar to the high-school classroom debate that led the teacher to suggest to "put the Bible on the shelf."

It was also out of this basic concern that marked my own personal context when I first read his article. As I mentioned above, when I first came across McDermott's article I was trying to write something myself as a reflection of the situation I had experienced during that summer working in the drug rehabilitation community. The Sunday lectionary readings for that particular week included a section of Paul's Second Letter to the Corinthians which included these verses:

> From now on, therefore, we regard no one from a human point of view; even though we once knew Christ from a human point of view, we know him no longer in that way. So if anyone is in Christ, there is a new creation: everything old has passed away; see, everything has become new! All this is from God, who reconciled us to himself through Christ, and has given us the ministry [διακονίαν *diakonian*] of reconciliation; that is, in Christ God was reconciling the world to himself, not counting their trespasses against them, and entrusting the message of reconciliation to us. So we are ambassadors for Christ, since God is making his appeal through us; we entreat you on behalf of Christ, be reconciled to God. For our sake he made him to be sin who knew no sin, so that in him we might become the righteousness of God (2 Cor 5: 16–21).

I am sure I had read those verses numerous times before, but this particular time the "helix" of my particular life experiences of having just returned from working with the men in drug rehabilitation and reading McDermott's article helped me see a deeper truth of this passage in a way I had not realized before. Yes, our formative identity is a new creation in Christ. Yet, I know that I have not yet been completely transformed, the young men I had just been working with were not yet completely transformed, and even those judged so harshly by Cardinal Siri and Father McDermott were not yet completely transformed. What was it then that God was calling us to do? To judge and

---

of a Repenting Heterosexist," in *Homosexuality in the Church: Both Sides of the Debate*, ed. Jeffrey S. Siker (Louisville: Westminster/John Knox Press, 1994) 179–94. I treat Siker's article at some length in my own chapter, "Scripture and Ethics: Core, Context, and Coherence," in *Moral Theology: Fundamental Issues and New Directions. Festschrift for James Hanigan*, mentioned above in fn. 20.

condemn one another? Or perhaps to be something else, namely, ministers ("deacons") of reconciliation and ambassadors of Christ? At the moment the helix of the Scripture intersected with the helix of my life experience so that I could see both in a new light.

The Bible is neither intended to be a rule book nor a technical manual of the moral life. Attention to core, context, and coherence can help us remain open to the Spirit of God that continues to speak to us through both the Scriptures and in the various signs of our times. Just as both exegesis and hermeneutics are ongoing processes, and not once-and-for-all established results, so too the Christian community's ethical use of Scripture must be somewhat open-ended. It is part of our Christian hope that we grow in our understanding and living of the Christian vocation—both individually and communally. The three Cs of Scripture and ethics, core, context, and coherence do not seem to be calling us to take God's place on earth as judge and scrutinizer of people's hearts. St. Paul expresses a similar sentiment: "It is the Lord who judges me. Therefore do not pronounce judgment before the time, before the Lord comes, who will bring to light the things now hidden in darkness and will disclose the purposes of the heart. Then each one will receive commendation from God" (1 Cor 4:4b-5). This does not let us off the hook of judgment, but it leaves the task of judgment in God's hands (cf Jer 17:10).

What God has placed in our hands instead is the ongoing mission of reconciliation. In this we are to be not just his ministers, but his ambassadors. As ambassadors it is not our role to devise God's policy, merely to implement it as best we can according to the light that the Spirit of Jesus gives us. In that light then, and guided by these three Cs of core meaning, context of the Scripture, and coherence both to the whole canon of Scripture and a theologically sound image of God as revealed in Jesus Christ, we can trust that the Spirit will lead us ever more deeply into the progressive revelation of God's merciful and compassionate love that we are called to accept and live in the concreteness of our lives in our morally complex world. While we do this in the community of disciples, in the last analysis we have to also do this alone, and thus we need to turn now to look at how the rational claim axis and the sacred claim axis intersect in the core of the human person, namely, in conscience.

4

The Sanctuary of Conscience: Where the Axes Intersect

Introduction to the Notion of Conscience

When I begin my courses and workshops in moral theology, I tell my students that everything the Church has to say on this subject can be summed up in one key sentence: always follow your formed and informed conscience.[1] Everything else, including both the preceding and following chapters, is really just commentary on this single moral imperative, which is termed the primacy of conscience. While the term conscience as such may not be a key biblical theme, nevertheless the basic idea is captured well in a number of places. For example, the obligation to follow one's conscience is the same as the obligation to follow the voice of God, as we see illustrated well in the post-Pentecost account (cf. Acts 5:27-32) of Peter and the disciples when they were ordered by the officials of the Sanhedrin not to preach any more about Jesus. Peter's response is a classic expression of the primacy of conscience: "We must obey God rather than any human authority" (Acts 5:29). Overall I would argue that it is here in the conscience of the

---

[1] Since conscience is such a key concept in moral theology, the amount of material available is vast. A helpful overview in the personalist tradition of post-Vatican II moral theology is given by Linda Hogan, *Confronting the Truth: Conscience in the Catholic Tradition* (New York: Paulist, 2001). Also helpful in fleshing out aspects of the contemporary Catholic understandings of conscience are the following titles: Richard M. Gula, s.s., "Conscience" in *Christian Ethics: An Introduction*, ed. Bernard Hoose (Collegeville: The Liturgical Press, 1998) 110–22; Bernard Häring, c.ss.r., "Conscience: The Sanctuary of Creative Fidelity and Liberty," chap. 6 in Id., *Free and Faithful in Christ: Moral Theology for Priests and Laity, Volume I: General Moral Theology* (Middlegreen, Slough, United Kingdom: St. Paul Publications, 1978) 224–301; Raphael Gallagher, c.ss.r., and Brendan McConvery, C.Ss.R., eds., *Conscience: Studies in Honour of Seán O'Riordan*, c.ss.r. (Dublin: Gill and Macmillan, 1989); and Dennis J. Billy, c.ss.r. and James Keating, *Conscience and Prayer: the Spirit of Catholic Moral Theology* (Collegeville: The Liturgical Press, 2001).

individual that the rational claim axis and the sacred claim axis intersect, and furthermore it is in conscience that the person brings all of the input from these four sectors together in his or her life.

As we shall see later in this chapter, the notion of conscience is closely intertwined with overall moral development, and the literature on this latter topic has grown significantly in the last two decades.[2] However, we will focus our discussion here primarily on the theological notions of conscience as they have come out of the manualist tradition and have been refined and developed in light of the teachings of the Second Vatican Council. Since Vatican II the primary metaphor used by the Church for conscience is to call it the sanctuary of the human person. In this sense sanctuary has two basic meanings: first, it is a holy place, a sacred space, because that is the most privileged location where the individual meets God. In a church it is the altar (and *not* the tabernacle) that makes the sanctuary holy since that is where God meets the assembled human community. So, too, it is within the interior of the conscience that the individual is, where, according to an old theological axiom, the individual is truly *solus cum solo,* that is, in a fundamental stance before God who alone is our absolute. Besides this sacred space where we meet God, there is another meaning of sanctuary that is actually rooted in this first meaning, namely, a safe place in which no outside authority, not even the legitimate officers of the law may enter justifiably.

This second aspect of sanctuary comes from the practice in the Middle Ages of the so-called "right of sanctuary," which meant that if an individual suspected of a crime could physically reach the church sanctuary before being apprehended, then the police could not enter and remove him or her. Certainly the person did not run for the church sanctuary because that was the best tactical location to mount an all-out strategic defense. Rather it was the moral tradition held by everyone in the community, including those charged with maintaining the law and order, that recognized that it is God, and not anyone

---

[2] Some texts that are helpful in the discussion on moral development would include the following: Owen Flanagan and Amélie Oksenberg Rorty, eds., *Identity, Character, and Morality: Essays in Moral Psychology* (London: MIT Press, 1990); Carol Gilligan, *In a Different Voice: Psychological Theory and Women's Development* (Cambridge, Mass. and London: Harvard University Press, 1982); Lawrence Kohlberg, *Essays on Moral Development,* 2 vols. (San Francisco: Harper and Row, 1981 and 1984); Charles Taylor, *Sources of the Self: The Making of Modern Identity* (Cambridge, Mass.: Harvard University Press, 1989); and Gerhard Zecha and Paul Weingartner, eds., *Conscience: An Interdisciplinary View: Salzburg Colloquium on Ethics in the Sciences and Humanities* (Dordrecht: D. Reidel, 1987).

else, who ultimately is the final and highest judge of each and every person (cf. Jer 17: 9-10 and 1 Cor 4: 3-5). Therefore, when we speak of conscience as being the sanctuary of the human person, we bring together both of these meanings and both are combined in this classic text on conscience from *Gaudium et spes*, Vatican II's Pastoral Constitution on the Church in the Modern World:

> Deep within his conscience man discovers a law which he has not laid upon himself but which he must obey. Its voice, ever calling him to love and to do what is good and to avoid evil, tells him inwardly at the right moment: do this, shun that. For man has in his heart a law inscribed by God. His dignity lies in observing this law, and by it he will be judged. His conscience is man's most secret core, and his sanctuary. There he is alone with God whose voice echoes in his depths. By conscience, in a wonderful way, that law is made known which is fulfilled in the love of God and of one's neighbor. Through loyalty to conscience Christians are joined to other men in the search for truth and for the right solution to so many moral problems which arise both in the life of individuals and from social relationships. Hence, the more a correct conscience prevails, the more do persons and groups turn aside from blind choice and try to be guided by the objective standards of moral conduct. Yet it often happens that conscience goes astray through ignorance which it is unable to avoid, without thereby losing its dignity. This cannot be said of the man who takes little trouble to find out what is true and good, or when conscience is by degrees almost blinded through the habit of committing sin (*Gaudium et spes*, #16).[3]

The sanctuary of conscience leads into the Roman Catholic notion of the autonomy of the conscience. "Autonomy" comes from the two Greek words *nomos* νομος ("law") and *autos* αὐτος ("self"). This means that the individual first discerns and then applies the law to her/himself. It does *not* mean that the individual "invents" the moral law for her/himself. The key aspect of moral autonomy is the sanctity of conscience since acknowledgment of and an obedient response to this moral voice is the locus of all moral goodness and badness. A person is morally good because he or she honestly strives to discern the good and do it, and to uncover evil and avoid or minimize it. It is primarily this stance or effort that determines a person's moral bearing— their overall moral goodness or badness, and only secondarily whether the actual decisions made and actions taken are objectively correct.

[3] The sanctity of conscience is also reflected in Vatican II's Declaration on Religious Liberty, *Dignitatis humanae* (cf. #3, 11 and *passim*) and is also repeated in the *Catechism of the Catholic Church* (cf. 1776).

If the conscience is not the ultimate moral authority *to be obeyed*, then whatever would be posited instead as that ultimate moral authority would of necessity be outside the person. To replace the authority of conscience as the ultimate voice of moral authority, even if it be the pope or the bishops, would open up a huge number of problems concerning authority and mature human action. Heteronomy, the imposition of the moral law from some outside source ("hetero" means "other" or "different" in Greek), is *not* the traditional Roman Catholic position. Whatever authority one believes is absolute is, in effect, the voice of God for that person, and if we allow any outside authority—no matter how respected—to supplant the person's individual conscience, then we are, in effect, making this heteronomous moral authority into God for that person. Making into a "god" that which is not truly God is idolatry, and it is possible to idolize even authority figures which are otherwise worthy and good in themselves. However, to relinquish one's obligation to follow one's conscience, which means seeking to follow what one honestly believes in God's voice, in favor of following the voice of an external authority, would be making that authority into a false god.

Even in the time of St. Thomas Aquinas, when the common theological belief was that outside the institution of the Roman Catholic Church there is no eternal salvation *(extra ecclesia nulla salus est)* the Angelic Doctor maintained that even if an individual were to be excommunicated from the Church for holding a position in conscience, that individual *must* follow his or her conscience, since the ultimate judge and savior is not any earthly individual or institution, but God himself (cf. *ST I-II*, q. 19, art. 5, reply to objection 1). Thus, when in conscience we meet God face to face is what the tradition called *coram Deo*, before God. In laying down this charge to follow one's conscience, even if confronted by the possibility of excommunication, Thomas was not consigning the individual to hell, but underscoring that the key moral relationship between God and the individual is held in conscience, and that if the person (even erroneously) sincerely believed God was asking him or her to do something, then acting out of that conviction would demonstrate faith in God and the concomitant fidelity of action that faith would inspire.

One of my colleagues was challenged once by a seminarian who put the issue this way: "I don't think we should follow Thomas Aquinas' teaching on conscience, since it would be better just to follow the Church's magisterium in everything and then we'll know we're doing the right thing." While most moral theologians today would not agree with this young man and would align themselves instead with *Gaudium et spes* and Thomas Aquinas on the primacy of conscience, there still is a certain uneasiness about trusting something in myself that frankly can lack full insight, or be blinded in so many ways, deceived by rationalization, or be dulled by vice and sin, or just be outright wrong. However, there is one theological school of thought that holds that in virtually every situation we should just follow the official teaching of the magisterium unreservedly, as expressed by the moral philosopher Germain Grisez: "For her members, the Catholic Church is the supreme moral authority under God. Catholics ought to conform their consciences to her teaching in every question, every detail, every respect."[4] Grisez says this must be so since "we believe that our Lord teaches in and through the Church and gives us the word of the Father. Hence, our submission to the Church's teaching is not submission to mere human opinions, but to the very word of God."[5]

While in no way seeking to attack or diminish the legitimate authority of the Church's magisterium, we have to point out a couple of critical difficulties with Grisez's position. First, as we noted in the preceding chapter, it is very difficult to discern in the concrete precisely what the "very word of God" might mean in a complex moral dilemma. As we saw in the last chapter, even the *ipsissima verba*, the very words of Jesus (e.g., about cutting off an offending organ), are not always literalistic infallible guides about what is truly human in a given situation. Second, Grisez moves too quickly from a premise with which we would agree ("we believe that our Lord teaches in and through the Church and gives us the word of the Father") to a conclusion which does not necessarily follow in each and every instance ("Hence, our submission to the Church's teaching is not submission to mere human opinions, but to the very word of God"). As history has shown in numerous instances, this is a condition that on more than one occasion is simply contrary to fact. The magisterium has held a number of opinions that over time it has come to realize were not only ill-suited to the particular historical context, but not really in accord with the progressive revelation of which Vatican II's Constitution on Divine Revelation,

[4] Germain Grisez, *The Way of the Lord Jesus. Volume One: Christian Moral Principles,* Chicago: Franciscan Herald Press, 1983) 566.

[5] Ibid., 570.

Dei verbum, speaks, or our ongoing growth in our understanding of what is truly human according to the natural law.[6]

Even with the assistance of the Holy Spirit, the magisterium is still made of individual human beings who are also subject to all the limitations of the human condition, including partial knowledge. In fact, *Dei verbum* clearly states that the "teaching office is not above the word of God, but serves it" (#10), and as Jesus reminds us no servant is equal to or above the Master (cf. Matt 10:24). Thirdly, as Cardinal Ratzinger noted in a statement quoted in chapter 2, but which bears repeating in this context:

> In the process of assimilating what is really rational and rejecting what only seems to be rational, the whole Church has to play a part. This process cannot be carried out in every detail by an isolated Magisterium, with oracular infallibility. The life and suffering of Christians who profess their faith in the midst of their times has just as important a part to play as the thinking and questioning of the learned, which would have a very hollow ring without the backing of Christian existence, which learns to discern spirits in the travail of everyday life.[7]

Besides the false equation with the word of God as being absolute and completely coterminous with each and every word of the magisterium, the deeper problem with this view is that it ultimately would result in interposing a third party between God and the individual. As one commentator has observed on this position, "it would seem, then, that Grisez advocates obedience to the pope or bishop even when the pope or bishop is wrong. If we carry that to its logical conclusion, we find that, according to Grisez, a person should conform with official teaching even when his or her conscience dictates otherwise."[8] A strict

---

[6] This is an area where the study of history is crucial. See, for example, John T. Noonan, Jr. "Development in Moral Doctrine," *Theological Studies* 54 (1993) 662–77, or his shorter article, "On the Development of Doctrine," *America* 180 (3 April 1999) 6–8. Noonan shows how the Church has developed its moral doctrine in five key areas: adultery, the death penalty, religious liberty, slavery, and usury. A helpful collection which shows how magisterial teaching has changed in a wide variety of areas is found in Maureen Fiedler and Linda Rabben, eds., *Rome Has Spoken: A Guide to Forgotten Papal Statements and How They Have Changed through the Centuries* (New York: Crossroad, 1998).

[7] Ratzinger, "Magisterium of the Church, Faith, Morality," in *Readings in Moral Theology*, no. 2, ed. Charles E. Curran and Richard A. McCormick, s.j. (New York: Paulist Press, 1980) 185.

[8] Bernard Hoose, *Proportionalism: The American Debate and its European Roots* (Washington, D.C.: Georgetown University Press, 1987) 112. In another article Hoose expands his critique, noting that "Grisez, in holding that Catholics should always obey the moral teaching of the magisterium, even when that teaching is possibly wrong, reveals something of great

interpretation of Grisez's view would seem in effect to reverse the Church's centuries-old tradition on the sanctity of conscience.

Recalling the Tradition quadrant of our sacred claim axis, it is the constant teaching of the Church that an individual always follow his or her conscience, even when that conscience might be in "objective" error on what is morally right. However, it is still a basic teaching of the Church that we are bound to follow our conscience faithfully in *all* of our activity even if our conscience be incorrect, incompletely formed, and we cannot rectify these failings. Of course, we should not minimize or overlook our obligation both to form and inform our consciences and here Church teaching is important, as well as the other "fonts" of moral theology, such as Scripture, theological reflection, etc. We will turn to the process of forming and informing our conscience shortly. Even in the case of a malformed or poorly informed, or so-called erroneous, conscience the *Catechism of the Catholic Church* states emphatically that no one must be forced to act contrary to his or her conscience, and that one must always follow his or her conscience. To deliberately act against one's conscience would be condemning one-self.[9] Yet while this freedom of conscience is not quite absolute, it is limited by the common good, since it would not grant anyone the "right" to follow his/her conscience in order to hurt seriously oneself or others (two clear examples would be suicide and murder). Thus, we see this absolute right of conscience socially contextualized and in conscience the sacred claim and rational claim axes do intersect.

To sum up this core teaching on the primacy of conscience, if conscience is removed or displaced as our interior moral guide then in the resulting vacuum some other exterior moral guide will illegitimately usurp this role. Our experience and human history have shown a wide array of potential usurpers, such as the state, political correctness, conventional wisdom, peer pressure, as well as any religious authority, including the magisterium of the Church. While these guides may have differing values and roles to play as exterior guides, none should

---

importance about his understanding of the human good and the place it has in his method of moral judgement. It would seem that rightness for him is dependent upon the fulfilment of certain basic goods, *except where such fulfilment would conflict with the will of God as expressed through the magisterium of the Roman Catholic Church* [emphasis in the original]." "Proportionalists, Deontologists and the Human Good," *The Heythrop Journal* 33 (1992) 184.

[9] Cf. the whole section of "Moral Conscience" in the *Catechism of the Catholic Church*, #1776–1802, but especially #1782 and #1790 for the points cited here.

ever be elevated to the role of highest guide (held by the interior conscience). To do so would violate the fundamental dignity and whole notion of human personhood, as well as call into question much of the whole philosophical and theological underpinnings of our understanding of morality.

Conscience in Manualist Moral Theology

While conscience is not primarily a scriptural term, there are certain aspects of "conscience" that derive from variant spellings of the Greek word συνε ίδησις found in the New Testament and rendered as *synderesis* and/or *syneidesis*. These were interpreted by scholastic theologians and Thomas Aquinas as referring to two slightly different aspects of conscience, namely, as a "habit" and as an "act" of moral judgment. The Greek terms were translated (and combined) in Latin as *conscientia*, and from that comes the English word "conscience." However, as the tradition developed there was unfortunately insufficient continued contact with Scripture and so the treatment of conscience became largely divorced from the New Testament themes of discernment and discipleship.

The traditional approach to moral conscience is an important part of the heritage, and since many theologians and lay people still work implicitly out of this background or in reaction to this heritage we need to outline it in brief. In the scholastic and manualist traditions conscience was called a "faculty," and this term referred to the capacity to do something. Thus, the faculty of speech gave one the possibility of communication, and the faculty of conscience gave one the possibility of using reason in moral reflection. However, this notion of conscience as faculty was unfortunately somewhat abstracted or extrapolated from the individual's whole personhood, as can be seen in the following definition taken from a widely used pre-Vatican II dictionary of moral theology: "*Conscience* is a judgment made by an individual concerning the morality of his actions. More precisely, conscience is a judgment of the practical reason deciding by inference from general principles the moral goodness or malice of a particular act."[10]

In the manualist tradition there were two kinds of judgment made in conscience. The first concerned the rightness or wrongness of an

---

[10] Giuseppe Graneris, "Conscience," in *Dictionary of Moral Theology*, ed. Francesco Cardinal Roberti and Pietro Palazzini, trans. from the 2nd Italian ed. under the direction of Henry J. Yannone (London: Burns & Oates, 1962) 295.

abstract action in itself, e.g., that plagiarism is wrong. The second judgment is whether the particular action being contemplated by an individual constituted that abstract action or not. In other words, does my use of someone else's insights in my term paper without giving a detailed reference citation constitute plagiarism? The first judgment refers primarily to the "objective" nature—the rightness or wrongness of the moral act in itself, and in the Latin this was called the *iudicium de actu ponendo* (judgment concerning the act to be undertaken). The second type of judgment was called *iudicium de positione actus*, literally, "judgment about the position of the act." This judgment is related more closely to the subjective judgment of the moral agent that this or that act will be "right" and therefore "good."[11]

Perhaps a concrete example might help us to see this abstract principle a bit more clearly. Bob is having some difficulty since he has partied a bit too long the night before the big English test. He has a splitting headache and doesn't feel he can do very well on the upcoming exam. Bob therefore asks his good friend John to take the test for him, and he assures John that since the class is extremely large, if John just sits in Bob's assigned seat all will go well. John realizes that doing well on this test will be very crucial for Bob's grade in the course and his larger career plans. He believes that since Bob basically knows the material to be covered in the test, if he sits in for Bob it really won't be "dishonest" or "cheating," but rather simply helping out a good friend who is temporarily indisposed. So John decides to go ahead and take the test for Bob. In John's mind, to use the traditional vocabulary, he considers the moral issue at hand to be a legitimate act of friendship. Taking the test for Bob is this act of friendship and John wants to be a good friend. Thus, the *iudicium de actu ponendo* (judgment concerning the act to be undertaken) is equated with helping out a friend, and the concrete way to help out his friend is to take the exam for him in this set of circumstances. But we would hold that John has in fact *mis*-judged the

---

[11] In the traditional theology this distinction allowed for the possibility that one could "err" about the objective moral nature of an act, and yet still be acting in good faith (or sometimes called good conscience). The "error" would be an error of judgment *de actu ponendo*. In acting in good faith though one could not "err" in the second sort of judgment though *de positione actus*. Thus, in summary we could say that the person believes that doing "X" is morally good: this is the *iudicium de positione actus*. If the person believed that "X" was not morally good, but did it anyway, this would be malicious. However, this "judgment" so far only has taken into account the "subjective" judgment of the moral agent about the action. The action itself could in fact be morally (or "objectively") wrong. This "objective" moral judgment is the *iudicium de actu ponendo* (judgment concerning the act to be undertaken).

actual act being undertaken (the taking of the test for Bob). John's judgment about the actual act is that it is an act of legitimate friendship when in fact it is an act of cheating and is morally dishonest.

The second type of conscience mis-judgment involved here, the so-called *iudicium de positione actus* or judgment about the position of the act, follows from the first mis-judgment. John wants to be a good friend and we would agree that this in itself is morally good. However, since John is mistaken about the actual moral meaning of the act he performs (taking the test for Bob), that is the root of John's moral error. It isn't that John has mistaken the basic notion that friendship is good and therefore helping out one's friends is morally good; he has instead misunderstood that to help out his friend *in this manner* is morally wrong since the act he has done, from a moral perspective, is not in fact an act of friendship but an act of cheating. John is acting in good faith, but John is still wrong and John's error is in misjudging the moral meaning of the act he performs.

This distinction is key to understanding the Church's traditional moral teaching on right and erroneous conscience, and the related concepts of vincible and invincible ignorance. As we have seen from the preceding discussion the manualists did not think it likely that someone would normally choose to do evil in full knowledge, and so they posited "ignorance" of the objective moral order as the cause for such an erroneous choice.[12] It wasn't that John was malicious and wanted to pervert the educational system that led him to take the exam for Bob; rather it was that John was ignorant about the real moral meaning of his playing exam switcheroo with Bob. The manualists held that if this ignorance could be overcome by the person's reasonable efforts it was termed "vincible," and the person was held to be morally accountable for his or her actions in this case. But if this ignorance could not be overcome even by a person's sincere efforts, then the ignorance was called "invincible" and the person was *not* held morally accountable for his or her actions, even though the actions themselves were still judged to violate the objective moral order. Admittedly this traditional model is excessively intellectualistic, and these are rather difficult concepts to digest all at once so we shall re-

---

[12] The manualists believed therefore that for a person acting in good faith, his or her *iudicium de actu ponendo* (judgment concerning the act to be undertaken) could be erroneous while at the same time the *iudicium de positione actus* (judgment about the position of the act) could not in principle be erroneous—i.e., a person who is acting in good faith will always try to do what she or he judges to be right.

turn to them again once we have finished outlining all of the relevant concepts in the manualist treatment of conscience.

"Certain" and "doubtful" were two conscience terms used in the manualist tradition, and this pair was described in terms of the degree of assent given by the person's conscience to the judgment made. A certain conscience was one in which the individual believed to be acting correctly (even if objectively this was not the case). A doubtful conscience described a situation in which the person was genuinely perplexed as to the morally correct decision. To use our example of John's taking the test for Bob, if John was morally convinced that this would be a good act of friendship then we would describe his conscience as "certain" (though still erroneous). If John, on the other hand, was perplexed as to whether taking the test for Bob would be the right thing to do, then we would describe his conscience in this instance as being "doubtful." The manualist tradition always held that one should try to resolve a doubtful conscience before taking action, and that in cases in which the person was morally perplexed as to the proper course of action he or she was advised to take appropriate counsel, such as talking to a priest in confession.

While this may have worked to some extent in theory, we must recognize that many times people simply do not take this amount of reflection before acting, and also in some critical instances there simply would not be time to get a second or third opinion. I do not think it is very helpful to consider these concepts of vincible/invincible and certain/doubtful as clearly differentiated and demarcated compartments so that in one compartment we have "certain" conscience and in another we have "doubtful" conscience. Rather I think it would be more accurate to visualize these types of conscience as range points along a spectrum. Thus, most of us move from doubt to certainty not all at once, but over time. Similarly, our ignorance does not come in two separate varieties labeled "vincible" and "invincible," but like every process of acquiring knowledge also will grow over time. Thus, what might be considered "invincible ignorance" at one point in human history (such as the notion that slavery was morally acceptable) will over time gradually shift so that if someone today were to hold the proposition that slavery could be morally good or even neutral, we would probably judge that person as being culpably ignorant. Nevertheless, invincibility and doubt are concepts that can still be helpful in nuancing (not dispensing from) moral culpability in a whole range of issues, both personal and social, such as technological advances with unforeseen effects, and/or involvement in aspects of structural evil and social sin.

In this context we should also raise what is called the principle of responsibility, which means that we do have to exercise a certain amount of caution and prudence in considering the possibility that some of our actions may have effects and ramifications that we do not clearly anticipate at the moment of our acting. In contemporary ethics the concept of relational responsibility ethics has developed into an important moral theory in its own right.[13] Even though we obviously cannot foresee each and every consequence of our actions, our historical nature teaches us that we should expect unforeseen effects. This realization should not necessarily paralyze us from action, but rather school us in greater prudence. The notions of vincibility, invincibility, certainty, and doubt also point to the great need for continuous conscience formation, information, and conversion. We can see these terms as inter-related aspects, grounded in the objective moral order, while recognizing our own sinfulness and need for ongoing conversion.[14]

The Enigma of a Certain but Erroneous Conscience

As we have stressed, the fundamental tenet of the primacy of conscience is that one must *always* follow one's conscience, and this includes even those cases when that conscience is wrong, or erroneous, about what is morally correct. Of course, one has a serious obligation to form and inform one's conscience, yet we need to probe a bit further into what may seem a bit enigmatic at first: if there is an objective moral order grounded in God's loving providence, and if the first principle of the natural law is to do and foster the good and avoid or minimize evil as far as possible, how is it that we should allow, much less exhort, people to follow their conscience even when we believe them to be wrong? This is an important point to clarify since one hears very often the phrase "I felt it was okay to do according to my conscience." I remember some years ago coming across a cartoon that

---

[13] See Hans Jonas, *The Imperative of Responsibility: In Search of an Ethic for the Technological Age*, trans. Hans Jonas and David Herr (Chicago: University of Chicago Press, 1985); and H. Richard Niebuhr's classic work, *The Responsible Self: An Essay in Christian Moral Philosophy*, with an introduction by James M. Gustafson (New York: Harper & Row, 1963).

[14] Pope John Paul II makes this same point of the need for ongoing conscience formation "to make it the object of a continuous conversion to what is true and what is good" *Veritatis splendor*, #64.

read "my conscience used to trouble me—but since then I've learned a lot of tricks to keep it quiet!" How do we avoid anesthetizing the true voice of conscience in our lives?

Let us return then to John's dilemma about whether or not he should take the test for Bob. If taking the test for Bob under these circumstances were in accord with the relevant objective moral norms the traditional vocabulary would call the judgment of John's conscience to be "right," since it was in accord with the demands of objective morality. However, most of us would probably say that John was not right in this case, and so his conscience-based judgment was in error. Now comes a further question: was John morally responsible for his action? This is where a consideration of vincible and invincible ignorance comes into play. John made a mistake in judgment and the manualists would attribute this judgment to moral ignorance. However, they would say that if the resulting error in judgment could have been overcome by a reasonable effort of reflection by John, then his resulting error was due to vincible ignorance, since the word "vincible" means "able to be overcome." In this case John would be morally responsible for his actions.

I suspect most of us (or at least most teachers) would conclude that if John had just thought things through a bit more he would have quickly realized that helping out Bob in this way would ultimately be to no one's true good, and that taking the exam under these circumstances would be morally wrong. The fact that John did not take enough time or effort to think this matter through does not remove the moral responsibility for his action, since his ignorance was vincible. Even though most of us probably would not use this particular set of vocabulary terms to analyze the situation, I suspect that nearly everyone would agree that John did not do the right thing in these circumstances and that he is morally responsible for his unethical choice. Most of us have encountered people claiming to act in good conscience when we suspect that this simply is not the case. Probably in a significant number of such cases, a person who does evil does so acting in bad conscience. It is just that the person has not taken care to inform his/her conscience adequately and yet has the freedom and ability to do so. We should acknowledge the very real human tendency to let ourselves off the hook. For example, a person who cheats on his/her taxes saying "everyone does it" or "the government knows this and has adjusted the tax rates accordingly" (an explanation I heard often while living in Italy).

What we see at work here is probably the biggest conscience problem for good people, namely, the dark side of the exercise of human reason which we call rationalization. So often we can deceive ourselves into thinking that if we can just come up with some "reasons" for our desired action, then the action itself must be "reasonable," and we trick ourselves into saying that we are then following our conscience. The traditional notion of vincible ignorance tells us that we can and should take great care and effort at arriving at moral decisions, especially when the easier way out seems so attractive. In this process we should seek to inform our conscience by carefully considering not only the particular case or problem at hand, looking at all alternatives, weighing consequences, but also honestly examining the positions and opinions of trusted moral authorities. Here is where outside authority, especially the teachings of the Church, do play an important role. Listening to these authority figures is opening our hearts and minds to the genuine possibility that we may not always have the moral wisdom necessary for making a good decision. This whole process of carefully informing our conscience and discerning what these authorities tell us is the virtue necessary to correct our vincible ignorance and combat the tendency of rationalization so that we can more consistently make better moral choices.

But what about the second kind of erroneous conscience, namely, that done due to so-called invincible ignorance? Pope John Paul II describes invincible ignorance as "an ignorance of which the subject is not aware and which he is unable to overcome by himself."[15] Strictly speaking an invincibly erroneous conscience is not connected with errors of fact that lead to evil results, such as "I thought the loaded gun was in fact empty when I pulled the trigger." This action certainly is evil, but not morally so, as we've discussed in chapter 2. Rather, invincible error concerns mitigating factors which are so serious that the person most likely cannot see his/her own error and the fault for the lack of such moral insight is not personally culpable. Invincible error and ignorance keep our acts from being truly "human" in the full moral sense.

Though this concept has been accepted for centuries by moral theologians, I have found that the task of trying to explain invincible ignorance and its related concepts of imputable guilt (i.e., moral innocence) is quite difficult indeed. It seems that the ultimate stumbling block for

[15] Ibid., #63.

many people is the troubling logical conclusion, which the manualistic tradition has taught since the time of Thomas Aquinas. It concludes that a person who acts in invincible ignorance and does something objectively wrong from a moral point of view incurs no moral guilt (the position of Thomas Aquinas), and might even be said to gain moral merit (the position of Alphonsus Liguori, doctor of the Church and patron saint of moral theologians). This seems to call into question the whole notion of an objective moral order for these sorts of people.

Before going further let us see if an analogy might clarify this enigmatic point about invincible ignorance not causing moral culpability. Probably most of us would admit that a doctor in the 1970s would not be either medically or morally negligent for missing the correct diagnosis when confronted by a range of symptoms that we now know to be classic indicators of AIDS. There really would be no way at that time for the doctor to diagnose the disease. The doctor would be ignorant, but the ignorance would be invincible, since at that time in history even heroic efforts on the part of the physician would not have uncovered the medical truth of the AIDS condition. Therefore due to this invincible ignorance, we would not hold the doctor to be morally culpable for the missed diagnosis. But if a doctor were to make the same mistake today we certainly would hold him or her medically and morally responsible. The ignorance in this case could be overcome by basic ongoing training expected of all physicians.[16]

Bernard Häring adds that invincible ignorance should not be interpreted as just a rational intellectualism, but rather we should look on it in light of an understanding of conscience that embraces the existential totality of the individual human person. Häring defines invincible ignorance as "a matter of a person to 'realize' a moral obligation. Because of the person's total experience, the psychological impasses, and the whole context of his life, he is unable to cope with a certain moral imperative. The intellectual difficulties of grasping the values behind a certain imperative are often deeply rooted in existential difficulties."[17]

---

[16] I am indebted for this excellent example to Charles E. Curran, *The Catholic Moral Tradition Today: A Synthesis* (Washington, D.C.: Georgetown University Press, 1999) 173.

[17] Bernard Häring, "A Theological Evaluation," in *The Morality of Abortion: Legal and Historical Perspectives*, ed. John T. Noonan, Jr. (Cambridge, Mass.: Harvard University Press, 1970) 140.

Connecting the Objective and Subjective Poles of Conscience

Another eminent moral theologian who would share Häring's insight is Josef Fuchs. In many important articles on the nature of conscience, Fuchs has tried to build on both the long-standing tradition of the primacy of conscience and the Vatican II affirmation of conscience as the privileged inner sanctuary where the human person most closely encounters God. One of Fuchs' major contributions to our understanding of what conscience is and how it operates is to note the relationship between the subjective and objective aspects found in individual human conscience. Fuchs notes that historically the "emphasis has been placed on the object-orientation of the conscience. This tells one *what* one has to do, providing ethical evaluations and formulations of ethical norms, and indicating the solution to problematic situations. In theology these elements are often considered as being 'the voice of God': hence, there is a general tendency in many cases to identify the conscience with practical reason."[18]

This view of conscience impoverishes its deeper nature and so, instead of using the manualist traditional term of conscience as a faculty of reason employed in judging relevant moral norms and corresponding actions, Fuchs chooses to speak of conscience as a "phenomenon." A phenomenon includes the traditional manualistic notion of conscience as a faculty that exercises right reason, but conscience obviously involves so much more than just making right (or wrong) judgments. For Fuchs, the deepest levels of a person's consciousness can never be fully plumbed either by the person him/herself, much less by others. God alone knows the individual human person completely. Yet human persons do realize in some incomplete and imperfect sense that they are moral beings and that therefore their lives are bounded to an extent by moral obligations that they may have not chosen for themselves. For example, I can choose to go or not to go to a museum next Sunday, but I am not free to choose to be or not to be a moral being. This aspect of moral being Fuchs calls "the deepest core of the conscience as personal subject."[19]

As we saw above with the brief discussion on rationalization, some confusion results in the understanding of the expression, "follow your

---

[18] Josef Fuchs, S.J., "The Phenomenon of Conscience: Subject-orientation and Object-orientation," ch. 8 in *Christian Morality: The Word Became Flesh*, trans., Brian McNeil (Washington, D.C.: Georgetown University Press; Dublin: Gill and Macmillan, 1987) 123.

[19] Ibid., 124.

conscience," and we need to keep clearly in mind what conscience actually involves. Fuchs says that the injunction to follow one's conscience is not first and foremost related to conforming one's actions to an understanding of what the objective moral order requires, but that fundamentally following one's conscience is basically related to the person as a subject him/herself. Of course, there is an object-orientation to our conscience as well, yet Fuchs cautions that it is "not possible to learn about objective and morally correct behavior and conduct in the world from external norms only but also from one's own convictions embedded in the conscience."[20] The problem has been to focus primarily on the object-orientation, the concrete moral choice made, and therefore to equate conscience with practical reason. However, this is putting the cart before the horse, since we cannot have an object-orientation unless we first have a subject, namely, the person who is actually making the concrete moral decision. To return to our two test-taking students, John and Bob, we cannot speak of John's choice to do the right or wrong thing (object-orientation) without first attending to the fact that John exists as a moral being before, during, and after his individual ethical actions. Fuchs would say that this understanding of conscience returns us "to the matter of the human being's deep-seated self-consciousness. Fundamentally, this consciousness is always present in every human self-realization, so that it concerns not simply the realization of one deed or another, but also, at the same time and very profoundly, the realization of one's very self."[21]

Fuchs would say that we strive for proper realization of ourselves because that is our core nature, in other words, who we are as authentic human beings. Striving for the proper realization in the world in which we live means we are ultimately seeking to be faithful and true to ourselves, being who we are made to be by God. Conscience then is the modality of that core nature that makes this particular way of being human possible. This is what Fuchs calls the subject-orientation of conscience and as such "conscience's genuine and therefore primary interest is the moral goodness of the personal subject as such. And it is solely this personal morality that is morality in the true and original meaning of the word. Every other use of the word is analogous, e.g., 'moral rectitude' in life, moral norms for acting, etc."[22] In other words, these other terms simply mean that we are seeking to be true to ourselves.

[20] Ibid.
[21] Ibid.
[22] Ibid., 125.

As the great English metaphysical poet John Donne (d. 1631) observed, "no man is an island, entire of itself; every man is a piece of the continent, a part of the main; if a clod be washed away by the sea, Europe is the less, as well as if a promontory were, as well as if a manor of thy friends or of thine own were; any man's death diminishes me, because I am involved in mankind; and therefore never send to know for whom the bell tolls; it tolls for thee."[23] This means that not just in death, but especially in life we cannot realize ourselves in total subjectivity alone. We have to go out of ourselves, and seek to live in the world with others. This fact brings us to the other essential aspect of conscience, the object-orientation.

As Thomas Aquinas argues, the desire to do and foster the good and avoid and minimize evil is inscribed on our hearts (the so-called *lex indita non scripta*), and in this vein Fuchs says that "on account of one's goodness one must seek in personal responsibility to act according to the appropriate call of the human objective world. Grounded in one's own personal goodness one strives for right behavior in this world, acting in the interests of the well-being of the human global community as an extension of the core of one's very self."[24] The relationship and interaction between the subject-orientation and object-orientation are the two poles of the human conscience, but just as the North Pole and South Pole are found in the planet earth, so both the subject-orientation and object-orientation poles of conscience are properly found *within* the human person. According to Fuchs' view, the object-orientation pole does *not* stand outside the human person. Though the faculty notion of conscience employed in the manualist tradition would seem to suggest that the objective moral order is "out there" somewhere, and conscience simply judges the appropriate moral norm and corresponding action, Fuchs would argue that since the objective moral order is ultimately grounded in the relationship God has with us, we do not find this moral order "out there" in an way external to us. The objective moral order is not an external entity like the periodic table of elements which could be grasped by a chemist's or physicist's experiment, or as an astronomer might measure how the moon stands in relation to the earth. Fuchs would argue that if the objective moral order is not "out there," then it must be "in here"—in the interior of the sanctuary of a person's conscience and therefore the

---

[23] John Donne, "Devotions on Emergent Occasions," no. 6.
[24] Fuchs, "Phenomenon," 124.

objective pole of conscience does not exist outside of the human person, but within. Perhaps a couple of diagrams may help illustrate this important insight.

This diagram shows conscience seen primarily as a faculty of making correct moral judgments. The objective moral order stands outside and somewhat apart from the individual person, while the person is called upon to respond to a concrete moral dilemma by judging the proper moral principle and its concomitant application in this or that particular situation. This view is a bit like doing a high-school chemistry experiment: you are confronted with an unknown substance that you then try to identify correctly, using the established experimental methods of testing you have learned to date, and bringing these results together with your knowledge of the periodic table of elements and the other laws of nature. In this analogy all of the various circumstances of the moral situation are like the observable properties of the unknown substance being tested, and the relevant objective moral norms are somewhat like the chemical properties of the laws of nature as embodied in the periodic table of elements.

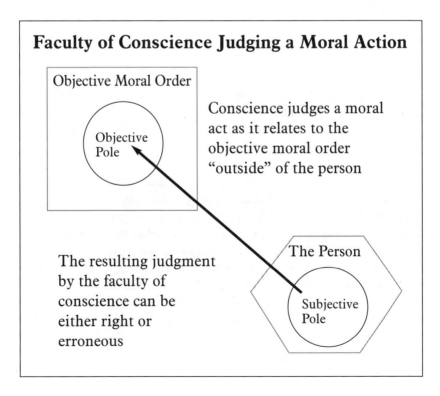

Faculty of Conscience Judging a Moral Action

Objective Moral Order

Objective Pole

Conscience judges a moral act as it relates to the objective moral order "outside" of the person

The resulting judgment by the faculty of conscience can be either right or erroneous

The Person

Subjective Pole

Following this model, the role of conscience then is to put these two together to come out with the morally right answer. Just like the high-school chemistry student doing the experiment, a moral misjudgment or error can be made. If this error is due to insufficient reflection (like the student doing a sloppy experiment), then this would be an example of vincible ignorance and the person would be morally culpable for his or her poor moral judgment. However, if our young chemists were faced with a complex compound that required more refined tools of analysis than were to be found in the high-school chem lab, or if the chemists were confronted with some brand new natural phenomenon they had not yet studied, then we would not hold them culpable for the resulting misidentification of the mystery compound or puzzling phenomenon. This would be equivalent to invincible ignorance. While the concept of invincible ignorance was accepted in the moral manuals, the concrete illustrative examples given were not generally helpful, and those that were supplied usually attributed the particular instance of invincible ignorance to some gross defect of moral upbringing, somewhat like a young man raised in the midst of a ring of petty thieves might lack the proper training to recognize the moral evil of stealing. However, the view was maintained that the objective moral order itself remained intact since it stood outside of the individual human person, as it is pictured in our diagram.

There is a problem with this diagram though as it tries to depict the full picture of conscience, since this schematization does not adequately resolve our enigma of just why someone should follow even his or her erroneous conscience. If getting the correct moral answer is paramount, and if the role of conscience is primarily to supply the individual with the correct moral answer, then if that conscience is faulty it should be either corrected or replaced by a faculty that will work better, such as trusting the external authority of a moral expert such as the magisterium of the Church. If this works in the exceptional cases of invincible ignorance then it is only a short logical step to surrender virtually all of our moral judgment to this same moral expert, adopting a view similar to that enunciated by Germain Grisez, that "Catholics ought to conform their consciences to her [the Church's magisterium] teaching in every question, every detail, every respect."[25]

While there may be a certain amount of intellectual and moral comfort in this approach, as we have seen in our discussion above,

[25] Grisez, *The Way of the Lord Jesus*, 566.

there still is one troubling element—this sort of surrender to an outside moral authority, no matter how expert or worthy of our respect, would mean that we would have to give up in effect the traditional Catholic teaching on legitimate moral autonomy and the primacy of conscience. Is there any way out of this conundrum? I believe there is if we return to the fuller notion of conscience expressed in Vatican II as the sacred place, the sanctuary, where the individual meets God in a most privileged way. For this understanding of how conscience operates, we need to replace our earlier diagram with another picture.

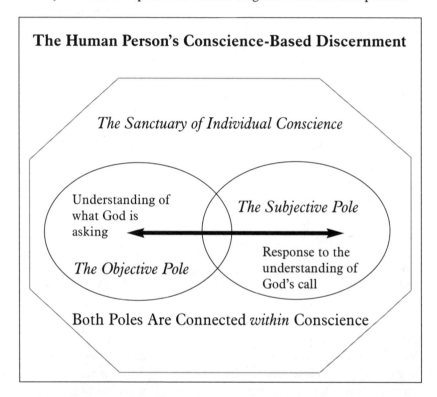

The Human Person's Conscience-Based Discernment

The Sanctuary of Individual Conscience

Understanding of what God is asking

The Subjective Pole

The Objective Pole

Response to the understanding of God's call

Both Poles Are Connected *within* Conscience

In this second depiction we see that the objective pole of moral judgment is also connected to the subjective pole, but that both poles are located within the individual's conscience-based moral discernment. It is here within the conscience that the individual first discovers and then responds to that law inscribed on the human heart by God. To repeat the words of *Gaudium et spes,* "Its voice, ever calling him to love and to do what is good and to avoid evil, tells him inwardly at the right moment: do this, shun that." This voice, this objective pole, is truly objective, but not in an "out there" external manner like the periodic table of elements is the objective pole to our high-school chemistry experiment. Rather, when individuals discern and respond to what they honestly (objectively) believe God is asking of them, then they are responding to this objective pole. This is so because, as our classic description of conscience in *Gaudium et spes* goes on to add, the human person has in his or her "heart a law inscribed by God [the *lex indita non scripta*]. His dignity lies in observing this law, and by it he will be judged" (*GS* #16). These words tell us therefore that even more important than getting the ethically correct answer is the authentic conscience-based process of moral discernment and response on the part of the individual. When individuals undertake this process, they are in effect answering what they honestly and "objectively" believe to be the voice of God in their heart, and it is this hearing and responding that connect the objective and subjective poles of conscience. Even if the person is ultimately wrong about his or her decision, if it "happens that conscience goes astray through ignorance which it is unable to avoid" (*GS* #16), nevertheless conscience does not lose its dignity.

Building on these insights from *Gaudium et spes*, we have a better understanding of how conscience operates, and this in turn helps us see more clearly the true nature of human morality. In this vein Fuchs concludes that "the personal subject's own decisions are either moral or immoral not on account of the subject either actually accepting or rejecting the 'morally correct' conduct of the object world, but because he either takes the necessary pains or fails to do so." It is the effort above all else that counts, and this means that for the individual his or her "personal moral goodness is not a case of someone acting in a morally correct way in our human world, but of acting according to what the conscience recognizes as being right." Moral goodness, since it is essentially personal, "is exclusively something existing within the subject (conscience), as is likewise the 'moral truth' and the 'moral decision' which exist and take place internally; the latter refers not to a truth 'in itself' but to a truth 'in myself.'"[26] In other words, what Fuchs is saying is that it is primarily the sincere effort and commitment to do what we honestly believe to be the right thing that makes us morally good, and not the actual right or wrong act performed in itself. Similarly, what

---

[26] Fuchs, "The Phenomenon of Conscience," 125. To bolster this argument Fuchs references Thomas Aquinas on this point in the latter's own discussion of Aristotle; cf. Thomas Aquinas, *In Eth. Nic.*, LVI 1,1, n. 1131.

makes us morally bad is the lack of this sort of effort, and not primarily the act in itself. Thus, in Fuchs' view getting the right (or wrong) answer in itself does not make us morally good or bad, but rather the effort we take, or do not take, to try to do the right thing or avoid the wrong thing. This seems like a simple enough conclusion in theory, but it is still the locus of considerable discussion and misunderstanding.[27]

This process takes place within the human subject, but it is not subjective in the sense that individuals make up what they consider to be moral, but simply try to respond as honestly as possible to what they believe God is objectively asking of them. Of course, not everyone always takes the necessary pains to respond honestly, such as the one "who takes little trouble to find out what is true and good, or when conscience is by degrees almost blinded through the habit of committing sin" (*GS* #16). It is important to bear in mind the effects of habitual vice and the deadening of both individual and collective conscience that results from such vice. Even when sincere efforts are undertaken, we do not always arrive at the morally correct answer, either individually or corporately. *Gaudium et spes* makes much the same point when it points out that in this process of responding in "loyalty to conscience Christians are joined to other men in the search for truth and for the right solution to so many moral problems which arise both in the life of individuals and from social relationships. Hence, the more a correct conscience prevails, the more do persons and groups turn aside from blind choice and try to be guided by the objective standards of moral conduct" (*GS* #16). In short, there is a reciprocal relationship between the objective and subjective poles of conscience that exists primarily within the human person. However, since persons are by nature social beings, their individual exercise of conscience likewise has to have a social dimension. It is this social dimension of conscience that has often been neglected and to which we should now turn.

Conscience and Culture as Modalities of Moral Living

As we noted above, conscience is one of the basic modalities in which we are human. If any member of the species we call *homo sapiens*

---

[27] One theologian who has written extensively on this issue is James F. Keenan, S.J. See especially Keenan's doctoral dissertation done under Fuchs, *Goodness and Rightness in Thomas Aquinas' Summa Theologiae* (Washington, D.C.: Georgetown University Press, 1992), as well as his article "Can a Wrong Action Be Good? The Development of Theological Opinion on Erroneous Conscience," *Eglise et théologie* 24 (1993) 205–19, which gives a brief historical overview of the tradition of this issue.

really lacked any sense of conscience at all, then it would be very difficult to call that individual a truly human person from a moral perspective because he or she would be incapable of the sort of basic moral reflection and action that goes into personhood. Calling conscience a modality means that it is more than just a faculty of the human person, since we could imagine a true human person who might lack a given faculty (such as the faculty of sight) and yet we would still believe that individual to be a person capable of moral agency. But if certain individuals were to have absolutely no sense of conscience, then we could not really consider them to be true moral persons since they would lack this absolutely essential element for moral life.

While conscience is a foundational modality or way in which we are human, there are other modalities as well. Sexuality is certainly one of these, as there is no person who does not have a core sexual identity, even if that person were to refrain from engaging in any and all direct genital activity for life. So much important work on probing the complex interrelationships between the notions of sex, sexuality, and gender has been done in recent years,[28] and some of the fruit of this research has influenced official magisterial teaching as well. The *Catechism of the Catholic Church* stresses that sexuality embraces all aspects of the human person in the unity of body and soul, and everyone regardless of their particular vocation or station in life, has to live out his or her sexual identity (cf. # 2332–33). This sexuality is part of the way in which we were created human and thus is a modality of being human which is much broader and deeper than sexual activity or even the gender roles we play. Certainly our modality of sexuality is given expression in the experience quadrant of our moral sources and thus has to come into play with our modality of conscience as well.

While much more has been, and still remains to be, said about sexuality, there is another modality of our being human that is less well developed in either traditional or contemporary moral theology. This underdeveloped theme is culture. Like sexuality, culture has been with us since the dawn of human existence, yet our understanding of how each operates and what each involves is only now beginning to unfold.

---

[28] While the bibliography here is vast, I would especially recommend Lisa Sowle Cahill's magisterial work, *Sex, Gender and Christian Ethics* (New York: Cambridge University Press, 1996), and Kevin Kelley's *New Directions in Sexual Ethics: Moral Theology and the Challenge to* AIDS (London: Geoffrey Chapman, 1998).

Part of the reason for this delayed attention to the role of culture in human morality is due to the understanding of the human person articulated from the time of the Greek philosophers through medieval scholastic philosophy and down through the flowering of the manualist tradition. This approach tended to focus on a conceptualization of "human nature" that focused on the supposed "essence" and tended to factor out all the non-essential factors (called "accidents" in scholastic terminology). So how are we to understand the interaction between nature and culture? One view that is too common, but ultimately seriously misguided, is that of the late Swiss moral theologian Franz Böckle who put it this way:

> Nature is now understood, on the one hand, as a necessary structure, which emerges all the more clearly the more the cultural superstructure is stripped away. It therefore becomes important for nature to be liberated and for all human activity to be consistently understood as natural. Alternately, nature can be viewed as mankind's pure and hypothetical original condition, preceding human history.[29]

While we probably could agree that a person's hair color is not crucial or essential to human personhood, if we are not careful in what we choose to disregard we may arrive at an abstraction that unfortunately bears no real resemblance to any actual human person, past, present, or to come. Can we strip away the "cultural superstructure" as Böckle suggests, and then get to core human nature? I would answer in the negative, and for some support would turn to the noted cultural anthropologist Mary Douglas who says that this precisely is what has happened too often when moral philosophy in its search for universal moral principles applicable to all peoples, embarks on that quest with a seriously skewed underlying understanding of both culture and humanity:

> According to this view, culture consists of many layers: peel off the top one and the next and the next, with every step toward conceiving a decultured human being we could be arriving at the moral principles which drive us all. But this superficially attractive idea presupposes an inner homunculus, the core rational being. It also presupposes this feral child, stripped of all cultural adhesions, to be the locus of moral principles.[30]

[29] Franz Böckle, "Nature as the Basis of Morality," in *Readings in Moral Theology, No. 7: Natural Law and Theology*, ed. Charles E. Curran and Richard A. McCormick (Mahwah, N.J.: Paulist Press, 1991) 392.

[30] Mary Douglas, "Morality and Culture," *Ethics* 93 (1983) 787. This article is a review essay of four books that touch on culture and morality: Adrian Mayer, ed., *Culture and*

I would argue strongly, along with Mary Douglas, that there is no such thing as "culture-less" human nature. We cannot strip the layers of culture away from any human individual or group in order to reach some pristine state of moral nature that would then shine forth unclouded by the accretions of particular cultures. What this means for the whole area of ethics is that we need to pay greater methodological attention to cultural particularity that in turn calls for greater respect for, and attention to, culture itself as a "morally relevant feature" of the highest order. It also means that we have to use a concept such as "human nature" very carefully since there is no model "human nature" that can somehow be employed to mold all ethically correct human behavior.

The term "human nature" is an abstraction. Abstractions are very important in our philosophical reflection since they help us to navigate from the particularities of our individual experiences to common notions of what constitutes true human flourishing, i.e., to move along the rational claim access from the Human Experience Sector to the Rational Reflection in the Normatively Human Sector. However, like every abstraction, the notion of "human nature" needs careful deliberation in deriving concrete judgments in regard to any actual, living, breathing human being or group of human beings.

I have written elsewhere at some length on this theme,[31] but to return to our discussion of conscience, I would argue that culture is also a basic modality of being human, and this cultural modality will play a critical role in how conscience works in every individual, since each and every person is enculturated into a particular culture. What moral difference could this make? To begin to answer that question adequately would take at least another book, so let me just offer some reflections on how a fuller understanding of culture as a modality of

---

Morality: Essays in Honor of Christoph von Fürer-Haimendorf (Delhi: Oxford University Press, 1981); Mary Midgeley, *Heart and Mind, the Varieties of Moral Experience* (New York: St. Martin's Press, 1981); Rodney Needham, *Circumstantial Deliveries* (Berkeley: University of California Press, 1981); and Peggy Reeves Sanday, *Female Power and Male Dominance: On the Origins of Sexuality Inequality* (New York: Cambridge University Press, 1981).

[31] See especially my articles "Cultural Particularity and the Globalization of Ethics in the Light of Inculturation," *Pacifica* 9 (1996) 69–86; "The Common Good in a Cross-Cultural Perspective: Insights from the Confucian Moral Community," in *Religion, Ethics & the Common Good*, ed. James Donahue and Theresa Maser (Mystic, Conn.: Twenty-Third Publications, 1996); "Through Thick And Thin: Teaching Ethics in a Cross-cultural Perspective," *Horizons* 27 (Spring 2000) 63–80, and "A New Pentecost for Moral Theology: The Challenge of Inculturation of Ethics," *Josephinum* 10 (2003).

being human may help us better understand how the modality of conscience works in those difficult situations which might involve what traditionally we termed invincible ignorance.

As we have already noted, the concept of invincible ignorance was well established in theory in the manualistic tradition, though how it could be judged in the concrete was often considerably more difficult to discern. Some of the classic examples given tended to center on some personal defect for which the individual persons were not themselves responsible and which it would be virtually impossible for them to overcome. In this context we might recall the character "Lenny" in John Steinbeck's novel *Of Mice and Men,* who due to his mental retardation had a much diminished ability to perceive "right" and "wrong" in his concrete actions. Though the evil that resulted from his actions was very real, Lenny himself could not be judged to be morally culpable for these actions.

But is there some sense in which our culture might function like moral retardation in certain areas of our lives? It might be easier to see what we consider this moral retardation in other cultures rather than in our own, so let me offer a cross-cultural example to illustrate this point. If we conclude that this sort of moral retardation or ethical blind spot exists in other cultures, it would be fair to assume that similar deficiencies are likely to be found in our culture as well. My example comes from a summer I spent working as a live-in counselor in a drug rehabilitation program a number of years ago in southern Italy. This program was actually modeled on the traditional Jesuit novitiate program, and in the average two-year treatment regimen the young men and women were weaned not only off their narcotic addictions but were re-enculturated into the matrix of relationships, values, family, and friends that would help sustain them in a life of recovered sobriety.

The particular group I was assigned to live with were men mostly in their twenties who had come for the most part from the very poor sections of Naples that were dominated in every aspect of life by the Camorra, which was the Neopolitan version of the Mafia. The Camorra was quite different from the picture of Mafia life in America that we might get from movies like *The Godfather* or shows like *The Sopranos.* This life was not the fast-track to riches, but for most of these young men the Camorra provided them with virtually their only chance of any kind of job, and the Camorra itself functioned much like a local government set in these poor neighborhoods in Naples. Raised in that sort of environment it was hard to see even the possibility of another way of living, and when the drug culture was added into the mix the resulting combination was truly lethal.

One day in one of the sessions I was directing, we turned to the topic of the vendetta. I was more than a little surprised when the men in my group all said they considered the vendetta to be an honorable thing to do. From their perspective it seemed to be truly moral. After all, they argued, the individual was asked to put himself at risk in order to protect the honor of the group, or to right some injustice that had been perpetrated on the group. Thus, they reasoned that the vendetta was really an act of self-sacrifice on the part of the individual for the good of the larger group. No matter how much we discussed this matter it seemed impossible to get these men to see the other moral side of the coin—that the vendetta was a perpetuation of the cycle of violence and that murder was a reprehensible assault on another's fundamental human dignity.

While I was somewhat shocked by this collective moral opinion, I knew from my daily life with these men that they were fundamentally good, kind, honest, and sincere in their efforts to try to rehabilitate themselves. Yet, this one moral blind spot remained. In retrospect I concluded that perhaps those men who had been raised in this sort of Mafia ghetto had so deeply internalized the cultural ethos of which the vendetta was a key part that they simply could not see the violence involved for what it was. We might call this an example of cultural invincible ignorance. If someone raised in that environment were to fulfill a vendetta, believing that this was a noble, moral action, how would we judge the action? Certainly the violence is morally evil, but how can we decide about the person's own moral culpability? Obviously that is a question that cannot be answered in the concrete, since none of us has God's ability to see into the human heart, not even our own. But, if we accept the notion of culturally contextualized invincible ignorance, then it might be possible to conclude that even in this sort of horrible situation the person who acted on this vendetta was not morally culpable for his actions.

Let us return to America and see if we can detect any cultural logs that might be lodged in our own eyes and therefore make it very difficult for us to see the moral situation for what it truly is. If this ignorance is truly invincible, it will be very difficult, if not impossible here and now, to uncover it so that all people will have an eureka experience and say "ah-ha!" now I see this issue for what it truly is. If we look back, however, at our country's history, I think we could admit to any number of serious cultural blind spots that people at the time did not clearly see, for example, racism, slavery, Jim Crow segregation legislation, the practice of child labor, exploitation of poor immigrants, and so on. Invincible error is very difficult to ascertain with complete assurance, and so again it is impossible to gauge with accuracy what might be the mixture of vincible and invincible ignorance in these sorts of situations. Therefore, we will have to leave it to God alone to judge the moral culpability or lack thereof.

If looking back at our own history and looking at the histories of other cultures, we can conclude that all sorts of cultural biases, blind spots, and radical misunderstandings conspired to produce this sort of invincible ignorance in the past, could the same forces be operating in the present, so that we cannot see the complex moral reality for what it truly is in God's eyes? Probably most of us could say "yes" in the abstract, but when we start to consider the concrete areas in which we might be seriously morally blinded, sharp disagreements are likely to arise. I suspect that some of the contemporary instances of cultural ignorance would involve many hot button issues such as abortion, ecology, capital punishment, war, economic rights for the poor, and a whole range of issues connected with the living out of our modality of sexuality. How can we resolve the moral rectitude of these issues once and for all? The very fact that these items are so highly charged and lead to positions sharply polarized might support my thesis that one or the other side of the debate simply cannot see some of the key moral elements that are crystal clear to their opponents. Certainly this was true in the past, if we look at an issue such as slavery, which has now been resolved. During the time of the abolitionist movement, vast numbers of our forebears simply could not see the moral rectitude of the anti-slavery arguments. Now, of course, we can. But this kind of growth into moral insight comes slowly, and as we argued in chapter 2, we probably can never say that we fully know on this side of heaven all that the natural law holds and calls us to.

In the year 1054 slavery was widely accepted; in 1854 it was widely, though not universally condemned; by 1954 it was universally condemned, yet the residual practices connected with slavery, such as segregation and racism, remained. Why were all of those practices tolerated, and even in many instances applauded, whether in 1054, 1854, or 1954? We have argued that at least in part this was due to the invincible ignorance of our culture at that time. Yet with time and considerable corporate effort, we have reached a level of insight on these issues which has lifted the veil of invincible ignorance on a particular issue. What will we see in 2054 as morally reprehensible that which is tolerated today? How is this development in our cultural traditions of moral wisdom achieved? With lots and lots of effort and moral energy expended over time our moral vision has been and will continue to be corrected. So while ignorance may seem to be invincible, this is not absolutely the case for all time, as both individuals and whole societies can grow in moral wisdom. Nevertheless, this acknowledgment of the existence of cultural invincible ignorance does help direct our attention to the crucial necessity of character formation and habits of good moral discernment, and this now brings us to the process of conscience formation.

The Spiral of Conscience-Based Moral Living

We are born with conscience, but it is not like a genetic code that stamps our moral character in the ways in which our genes might condition and influence our biological development. Certainly we have seen by now that conscience is very complex, but we can describe a number of key aspects in the way conscience is formed and the way in which it operates in the process of moral living. At the risk of over-simplification, I think we can consider what I call the spiral of conscience-based moral living. A spiral suggests both a certain circularity in the process of conscience development as well as an ongoing and upward progression as we grow in moral wisdom and skill in putting this wisdom into practice. The starting point of our conscience spiral is the basic formation phase. All of us first learn our core moral values from our family members, especially our parents. As time goes on other voices, including the values and practices of our culture, broaden this basic foundation.

I have often used my observations of my young niece Julia to see how conscience is first formed and put into practice. The first Christmas I was home Julia was about eighteen months old. My sister Ann had the Christmas tree up in the living room, but most of the ornaments were hung at waist level and above. Every time Julia would head for one of the bright baubles, Ann would say "No, Julia, that's hot!" and Julia would back away. While this dual preservation of child and Christmas tree probably is not a complex moral issue, it does illustrate that our moral character builds on certain core values that we aim to preserve as well as moral authorities we have learned to respect and obey. Julia knew what the word "hot" meant, but, precocious though she was, the term "breakable" was not yet in her operative vocabulary. She also knew that mom was a person who could be trusted, and in any event should be obeyed lest Julia incur a time-out. All of us begin our moral formation in this manner.

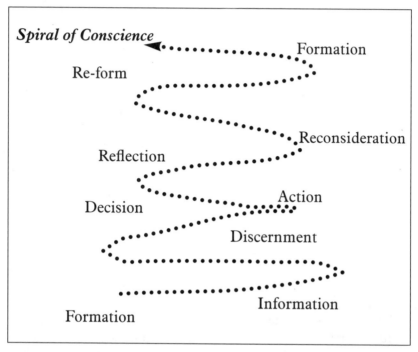

The next Christmas Julia was a year older, bigger, and wiser, and at age two and a half very involved in all the holiday celebrations. My sister once again had the tree up in its usual place, but this year the ornaments were more evenly distributed, though I noted that the more fragile keepsake decorations tended to cluster on the upper branches. Julia would investigate a number of the ornaments on the lower branches and Ann would simply say, "Julia, be careful—that could break." In my analogy of the conscience spiral I would call this the information phase. Julia was given more freedom to engage the ornaments than she had the year previous, but she was also given more detailed and appropriate information—as most parents quickly discover, "that's hot" is not a behavior control device that can be employed for very long. As Julia grew she was able to make better formed and informed decisions. For example, she learned that Christmas ornaments were not really hot, and that there was a difference between the plastic French horn ornament from Walgreens and the cherished handmade egg shell ornament that her mother had received as a child. Julia learned that with proper care she could admire, touch, and hold even this fragile egg shell ornament. Analogously it is this sort of growth that we all experience as we grow in our moral wisdom and put it into applied practice in our daily lives.

Informing our conscience is both ongoing and important, but the process of informing conscience is not like driving up to a gas station and simply filling our tank with moral knowledge. There are many sources that provide us with moral information, and at times these sources compete for our acceptance and conflict in what they seek to tell us. This leads us to the next indispensable phase of our spiral of conscience-based moral living, namely, moral discernment. Before we can move to discernment, we need to have adequate information to weigh.

This is a step that often gets underdone, or overlooked entirely. There is no shortcut to getting the kind of moral information we need. Here we want to recall our methodology of utilizing the four basic sectors of our moral theology since all of them will probably have some contribution to make. Ignoring any core sector will probably lead to a skewed moral analysis since we will be missing some important input. I remember when I was in high school one of the Jesuits on the faculty spoke to us on a certain contested social issue and said that instead of trying to get a variety of opinions on this issue, we should just go to the person who had the truth and listen to him—and he then made it clear where we could easily find the truth locally! His advice made a big impression on me at the time, but not for the reason he was hoping for. I had had enough religious education by that point to realize that the process of finding moral truth is not analogous to analyzing an unknown chemical compound or figuring out a difficult problem in calculus. If this were the case then my old Jesuit teacher's admonition would have made more sense, but alas, there is no textbook of moral truth that has the answer key in the back of the book— not even this one!

I mention this anecdote because often certain moral authorities do seem to present themselves as if the full splendor of the truth were contained in their utterances, and this kind of moral certitude is virtually impossible for any person or institution to achieve. We need to develop the good moral habit of seeking out information from a wide variety of sources, even if some of what we receive conflicts with other voices we hear. In this same vein we should be especially sensitive to the natural human tendency to seek out and listen primarily to those voices we like to hear. We should strive to develop a corrective to this human trait by taking extra efforts to understand other voices that may at first go against some of our feelings, but that still may have something important to say to us. This involves the methodology of moral discourse and we will discuss this in greater detail in the following chapter.

Once we have taken sufficient effort to gather an appropriate amount of information on the issue at hand comes the often difficult task of trying to sort through all this material. This is the step of discernment and I use this word quite deliberately. In the tradition of Christian spirituality, discernment means opening up the decision-making process not only to rational deliberation, but situating the decision in such a way that we seek to do not just our will, but we try to be open and sensitive to God's own Spirit present in our world.[32] After all, this is really what conscience-based moral living is all about, namely, trying to respond as honestly as possible to what we believe God is asking of us. In this process we can rely on the help and assistance of others, especially those sources we have come to recognize as normally trustworthy founts of moral wisdom. But in the last analysis it is each of us, in the inner sanctuary of our consciences, who has to bring this process to the next step. This means coming to some sort of decision about what we shall actually do.

Sometimes the moral decision comes easily, and at other times it comes only after a good deal of effort, and even anguish. Yet, the moment comes when the deliberative stage must lead into the action stage. Thus, we have to come to a decision and then do our best to put it into action in a prudent and practical manner. Decision and action are the next two points on our spiral of conscience-based moral living, and some might think that once we have come to a decision and actually acted upon it our process is finished. However, there is a very long tradition of conscience that tells us this is not so. Probably every one of us has had experiences in which we convinced ourselves that an action we had decided upon and were about to perform was the morally correct thing to do, only to discover shortly after the action was completed that our feelings about the rectitude of our action had changed considerably. This, of course, is due to the recognition on our part that

---

[32] Richard Gula's *Moral Discernment* (New York: Paulist Press, 1997) is a very helpful short book for relating this understanding of discernment to conscience and the moral life.

somehow we had short-circuited the moral decision-making process and had come up with a bad decision. As we have argued above, often the strong tendency to rationalization is the culprit for the moral missteps.

What do we do then? I have a cartoon I sometimes use in workshops that shows a middle-aged man in the midst of a physical exam who is complaining to his doctor that his conscience is troubling him, and he wonders if the doctor can't give him something to stop those bothersome symptoms! We can all catch the humor in this exchange, and yet, just as in many medical cases, it is important *not* to anesthetize the pain, so too in our moral living in these sorts of cases the so-called prick of conscience can give us the necessary push to continue along to the next stages in our conscience spiral, namely, reflection and reconsideration. However, it is important again to develop this habit of reflection on all important moral decisions and not just those that immediately bother us. If we take the reflection stage seriously, we must examine not only the decision itself but the whole process of information gathering, weighing this in discernment and then formulating a decision and putting it into concrete action. Even with actions that seem to be right and have had good results, the stage of reflection may confirm the value of this process for the future, or it may lead us to reconsideration of what was done so that in the future we might do things a bit differently.

On the other hand, if our reflection stage leads us to regret our decision, then a reconsideration of what led us to this decision in the first place will be particularly helpful in trying to rectify what went wrong. This rectification or confirmation stage is what I call "re-form," and it completes one whole circuit of the spiral but does not bring us back exactly to our starting point. The Greek philosopher Heraclitus observed that we can never step into the same river twice, and this is true in our conscience-based moral life as well. If we have gone through all of these stages, then the "re-form" stage will be an important aspect in our ongoing conscience formation. This in turn will help move us forward through the various stages of information, discernment, decision, action, reflection, reconsideration, and reform again and again.[33]

I must admit outright one weakness of this model. It still is very intellectual and rationalistic and seems to suggest that conscience is mostly about coming to the right answer. However, following Fuchs'

---

[33] Timothy O'Connell has a well-known notion of Conscience 1, as a human characteristic sense of value, Conscience 2 as the process of moral reasoning this characteristic

insights, conscience is really much more about the moral striving to seek out and do good and avoid or minimize evil than it is about always getting the right moral answer. In this whole process of moral striving, we have to pay attention to the non-intellectual sides of ourselves, especially our emotions, passions, and the other aspects of our psychological, social, and cultural development. All of these play a crucial role especially in the sectors of experience and tradition in our moral methodology, and though we do not have the time to go into them further here, we must do this homework before we can say we have looked adequately at all aspects of conscience development.[34]

Another weakness I acknowledge is that this model may strike us as overly optimistic, since it would seem to suggest that in one way or the other our moral development and progress will continue along the path of greater wisdom and perfection. Regrettably life is not always that way. At each stage of this spiral there are particular obstacles that may hinder, mislead, or even block the authentic conscience process individually or collectively. These obstacles can even produce a real rupture in our moral development.

Therefore we have to acknowledge that the upward spiral has an evil twin—a downward spiral of moral disintegration in which the process of moral development is reversed and individuals become

---

requires, and Conscience 3, the event contained in the actual reflection itself. While O'Connell's articulation has been well-received by professional theologians, I have found it a bit more difficult to explain effectively in classroom and workshop venues, and so prefer to use my own model of the spiral of conscience here. O'Connell's exposition of conscience is found in ch. 9 of his *Principles for a Catholic Morality,* rev. ed. (San Francisco: Harper and Row, 1976, 1990) 103–18.

[34] To flesh out some of these important themes, I would suggest the following excellent books. Sydney Callahan, *In Good Conscience: Reason and Emotion in Moral Decision-making* (San Francisco: Harper & Row, 1991) in which she discusses the role and function of conscience and emotions in the context of American society, taking into account new psychological understandings of self, emotion, reason, intuition, problem-solving, and developmental change. Also very helpful is the work of Walter E. Conn, *Christian Conversion: A Developmental Interpretation of Autonomy and Surrender* (New York: Paulist Press, 1986), who brings together both theological voices such as Bernard Lonergan and developmental psychologists such as Lawrence Kohlberg. Charles Shelton, S.J., has written extensively on adolescent psychology and his *Morality of the Heart: A Psychology for the Christian Moral Life* (New York: Crossroads, 1990) presents the thinking of leading developmental psychologists such as Hoffman, Kohlberg, Hann, and Gilligan, along with aspects of psychoanalytic theory, the cognitive sciences, theology, and the arts. Shelton uses the heart as the central and unifying metaphor for morality. Finally, William C. Spohn, in his "Passions and Principles," *Theological Studies* 52 (1991) 69–87, reviews and discusses recent moral literature that stresses aspects of the emotions and their involvement in morality. He looks at the emotions using the criterion of "appropriateness" for moral assessments and strategies and as well as the "education" of the emotions themselves.

increasingly self-centered and shut themselves off from others, especially those who do not share or support their own views. This is a tragic occurrence, and yet our faith tradition tells us that no one up to the very moment of death is ever definitively lost. Obviously this theme involves our understanding of sin, which deserves at least a book of its own. We have to take sin and moral failure seriously, and in the concluding chapter I will offer some brief reflections on this troubling reality which both mars and further complexifies our moral world. However, let us now turn back to the first parts of our conscience spiral and take another look at how the individual stages of information, discernment, decision, action, reflection, reconsideration, and reform can aid and be aided by outlining a Christian mode of moral discourse for dialogue among ourselves and with others in our morally complex world.

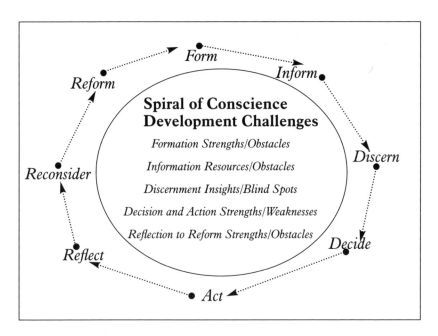

5

Modes of Moral Discourse:
Navigating Towards a Common Ground

When I give a workshop or adult education presentation on moral theology, I usually wear a sweater given to me a number of years ago by a former workshop attendee. The sweater has three colors neatly divided into panels: black, white, and grey. I always tell my workshop participants that even though this is the way we often seem to see our moral world, in reality it is virtually never quite so simple in terms of either color or organization. We can neither divide the morally relevant features, the related moral norms and principles, nor the people involved into neat little compartments labeling the "good" white, the "bad" black, and/or the "ambiguous" grey. Life and therefore morality are not monochromatic, and any moral evaluation that would seem to suggest such a simple dichotomy should be suspect. Our moral analysis has to capture a wide variety of colors, textures, and hue, while trying to weave together from an assortment of loose threads a tapestry that really does promote the human flourishing of all people and thus give God true praise.

As the Church Father St. Irenaeus put it, *Gloria Dei vivens homo:* "the glory of God is the human person fully alive." Conversely, St. Thomas Aquinas described sin as offending God only because it hurts us, God's precious creation.[1] Translating both of these sentiments into moral action resonates with another famous patristic dictum, *Ama* (or *dilige) et quod vis fac:* "Love and what you will, do." This last phrase is often rendered as "Love and do what you will," but both the literal

---

[1] For the Irenaeus reference, see his *Adversus haereses* ("Against Heresies"), bk. IV, ch. 20, sec. 7. For the reference to Thomas Aquinas, see his *Summa contra gentiles,* III, 122: *Non enim Deus a nobis offenditur nisi ex eo quod contra nostrum bonum agimus* ("God is only offended by us because we act against our own well-being").

and truer sense is better uncovered if we reverse the usual word order of the second part of the imperative. If we truly are guided by love, then the things we intend and want to do will likewise be in accordance with charity, which is the highest moral virtue since it reflects God's own in the best possible way (cf. 1 John 4:7-21).

Important as the theological insights of the above paragraph may be, clearly we need much more guidance in our efforts to navigate through the difficult and even dangerous areas of our lives, whether in the mundane details of everyday living or the more momentous decisions that confront us in crisis situations. In the manualist tradition the way in which moral principles were read, analyzed, interpreted, and applied to a concrete situation was called "casuistry," which comes from the Latin word *casus* which means "case." Since the primary goal of the education in moral theology was to help priests in the confessional, these cases were often called "cases of conscience" because they were connected to helping a person in a complex situation come to a sound conscience-based decision. Casuistry has gotten something of a bad reputation since the time of the Jansenist reaction to what was perceived as moral laxism. Most people are vaguely acquainted with the French philosopher Blase Pascal's caricature of the Jesuits and their method of moral casuistry, as presented in his well-known *Provincial Letters*, yet far fewer really understand the history in depth, nor the deeper issues involved.[2] If we are agreed that while "love and what you will, do" may be helpful as a general guide, we also recognize that we need a more probing analysis of what is going on in our morally complex world if we are to concretize in a meaningful way all that is involved in seeking to do and foster the good and minimize and avoid the evil.

The next chapter will consider how we might approach the application of casuistry in a pastorally sensitive manner, what I call casuistry with a human face. We also need to look more carefully at how we can and should dialogue with others on contested moral issues that, because they are often so contentious, get overly simplified in the

---

[2] There is a considerable amount written recently that gives a deeper analysis of both casuistry and its critics. See Albert R. Jonsen and Stephen Toulmin, *The Abuse of Casuistry: A History of Moral Reasoning* (Berkeley: University of California Press, 1988); James F. Keenan, S.J., and Thomas A. Shannon, eds., *The Context of Casuistry* (Washington, D.C.: Georgetown University Press, 1995); Richard B. Miller, *Casuistry and Modern Ethics: A Poetics of Practical Reasoning* (Chicago: University of Chicago Press, 1996); Terence Kennedy, C.SS.R., "Casuistry and the Problem of Pragmatism," *Australasian Catholic Record* 69 (1992) 67–77; and James F. Keenan, S.J., "The Return of Casuistry," *Theological Studies* 57 (1996) 123–39.

process of debate. So we need to step back a bit from our emotions and see what sorts of criteria should guide us as we enter into this area of moral discourse. My operative premise is that in our morally complex world we should not seek first to divide and conquer, but rather to unite and reconcile. If the latter strategy is adopted, we must seek to discern and then broaden the common ground in our contemporary moral debates.

Six Cs of Moral Discourse

In order to work towards building this sort of common ground, I propose first a set of six hallmarks of Christian moral discourse and then build on these to look at how some of the various modes of moral reasoning will help develop more holistic responses to many of our moral challenges.[3] In short, I propose that our moral discourse should be able to demonstrate the criteria of (1) comprehensiveness, (2) comprehensibility, (3) coherence or consistency, (4) credibility, (5) being convincing, and (6) being Christian. Let me explain each criterion in reference to a particular hot contemporary moral debate.

Probably no moral debate has proved more divisive in our country in the last generation than that of abortion. Very often the debate seems to be occupied by sharply divided and polarized positions, "pro-choice" or "pro-life," which do not easily admit even the possibility of a common ground that might provide a forum for a constructive dialogue on the issues themselves, much less development and acceptance of a common policy to resolve the concrete issues that gave rise to the initial debate. Even the names chosen for the rival positions would seem to allow that only one position could ever be truly moral—pro-life or pro-choice—the choice for one side seems to incur vilification by the other. Thus, no dialogue is possible because the positions already seem to be well-known, and each side has already excommunicated the other from the arena of authentic human moral discourse.

I would argue that if we could discuss an issue such as abortion, using rules for moral discourse that are agreed upon by most, if not all, parties to the debate, then we stand a much better chance at moving forward to establishing not only a common ground, but also we can begin to strategize realistically on responses in common to eliminate the need for abortion or tackle whatever other issue we're addressing.

---

[3] I have outlined these evaluative criteria in greater depth in my "Life Matters: 6 C's of Moral Discourse," *New Theology Review* 15 (May 2002) 48–59.

Many of us remember President Bill Clinton's position on abortion as hoping to keep it "safe, legal, and rare." While there is still considerable disagreement on the middle point (legal), most people would not be against trying to keep *any* medical procedure "safe," and similarly most would agree that a great tragedy such as abortion should be minimized as far as possible. Even the most ardent pro-choice feminist position does *not* tout abortion as a positive good in itself or that the number of abortions performed should be multiplied rather than diminished. In this vein, as Richard McCormick has astutely observed, "When we view abortion, for example, as a matter of individual choice, it divides people. Seen as a social problem, it could bring them together. Nearly everyone would agree that the conditions that lead to abortion (poverty, lack of education, broken families, lack of recreational alternatives and similar conditions) should be abolished."[4]

Not even a seminary setting is exempt from this sort of intramural polarization, as a group of us discovered when we invited Serrin Foster, the president of "Feminists for Life of America" (FLA, www.feminists-forlife.org), to the Graduate Theological Union (GTU) in Berkeley, the theological consortium which includes the Jesuit School of Theology-at-Berkeley (JSTB), the theologate in which I taught at the time. Our GTU group was called "Life Matters," and we sought to build on the late Cardinal Joseph Bernardin's notion of working towards the "seamless garment" of a consistent ethic of life in which we sought to build support for all pro-life initiatives, whether these be related to ending the death penalty, working for peace, or trying to make abortion unneeded and therefore unwanted. For the Feminist for Life event, we distributed to the faculty, staff, and student mail boxes a double-sided flyer that gave on the front side the basic facts of the date and time of the talk, along with Ms. Foster's explicit invitation to dialogue with those who might hold pro-choice positions. The back side of the flyer employed a FLA poster of a picture of Susan B. Anthony and a quotation from one of her writings in which Anthony unequivocally states her pro-life/anti-abortion position, calling it injurious for women. One of our JSTB's development officers responded very angrily to our flyer, demanding that no further material of this nature be placed in her box, and terming our "use" of Susan B. Anthony "utterly offensive," adding that many women on our campus would likewise be offended. I suspect our school

---

[4] Richard A. McCormick, s.j., "Value Variables in the Health-Care Reform Debate," *America* 168 (29 May 1993) 13. This article is also found in McCormick's *Corrective Vision: Explorations in Moral Theology* (Kansas City: Sheed & Ward, 1994).

official was right, i.e., that probably a number of women might have been upset with even the suggestion that there could be a pro-life feminist position, and therein lies a good part of the challenge—trying to get past the all-or-nothing battle approach.

My former colleague, of course, has many allies, and it often seems that even to suggest another perspective means that one is somehow against women and their well-being, as is seen in the comments of the well-known novelist Mary Gordon, who states quite frankly that "I have always felt it a safe proposition that whatever position the Vatican takes on the sexuality of women, I'm in a good place on the other side."[5] To be fair to them, there are lots of people on the other side who would adopt the same basic logic, but simply switch sides. Proponents on the other side of the debate are often guilty of many of the same techniques and/or of gross over-simplification of the abortion issue. Even killing of abortion providers has been justified in these words by one abortion clinic demonstrator: "Put it this way: Do you know about Adolf Hitler? Can I make an analogy here? Someone has to pay for sin. Praise the Lord!"[6] Any efforts to promote a feminist ethics might be seen by these people as nothing more than a thinly disguised agenda to destroy the family by adopting a totally irresponsible libertarian sexual ethic that utilizes abortion as a drastic, though effective means of post-coital contraception. It just seems a clear-cut black and white issue, with each side claiming to wear the white hats.

Medical ethicist Daniel Callahan calls this sort of approach the "ethics of advocacy," which he describes as an analysis characterized not only by a direct attack on the veracity of certain facts, but often results in a definite manipulation of which facts are "relevant" to the debate.[7] For example, one journalist, Frank Bruni, referred to the February 1997 issue of *Ms.* magazine that raised the issue of whether there is a linkage

[5] Mary Gordon, "Baby M: New Questions about Biology and Destiny," *Ms.* (June 1987) 28, as cited in Anne Patrick's *Liberating Conscience: Feminist Explorations in Catholic Moral Theology* (New York: Continuum, 1996) 55.

[6] Bob Talbot, an abortion clinic picketer in Redding, California, as quoted in the *San Francisco Chronicle* (4 May 1999) A-13.

[7] See Daniel Callahan, "An Ethical Challenge to Prochoice Advocates: Abortion and the Pluralistic Proposition," in *Bioethics*, ed. Thomas A. Shannon, 4th ed. (New York: Paulist Press, 1993) 21–35. Callahan's article originally appeared in *Commonweal* 117 (23 November 1990) 681–87. Interestingly, Callahan has argued for a modified pro-choice position, which his wife, the well-known psychologist Sydney Callahan, pronounces as being ultimately incoherent. Also very illuminating along these same lines is Cynthia Gorney's *Articles of Faith: A Frontline History of the Abortion Wars* (New York: Simon and Schuster, 1998) which takes an even-handed look at both camps in the abortion debate.

between abortion and breast cancer. Bruni noted that while this statistical evidence was reported in the article in *Ms.*, it was quickly deflected as being of no real significance. Commenting on this sort of "ethics of advocacy," Bruni remarked that "no sooner does abortion receive a tiny, possibly insignificant bruise than a fresh coat of makeup is applied to its cheek."[8]

Now, the use of such cosmetic argumentation is not confined to those with whom we might disagree on key ethical issues. The real issues connected to the tragic choice of abortion in order to deal with an unplanned or unwanted pregnancy go far beyond bumper-sticker analysis, regardless of whether the bumper sticker proclaims a sentiment such as "It's a child, not a 'choice'!" or "Keep your rosary out of my uterus!" If we are going to be both fair in debate and sincere in our efforts to seek the whole truth in a moral issue so we can respond to it in an adequate and effective manner, then we must be wary of our own attempts to paint over unwelcome or troubling aspects of that issue. This commitment to a thorough-going moral analysis furnishes the first hallmark of Christian moral discourse, namely, that it be truly comprehensive. The comprehensive criterion seeks to help us answer the question of why people actually choose abortion.

I certainly do not pretend to have all the answers to this question, but I believe that I can put forward some reasons drawn from my own experience as a priest, retreat director, and counselor. I have been involved for a number of years in helping out in a post-abortion healing ministry call "After the Choice."[9] I have listened to dozens of very painful stories told by both women and men about the decision to have an abortion. Sometimes this decision was agonizing at the moment it was made; sometimes the pain built up in the months and years afterwards. In each case it was clear that virtually no one happily or easily chose abortion as the first response to an unwanted pregnancy. Instead, abortion was usually reluctantly accepted only because it seemed to be the last resort to an otherwise insoluble dilemma. Sometimes the main problem was simple lack of emotional support by one's spouse, partner, or family. Lack of personal maturity is often a reason people put for-

---

[8] Frank Bruni, "The Partial Truth Abortion Fight," *The New York Times* (9 March 1997) E-3.

[9] See James T. Bretzke, S.J. and Monika Rodman, "After the Choice," *America* 181 (6 November 1999) 14–19. See also Michael T. Mannion, *Abortion & Healing: A Cry to Be Whole*, 2nd ed. (Kansas City: Sheed & Ward, 1986). This book contains a chapter on "Project Rachel," a post-abortion program widely used in Catholic dioceses in the United States.

ward, since they feel that they just are not ready to be good parents and to bring a child into the world under these circumstances would be just one more act of irresponsibility. Other times it was because of financial problems or the feeling that one more mouth to feed at this point in time would seriously harm all. I have yet to hear any woman say that she chose abortion because she considered it be her basic right of reproductive choice, or that she saw this as expressing a principled commitment to feminist ethics. Such arguments can be heard in a variety of fora, but I have yet to hear them voiced in the privacy of a retreat, counseling session, or confession.

Therefore, if we hope to develop helpful moral discourse regarding a hot-button issue like abortion we need to get beyond the bumper-sticker rhetoric and honestly seek to look long and hard at why people actually feel they have to choose abortion. If we are comprehensive in this analysis, then we can see just what the morally relevant features are and how these interact in the moral response made. If we want to influence or respond to this sort of real moral issue, we need to be more certain that we have a fuller picture of what is actually going on. The key here is an effective pastoral response, not winning an emotionally charged debate. In a debate we may wish to ignore or downplay some of the more telling points of the opposing side. But in a situation that aims at an effective response, we need to take into account all the morally relevant features and principles, even if this makes our response less black and white. While this seems like a simple enough position, it is clear from looking at the rhetoric involved in so many moral debates that rarely do the various sides involved seem to aim squarely at fulfilling the first criterion of our moral discourse by trying to present as comprehensive picture as possible of everything that is involved in the particular issue.

The second criterion I suggest for our moral discourse is to consider more carefully that what we say and how we frame our discourse be truly comprehensible to our target audience. Again, at first hearing this seems to be such an obvious criterion that it might seem almost trite. Yet, it is clear from experience that many moral debates and arguments are cast in terms the target audience is likely either to misunderstand or not understand at all. This second criterion of comprehensibility does not mean that the arguments and positions advanced are necessarily "wrong." Rather, because they are not adequately understood, they simply are not received by some of those to whom the discourse is directed. For example, in the case of abortion much of the traditional argumentation of the Church, such as the Congregation for the Doctrine of the Faith's "Declaration on Procured Abortion," *Questio de abortu,* has been formulated in terms of the natural law and uses terms such as "direct" and "indirect" and "intrinsic evil."

The language of "law" governs the whole Declaration and here I think "law" might be misunderstood by some as referring to a Church law, rather than an understanding of human flourishing grounded in what we discussed in chapter 2 as the natural law. Therefore, some people might believe that if the Church wanted to it could simply change its position on abortion the way it changed the discipline of not eating meat on Friday. While the Declaration does anticipate and reply to certain objections to its arguments, nevertheless one might ask if these objections have been sufficiently grasped and taken seriously in all their complexity, and/or if the replies provided will be fully comprehensible and convincing to those to whom they are supposedly directed.[10] To raise this issue is not to dissent to the teaching itself, but simply to question whether the teaching has been formulated and expounded as well as it might be.

To call a "direct abortion intrinsically evil" is a statement that as a moral theologian reasonably well-versed in the philosophical and theological tradition I believe to be essentially true. But my experience as a teacher and confessor leads me to strongly suspect that the vast majority of people we might be trying to reach with those four words would not understand correctly at least two of them, if not three (namely "direct" and "intrinsically evil"). Of course, it is always difficult to leave the jargon and the underlying philosophical and theological concepts with which one is familiar, and which seem to make so much internal sense when employed within one's own language framework. The second criterion of comprehensibility really does put the burden on those of us constructing our moral discourse to speak in a way that can be understood by a broader public that has not had the experience of an in-depth study of scholastic philosophy and theology.

Once we learn to speak in a manner understandable by our target audience, we have to take pains to pass the next criterion of moral dis-

---

[10] The document then moves to a discussion of the inter-relation between morality and law in reference to legislation covering abortion. It concludes by calling Christians to "heroism" if necessary "in order to remain faithful to the requirements of the divine law" and does concede that while one can never approve of abortion "it is above all necessary to combat its causes." For the complete text, see *Questio de abortu* ("Declaration on Procured Abortion") 18 November 1974 in *Vatican Council II. More Post-Conciliar Documents,* ed. Austin Flannery, O.P. (Collegeville: The Liturgical Press, 1982) 441–53.

course, which I call coherence or consistency. This criterion has two aspects. Internal consistency or coherence requires that the arguments, principles, and analysis applied hold together logically. For example, we cannot logically say that all people are created equal in one breath, and then in the next maintain that a certain part of the human population lacks equal rights because of differences in race, creed, gender, economic or social position, and the like. It took our nation a long time to realize that this sort of internal inconsistency weakened the impact of our moral arguments for the fundamental value of democracy. So we need to take a close, honest look at our moral discourse to see if the internal argumentation really is logically consistent.

Just as important, if not more important in the public domain, is the demand that our moral discourse be externally consistent as well. By external consistency or coherence I mean that the positions we adopt on one moral issue are consistent with similar or analogous positions on other issues. Many problematic examples of lack of external consistency could be given in reference to the abortion issue, so let me cite just a couple that I have come up against repeatedly. The argument that abortion is intrinsically evil is grounded in the presumption that all life is inherently valuable since it comes from God and we are made in God's own image, the *imago Dei*. Therefore, there is a certain lack of consistency if we zealously oppose the ending of human life at its inception, but strongly support the legitimacy of putting others to death through capital punishment. If it is the life of the person made by God in God's own image that is sacred, and if we believe that God holds all human life as precious, then it is only logical to expect that those who label themselves as strongly pro-life in the sense of being anti-abortion are just as strongly against the death penalty. This certainly is the argument made forcefully by Pope John Paul II in his encyclical on the Gospel of Life, *Evangelium vitae,* and one might think that at least Catholics would take seriously the Pope's arguments here, but both polls and politics show us that this regrettably is very often not the case.[11]

[11] This "incoherence" amongst Catholics who support pro-life measures on one hand, but fail to lend similar backing to ending capital punishment has been studied by Fordham sociologist James R. Kelly, who notes in a recent article that there does seem to be some increase recently for the Church's position against the death penalty. See his "Pro-life, Anti-Death Penalty?" in *America* 182 (1 April 2000) 6–8. For further evidence of the resistance of the conservative wing to this papal teaching, see Carl H. Horst, "The Death Penalty and Church Teaching," *Homiletic and Pastoral Review* (June 2000) 63–65. Horst, deputy attorney general in San Diego, argues that for the pope to state a general principle is acceptable, but

While it is true that abortion and capital punishment are not identical issues, and perhaps from a narrow position of internal consistency one could be both anti-abortion and pro-capital punishment, if we ask ourselves if this position is consistent in the broader, external sense, I think we will begin to see real problems. In the same way, if we hold human life to be so sacred from the moment of conception that we want to do all we can to safeguard and nurture it, then from the position of external consistency we need to make sure that our social welfare policies and economic opportunities make it easier for a mother *and* father to bring this child into the world and raise and nurture the child. Here we see how the consistency criterion reflects the comprehensiveness criterion, as we seek to understand, and then effectively address, all the factors that might go into someone's decision not to carry a child to term.

Once we have taken sufficient account to construct our moral discourse so that it is comprehensive in relation to the actual issue, comprehensible to the target audience, and coherent and/or consistent internally and externally with similar usages of moral principles in other issues, then we probably have already presented an argument that would pass the next criterion, namely, being credible. The most basic aspect of the credibility criterion is that it is able to be believed by people of sound mind and good will. This credibility criterion does *not* mean that *all* such people will in fact be convinced by this argument, but the credibility aspect does move us explicitly out of the circle of our supporters into the wider arena of dialogue with others who may not be of like mind. Moving into this wider dialogue requires us to adopt a certain approach to our moral argumentation. First, we should strive to state our positions and their underlying positions as clearly and cogently as possible. This much should be obvious. But the credibility criterion further requires us to treat others in the debate in a credible manner, especially those who may not agree with us. This means extending to them the basic respect we owe to all people, and we also extend this respect to their arguments as well. This does not mean that we simply accept them as true, but rather that we seek honestly to understand the arguments being made on their own terms.

---

that the application of the principles leaves room for different interpretations and that "no bishop, priest or layman may add his prudential judgments to the list of the Church teachings and enjoin them as obligatory" (64). Horst also draws a distinction between the papal condemnations of abortion, euthanasia, and capital punishment, noting the first two are "intrinsically evil" while capital punishment is not. I would suggest that in terms of convincing moral discourse this position might falter in light of my consistency criterion.

While caricatures may have a certain grain of truth in them, they are never fully credible, and we do a disservice to ourselves as well as those with whom we are seeking dialogue if we engage in, or leave unchallenged, caricatures of any position. Vilification of those with whom we disagree, even on life or death issues, is seldom a very effective means of winning them over to our side of the debate! I mention this last point explicitly because in certain contested areas of the abortion debate, this sort of mutual vilification seems to be more the rule than the exception. Thus, those who adopt a pro-choice position are probably not best described as bloodthirsty, murderous maniacs with a specialization in infanticide. Similarly, those who argue for a pro-life position are not necessarily cold-hearted reactionary patriarchal anti-feminist oppressors of women. Often a complex debate like the abortion issue will have many positions, not just two. Therefore it would not be credible to lump all those who hold a pro-life position with the extremists who advocate killing abortion providers anymore than it would be fair to associate every person who holds a pro-choice position with the most radical wing of feminism.[12]

Since many points in the abortion debate are disputed, we must take care not only to state our own position clearly but also to report accurately the counter-arguments and positions of those with whom we disagree. In his *Spiritual Exercises* St. Ignatius of Loyola outlines the principle called the *Presupputio* ("presupposition") that might be helpful to us in these sorts of debates. Ignatius first calls for us to take an initial stance of trying to give the best possible interpretation to another's statement, rather than to condemn it out of hand. If this benign stance still does not seem to render the other's position acceptable in our eyes, then before moving to condemnation Ignatius counsels us to ask the other person(s) how they understand their own position, to see if clarification cannot be found there. Only after all these steps have been exhausted does Ignatius suggest that we try to correct the other—but always with love.[13] If more of us practiced this principle in our moral dialogue, I think we would become much more effective than by adopting an

---

[12] An example of just this sort of unhelpful vilification can be found in Donna Steichen's *Ungodly Rage: The Hidden Face of Catholic Feminism* (San Francisco: Ignatius Press, 1991).

[13] This well-known Ignatian principle is found at #22 in the introductory annotations of the *Spiritual Exercises*. For a good contemporary translation and commentary on this text, see Ignatius of Loyola, *The Spiritual Exercises of St. Ignatius: A Literal Translation and a Contemporary Reading*, adapted by David L. Fleming, s.j. (St. Louis: Institute of Jesuit Sources, 1978). The *Catechism of the Catholic Church* in #2478 cites this text of this principle in full to explain the principle of avoiding rash judgments.

opposite policy of pugnacious polemicism. I would translate Ignatius'
Presupputio in this rule of thumb in dealing with opposing arguments:
just ask if the proponents of a position would accept our rendition of
their argument and our recapitulation of the major points in dispute. In
other words, can we state their position fairly, completely, and honestly?
Can they do the same for our arguments? If we can get this far in our dialogue, then we have come a considerable distance indeed.

Besides openness, sincerity, charity, and reasonableness, credibility
also requires a certain amount of evidence to ground and demonstrate
one's positions. As we saw in chapter 2, the Church has often based
much of her teaching on moral matters on the natural law and in this
regard has called herself an "expert" in humanity.[14] Claiming expertise
in any field logically requires verification of one's credentials, usually
by other human "experts" in these same given fields. An affirmation
of expertise that cannot be verified through normal human means
stretches the limits of genuine credibility. Thus, if we hope to be credible witnesses in any moral debate, we should seek first to establish
our expertise through input, confirmation, testing, and/or debate from
other recognized experts in these fields. If others perceive in us a reluctance or refusal to dialogue over these issues, instead of strength-
ening our credibility, rather the opposite reaction is likely to occur.

This verification of claimed expertise in humanity is frankly a
problem that the magisterium of the Church encounters on more than
one occasion. Certainly it would be grossly unfair to suggest that the
Church never dialogues or refuses to consult other experts. Yet, there
is a certain fairly wide-spread perception that in matters of abortion
and sexual ethics, the magisterium's (or our own!) process of consultation is not as wide as it might be, and that often the opinions of
those consulted are known in advance, and so the process of consultation leaves itself open to the charge of a somewhat orchestrated ratifi-
cation process, rather than to genuine information gathering. As the
noted moral theologian Lisa Sowle Cahill has lamented: "The repeti-
tion of time-honoured dicta in no way guarantees credibility. The
Church must speak to the modern world with sympathy, with genuine
understanding of the situations to be addressed, and with willingness
to learn new lessons, even to reformulate its moral wisdom."[15]

---

[14] Cf. Pope John Paul's *Sollictudo Rei Socialis*, no. 41, which in turn refers to Pope Paul
VI's *Populorum Progressio*, 42; and the *Catechism of the Catholic Church*, #2032 and #2036.

[15] Lisa Sowle Cahill, "Current Teaching on Sexual Ethics," in *Readings in Moral Theology No. 8: Dialogue About Catholic Sexual Teaching*, ed. Charles E. Curran and Richard A.
McCormick, s.j. (New York: Paulist Press, 1993) 534.

Actually what Cahill calls "credibility" here is what I mean by the fifth criterion of being "convincing." First of all, being "convincing" does *not* mean being coercive! One who "wins" an argument by force rarely, if ever, convinces the other of the truth of one's position. To convince someone properly means to bring them to belief—to a conviction that the arguments or positions advanced are more than merely credible—they are in fact true and require commitment by all who accept and serve the truth. However, we cannot hope to win an argument simply by stating our position and trying to silence or belittle the counterarguments. Therefore, if we seek to be truly convincing this must usually be done in full light of the counter-arguments put forward by those who do not accept our position. When I teach the abortion issue in my courses on contemporary moral problems, I usually ask my students to read and critically engage pro-choice feminist arguments such as those offered by Beverly Wildung Harrison precisely because these arguments are very convincing to a wide audience, even if these have failed to convince me personally.[16] Only after having those arguments clearly understood can we attempt to engage and answer them.[17] If we trust in the inherent reasonableness and truth of our position, then we have nothing at all to lose and much to gain by opening our discussion to a fair examination of counter-positions. I believe that this is the best way to convince others.

We have to seek to convince not only the head, but more importantly the heart. The fifth criterion challenges us to look also at the affective dimension of our moral being. Hot-button issues often seem more emotional than rational, and if we hope to engage the issue in its entirety, we must grapple with what makes this issue so highly charged. Reasons of the heart are usually more persuasive than those that speak only to the head, and thus our moral discourse must speak convincingly to the heart if we hope to move people to genuine

---

[16] See especially Harrison's *Our Right to Choose: Toward a New Ethic of Abortion* (Boston: Beacon Press, 1983) and/or her provocative essay, "Theology and Morality of Procreative Choice" (with Shirley Cloyes) in *Making the Connections: Essays in Feminist Social Ethics*, ed. Carols S. Robb (Boston: Beacon Press, 1985) 115–34.

[17] For one attempt at just such an answer to pro-choice feminist arguments, see Sydney Callahan, "Abortion and the Sexual Agenda: A Case for Prolife Feminism," in *Readings in Moral Theology No. 9: Feminist Ethics and the Catholic Moral Tradition*, ed. Charles E. Curran, Margaret A. Farley, R.S.M., and Richard A. McCormick, S.J. (New York: Paulist Press, 1996) 422–33. See also Frederica Mathewes-Green, *Real Choices: Listening to Women, Looking for Alternatives to Abortion* (Ben Lomond, Calif.: Conciliar Press, 1997).

conviction of our position. Attention to the affective dimension will also complement the cultivation of the virtues necessary to carry one's convictions into practice.[18]

While all of the above criteria and the comments made about them could apply to secular moral discourse operating along the rational claim axis, there is one last criterion that is explicitly faith-based in what we have called the sacred claim axis, namely, how is our moral discourse truly Christian? In other words, just what is it that makes our ethics "Christian" in distinction to some other adjective? Is it merely the ethical positions that the majority of Christians or Christian denominations hold? Is there some deeper and more essential connection in which the adjective "Christian" functions normatively not only to describe but also in some important sense to determine the content of the ethics? This question returns us to the part of the debate between the Moral Autonomy School and the Faith Ethics School touched upon in chapters 2 and 3. At this point I must confess that I align myself more with the latter group, even though I recognize and accept many of the facets of the Moral Autonomy School, especially the emphasis on the primacy of conscience. But after all is said and done, I believe that in some essential way our faith does make a critical difference to our ethics. I do not hold that Christians have some claim to "higher" moral knowledge or behavior that is not open to non-Christians, but rather simply the claim that Christians are bound to take seriously what I have termed the "sacred claim," which is found in the story and message of Jesus Christ that both speaks to and exercises a normative claim on Christians in a way that would not necessarily bind those who do not profess faith in him. This sacred claim can be very powerful because it speaks in a compelling way to our convictions, or what *ought* to convince us. Methodist ethicist Stanley Hauerwas has long argued that our abortion arguments fail because they do not bring the religious claims sufficiently into the discussion. He avers that abortion should be treated not as a "political"

---

[18] For a helpful essay on this point, see James A. Donahue, "The Use of Virtue and Character in Applied Ethics," *Horizons* 17 (1990) 228–43. See also William C. Spohn, "The Reasoning Heart: An American Approach to Christian Discernment," *Theological Studies* 44 (1983) 30–52. Spohn's essay is also found in *The Reasoning Heart: Toward a North American Theology*, ed. Frank M. Oppenheim, s.j. (Washington, D.C.: Georgetown University Press, 1986) 51–72. Spohn suggests an approach to Christian discernment based on the thinking of some American theologians that stresses the normative contribution of biblical symbols and distinctive Christian affectivity in guiding moral evaluation.

issue in the liberal political arena but as a religious issue calling for a faith-based response from Christians.[19]

If my basic position is correct, then our moral discourse must take into account the *Christian* nature of our moral life, not only in terms of abstract theory but in concrete applications that shape the responses we make in our daily lived moral lives. The Christian criterion is a different logical order than our first five criteria in that it is more content-driven than simply outlining certain rules for moral debate. This Christian content is critical though, and I believe there are a number of important biblically grounded themes we ought to include and integrate better into our moral discourse. I would propose that our moral theological discourse incorporate at least the following ten interrelated themes: (1) God's creation, which is essentially good; (2) God's grace, which is the first, middle, and last word of our moral lives; (3) the reality of sin, to which we are subject, and in which we are all personally involved; (4) forgiveness, which marks the divine response to the dynamic of sin (as well as the requirement of humans to do as God does, as we see in The Lord's Prayer) and which, therefore leads necessarily to (5) conversion and reconciliation; (6) the Cross of Christ, which stands as our paradigmatic symbol of who we are in relation to (7) redemption, which is the mystery of God's salvific will for sinful humanity; (8) the resurrection of the body, which symbolizes the destruction of the power of sin and death, as well as our final "end" for which God has created us; (9) eschatology, or the realization of both the present in-breaking of God's kingdom with its values into our human history as well as the ultimate promise of a truly brave new world yet to come; and (10) the Christian moral community of discipleship, which is how we are called and initiated into our life in the Lord, and which is therefore not merely the locus but also the focus for all aspects of our lives.

Development of these ten themes would require at least another book, but following up on this last point helps us to realize that in terms of the abortion debate, like every moral issue, the key question must in some essential way always involve this Christian call to discipleship. Moral theologian James Gaffney makes a similar point in a story he relates about a discussion between two students he had in an undergraduate theology class. One was a young woman who stated

[19] Stanley Hauerwas, "Abortion: Why the Arguments Fail," ch. 12 in his *A Community of Character: Toward a Constructive Christian Social Ethic* (Notre Dame, Ind. and London: University of Notre Dame Press, 1981) 212–29.

that she was pro-choice. However, when a fellow classmate asked her if she believed that Jesus would be pro-choice, she said "no" and then recognized that she would have to change her own view on permitting case-by-case abortions in non-life-threatening circumstances upon realizing that Jesus would not have condoned such a position.[20] As I have already stated in chapter 3, I am *not* arguing here that we adopt a "WWJD?" (What would Jesus do?) approach to Christian moral reasoning; the problems and limitations of such a simplistic approach are well-known and require little additional discussion here. However, along with Gaffney and Hauerwas, I am simply noting that Christian discipleship does have a sacred claim on our moral reasoning, and we must take both our discipleship identity and its concomitant moral claims more into account in our approach to ethical issues than we might have in the past.

To return to the abortion demonstrator cited above who justified attacks on abortion providers and clinics with the words, "Someone has to pay for sin. Praise the Lord!" I would argue that this individual has failed the Christian criterion miserably. He is right, someone has to pay for sin, but our faith tradition tells us that sin has been "paid for," and furthermore the person who has made this payment in full is Jesus Christ. If we are truly to "praise the Lord," it cannot be done by aggressively attacking others physically or verbally. The Christian criterion reminds us that compassion, mercy, and forgiveness are not attributes reserved for Jesus alone, and so if we are truly disciples in his name, then we must practice daily these virtues in all aspects of our lives. There is much in the official church teaching that speaks of compassion, patience, forgiveness, and reconciliation, but unfortunately these teachings often do not get the attention they deserve. Even in the case of abortion, Pope John Paul II presents a more nuanced compassionate view of the complex factors that may have led a woman to choose abortion:

> I would now like to say a special word to *women who have had an abortion*. The Church is aware of the many factors which may have influenced your decision, and she does not doubt that in many cases it was

[20] The discussion of this exchange is found in James Gaffney's article "On Paranesis and Fundamental Moral Theology," first published in *The Journal of Religious Ethics* 11 (1983) 24–34, and also found as ch. 10 in Gaffney's *Matters of Faith and Morals* (Kansas City: Sheed and Ward, 1987) 134–51. This article, which I have referenced in ch 3, gives a very convincing counter-argument to Bruno Schüller's position that Scripture is really not all that important in Christian ethics.

a painful and even shattering decision. The wound in your heart may not yet have healed. Certainly what happened was and remains terribly wrong. But do not give in to discouragement and do not lose hope. Try rather to understand what happened and face it honestly. If you have not already done so, give yourselves over with humility and trust to repentance. The Father of mercies is ready to give you his forgiveness and his peace in the Sacrament of Reconciliation. You will come to understand that nothing is definitively lost and you will also be able to ask forgiveness from your child, who is now living in the Lord. With the friendly and expert help and advice of other people, and as a result of your own painful experience, you can be among the most eloquent defenders of everyone's right to life. Through your commitment to life, whether by accepting the birth of other children or by welcoming and caring for those most in need of someone to be close to them, you will become promoters of a new way of looking at human life (*Evangelium vitae*, #99).

The last word then is not "somebody has to pay for sin," but a recognition that oftentimes for a variety of reasons we make choices that later on we come to regret, and that it is the ongoing efforts to live our lives as best we can that counts most in the eyes of the Lord. Hopefully our moral discourse should be first and last a word of hope and encouragement along these same lines. While much more could be said in spelling out the ramifications of the "Christian" criterion, let me emphasize that this sixth Christian criterion does not aim to replace nor supersede the previous five criteria of comprehensiveness, comprehensibility, coherence, being credible, and convincing. Rather, the last criterion of being Christian is simply meant to be the integrative organizing symbol of the whole of our Christian moral discourse.

Varieties of Moral Discourse

While the above six criteria for moral discourse will be helpful in working toward a common ground for addressing ethical issues, they do not by themselves envelop all the aspects of moral discourse used in a pluralistic society. James Gustafson has outlined four basic types of moral discourse that are widely used in our contemporary world, and he makes two basic methodological points regarding these types.[21] Gustafson's first observation is that each of these types of discourse has a special perspective to offer which the others lack. Building on

[21] James M. Gustafson, *Varieties of Moral Discourse: Prophetic, Narrative, Ethical, and Policy* (Grand Rapids, Mich.: Calvin College and Seminary, 1988).

this point he then concludes that no one variety of moral discourse is a stand-alone mode. Since all four have special insights and perspectives, they should be used in an integrated fashion. Gustafson labels his four varieties of moral discourse as prophetic, narrative, ethical, and policy, and he states clearly that each has its particular strengths and weaknesses.

The basic feature of Gustafson's first variety, prophetic discourse, is its passionate "indictment" of the current situation. The way in which the biblical prophets usually spoke pointed at what they considered to be the root causes of the waywardness they observed, be it religious, moral, or social. Only rarely did the prophets attack certain policies or specific instances of wrong-doing (Nathan's denunciation of King David would be an exception to this rule, cf. 2 Sam 12:1-25). The point of prophetic denunciation was not to aim at definite policy recommendations or pragmatic matters of technique or social strategy, but rather to move the hearts of the listeners to admission of guilt and a commitment to change and conversion. It is this aim that leads the prophets to adopt language and symbols of harlotry and infidelity, what Gustafson calls "passionate language," since the biblical prophets "did not establish their indictments on the basis of statistical analyses; they did not use moral arguments of a philosophically rigorous sort. They used language, metaphors, and symbols that are directed to the 'heart' as well as to the 'head.'"[22] Rational, abstract ethical analysis may be more rigorous in its analysis of the myriad factors involved in a moral problem, but it lacks the punch and urgency of prophetic discourse.

In addition to indictment or denunciation, another aspect of prophetic discourse is its usage of either utopian or eschatological ideals. Such discourse "portrays an alluring vision of the future, of possibilities for life in the world in which the forms of strife and suffering we all experience are overcome."[23] Gustafson notes that this serves an important purpose since it gives us hope in the midst of despair and "lifts the eyes and the aspirations beyond what hard realists see as possible to the possibilities that lie beyond . . . grounded in deep theological convictions: the breaking of the bondage of death in the accounts of Jesus' resurrection, the assurance of the coming Kingdom of God in which peace and justice will reign forever."[24]

[22] Ibid., 11.
[23] Ibid., 13.
[24] Ibid., 14.

What Gustafson terms prophetic discourse is used on both sides of the abortion debate, and yet this discourse lacks the complexity and depth to address even the comprehensiveness criterion that we set as the first of our six criteria for moral discourse. Therefore, as compelling and important as prophetic discourse can be, it does not replace the need for a more developed moral theory, including moral norms and the casuistry needed to read and apply them to concrete situations.

This is the mode of moral analysis Gustafson calls "ethical discourse," but before he takes up that particular genre he points to another variety of moral discourse that is also very powerful, namely, what he terms "narrative discourse." Gustafson sees the functional roles of narrative discourse played out in the moral agent and moral community. Narratives give us a sense of who we are as a community and these narratives sustain this particular moral identity by recalling our history and shared traditions, whether they come from Scripture or the lived experiences shared throughout time of the community. These narratives help shape the ethos of our culture, and this ethos in turn profoundly affects "the way we interpret or construe the world and events and thus affect what we determine to be appropriate action as members of the community. Narratives function to sustain and confirm the religious and moral identity of the Christian community, and evoke and sustain the faithfulness of its members to Jesus Christ."[25]

Like prophetic discourse, narratives can be very powerful because they touch us at the core of who we think we are. For example, one of the major reasons Martin Luther King, Jr. was ultimately successful in ending Jim Crow segregation in the South was that he was able to convince us that such practices simply could not ring true with the narrative of who as Americans we believe ourselves to be. Our narrative, expressed in the rendition of our story of our nation's beginnings and enshrined in sacred texts such as the Declaration for Independence and the Gettysburg Address simply could not also contain in a coherent fashion the counter-narrative of discrimination and segregation. What King did was force us to choose which narrative we wanted to be our true story: the narrative of freedom and liberty for all, or the sordid tale of racial violence and segregation. King was also able to use prophetic discourse effectively, especially in the eschatological ideals he presented in his well-known "I Have a Dream" speech delivered at the steps of the Lincoln Monument during the March on Washington

[25] Ibid., 20.

in 1963. But it really was the effective use of a national narrative that accounts for King's broad success throughout American society. Here we do *not* find the moral calculus of casuistry.

Narrative discourse is compelling, but it does not deal particularly well with genuine ethical quandaries. Yet, as Gustafson notes, narratives "can provide nuanced and subtle illumination both of what is at stake and of what conduct might be most appropriate. Ethical casuistic argument brings choice to a focus by distinctions and arguments; narrative evokes the imagination, stimulates our moral sensibilities and affections. Its conclusion is not as clearly decisive, but it enlarges one's vision of what is going on; one acts in its 'light' more than in conformity to it—as one does to a casuistic moral argument."[26]

As a methodology narrative discourse often uses an analogy, looking at the story in the narrative and then drawing conclusions for appropriate action in the circumstances at hand. Thus, King was able to use the American narrative of a land of equal opportunity for all to critique the practices of racial segregation in the Jim Crow South. In using the Bible the narrative methodology tends to operate in the ways William Spohn has outlined in his *Go and Do Likewise: Jesus and Ethics*, which we touched upon in chapter 3. In many ways the narrative mode of moral discourse resonates with our moral character and gives us a privileged window into our human nature precisely because it reflects better the ways in which we see ourselves as human beings. Few of us identify with an abstract, essentialist understanding of what it means to be truly human, but we all can relate to how a story shows us what, or what is not, genuinely worthy of being called human.

Important and compelling as narrative discourse is, it is nevertheless insufficient as either the primary or solitary mode of moral discourse. While it is true that as Christians we are a story-formed people, to echo Stanley Hauerwas, yet the Christian story is not the only plot in which we have roles to play. We are characters in many stories and in a pluralistic society we need to both recognize and live according to that complex reality.[27] Critiquing both of the first two va-

---

[26] Ibid., 21.

[27] See especially Hauerwas' *A Community of Character: Toward a Constructive Christian Social Ethic* (Notre Dame, Ind. and London: University of Notre Dame Press, 1981). The bibliography connected with narrative ethics and narrative theology is vast. For those who wish to pursue this theme further, I would recommend in particular the following works: Roger G. Betsworth, *Social Ethics: An Examination of American Moral Traditions* (Louisville: Westminster, John Knox Press, 1990). Betsworth focuses on four cultural narratives that have shaped the American ethical images of itself and the world: the biblical story, the

rieties of discourse Gustafson points out, "Symbolic prophetic indictments need to be checked against facts and figures and political analysis. Perceptive intuitions informed by parables need to be checked against more rational analysis, and we all belong to several communities. To live by the story of only one might impede our capacities to communicate with those with whom we share moral responsibilities who are informed by different stories and different communities."[28]

When all is said and done, there is no substitute for careful and close ethical reasoning that takes into account all of the morally relevant features and concomitant moral principles that should inform each aspect of our evaluation of our moral landscape. This is a landscape inhabited by peoples of many different faiths, non-faiths, cultures, etc., and ethics has traditionally played an important role in bridging what otherwise could be huge chasms. The crucial role of ethical discourse is one strong point highlighted by the Moral Autonomy School against the approach of the Faith Ethics School, since in a pluralistic and increasingly global society we cannot presume either a common sacred canon, such as the Bible, or a shared community history expressed in narrative. As Gustafson observes, if we are to aim at a common ethical ground, "should that not be supported by arguments and groundings that all human beings can share, rather than those that make particular appeals to the Bible, to Christian theological themes, and to the faith of Christians?"[29] Certainly this is the approach that the Catholic moral tradition has used extensively in its sexual and social ethics, grounding both in the natural law.

Yet, even this rationally based ethical discourse cannot stand alone as our only approach to moral analysis, as Gustafson notes:

> It does not have the capacities that prophetic discourse has vividly to point to some devil, some root of evil that must be extricated, to some deep loyalties and beliefs that systematically distort human life and human community. Nor does its vocabulary move persons with a sense of urgency. Ethical discourse cannot shape the ethos of a community in the way that narratives can, in part because its language and symbols are abstract and do not have the evocative power to sustain and cultivate

---

American gospel of success, the idea of well-being, and the global mission of America. John R. Donahue, s.j., *The Gospel in Parable: Metaphor, Narrative, and Theology in the Synoptic Gospels* (Philadelphia: Fortress Press, 1988); Stanley Hauerwas and L. Gregory Jones, eds., *Why Narrative? Readings in Narrative Theology* (Grand Rapids, Mich.: Eerdmans, 1989).

[28] Gustafson, *Varieties of Moral Discourse*, 26.

[29] Ibid., 34.

the nourishing common memories of a community. Its casuistic forms aid precision, but they can excessively delimit what ought to be taken into account in a good moral choice. A narrative, at the point of a choice, might help persons see themselves and circumstances in a broader context of time and history; it might enlarge the perception and imagination so that features are included that the concepts and procedures of casuistry conceal.[30]

Traditionally most of the moral analysis done by professional theologians has utilized the ethical mode of discourse, while people in their everyday lives probably have instinctively relied on some combination of the prophetic and narrative modes of discourse. Combining all three would give us a fuller framework and stronger tools for analysis, but even these three taken together still lack an important element—namely, the transition from moral evaluation into effective concrete action. There still is one mode of moral discourse not yet treated, and yet it is absolutely crucial if we hope to realize our ethical aspirations. This last mode is what Gustafson calls policy discourse, and regrettably it has been often overlooked and/or undeveloped by professional ethicists. Effective policy discourse cannot be done in isolation in the classroom or pulpit, since a key feature of it is that it is both formulated and put into action by the same people who have both the power to put their ethics into practice, as well as the responsibility for the consequences of those choices. Policy discourse is practiced most often by those in politics and the art of politics is the art of compromise, of seeking to do what one can and to accept that which one cannot change.

Compromise is not a virtue for prophets, but there is a long and noble tradition of this principle in Roman Catholic moral theology. Pope John Paul II has reiterated this Catholic principle explicitly in *Evangelium vitae* when he says that politicians may support abortion legislation that might still allow for the practice, but which seeks nevertheless to limit it, or make it less likely to be chosen.[31] Compromise also

---

[30] Ibid., 42–43.

[31] "When it is not possible to overturn or completely abrogate a pro-abortion law, an elected official, whose absolute personal opposition to procured abortion was well known, could licitly support proposals aimed at *limiting the harm* done by such a law and at lessening its negative consequences at the level of general opinion and public morality. This does not in fact represent an illicit cooperation with an unjust law, but rather a legitimate and proper attempt to limit its evil aspects" (*Evangelium vitae*, #73). The Congregation of the Doctrine of the Faith's 2003 "Doctrinal Note on Some Questions Regarding the Participation of Catholics in Political Life" reaffirms this same point. For the text, see http://www.vatican.va/roman_curia/congregations/cfaith/documents/rc_con_cfaith_doc_20 021124_politica_en.html.

takes seriously the starting point and ending point for all concrete moral action, namely, the conditions in which we find ourselves here and now. It is in light of, and within the parameters of these conditions that policy discourse is developed and moved forward, and as Gustafson notes, these conditions "both limit the possibilities of action and enable them."[32] While both prophetic and ethical discourse might pose as the key moral question, "what ought we to do?", policy discourse usually begins with the present tense and asks what is going on in the here and now. This has to be the starting question for formulating concrete policies since that which "is desirable is always related to what is possible; it is always under the constraints of the possible. And a critical factor of judgment is precisely *what is possible*" (emphasis in the original).[33]

It should be clear by now that policy discourse has definite strengths which the other modes of discourse might lack. The primary strength of policy discourse is that in the last analysis it does seek to get things done. While policy discourse is less captivated by prophetic denunciation or utopian idealism, it does try to move forward—even if the steps be small and the progress slow. Yet, of all the modes, policy depends most on the others, especially ethical discourse. A policy not grounded in some solid ethical analysis and guided by appropriate moral principles would be just pragmatism pure and simple. Yet, the pragmatic dimension is crucial and as Gustafson notes, policy discourse "works within limited visions, limited frames of reference. It accepts certain conditions which from prophetic and ethical perspectives could themselves be judged morally wrong, or at least morally inadequate."[34]

Policy discourse is more than a necessary evil, it is in fact a positive good, and if we hope to put our moral principles and ethical aspirations into fuller practice, then we need to develop better our expertise in this mode of moral discourse. The other three modes are also important. I would simply add that we need to develop a sensitivity or awareness for the modes and varieties of moral discourse at work in a given argument, or with an author, issue, or approach. In working to integrate better this awareness of the varieties of moral discourse and their respective strengths and weakness, I believe our six criteria of comprehensiveness, comprehensibility, consistency, credibility, being convincing, and Christian also must play a crucial role. Obviously this is not the last word on the subject, and we still have a lot of homework

[32] Gustafson, *Varieties of Moral Discourse*, 47.
[33] Ibid.
[34] Ibid., 51.

to do to develop and practice our expertise in using these modes of moral discourse. However, we need to draw this chapter to a close and move on to another dimension of living in a morally complex world, namely, how to help others in navigating this terrain so that the good can be truly done and fostered and evil minimized and avoided. In the next chapter we will turn to just such a pastoral analysis and application in a moral situation.

6

Navigating in the Morally Complex World: Casuistry with a Human Face

If the preceding chapters have been helpful in approaching moral theology in ways that give sufficient recognition of and attention to the complexities of the real world, then it seems a good way to finish this introductory exploration by applying some of the principles and methodology to an analysis and response to some representative moral cases. In the history of moral theology such applications were based on an exposition of a *casus* (Latin for "case"). The relevant moral features of the case were listed, and these were then read in light of what were considered to be the appropriate moral principles, which when applied to the case were considered the morally correct thing to do.

This whole methodology led to the rise of what is called "casuistry," or case analysis. Even in the height of the manualist tradition, the casuists recognized that the individual had to follow his or her conscience and that it would be technically impossible to foresee every possible set of variables so that the answer in one concrete case could easily and inevitably be applied to other cases, even if they initially appeared very similar. In fact, such cases were often called "cases of conscience" since the key moral problem centered on precisely what an individual should do in good conscience in this or that moral dilemma. Nevertheless, even if the particularities of an individual's circumstances and the sanctity of his or her conscience were acknowledged in the abstract, the old moral textbooks did tend to structure their presentations in such a way that one really could come to moral conclusions that were certain in much the same way one could arrive at a proof in geometry. As we noted in the last chapter, casuistry has often been derided from the time of Pascal to the present, but my

contention is that we must move from the abstract level of moral principles into the concrete realities and complexities of our everyday
lives. So we need a casuistry, but with a truly human face. By this I
mean if our casuistry is to be authentic it simply must take adequate
account of the human individuals involved, whether on the giving or
receiving end of pastoral care. As part of this adequate attention to the
pastoral reality, I suggest outlining a certain manner of thinking
through what would be the best pastoral approach in this or that particular situation. Pastoral application to a concrete situation involves
discerning the best responses to real people by taking into consideration everything we can reasonably learn about them in a manner that
is fully respectful of the individuals involved, as well as faithful to our
understanding of how the objective moral order can be best instanti-
ated in *this* "here and now" context.

Who counts as a potential "pastoral minister"? This term is *not* limited simply to ordained clergy or those who are working in an official
capacity such as a counselor or chaplain. Every member of the Christian community of disciples is called upon at one time or another to
care for others, and thus by virtue of our baptism, which ordains us all
into the priesthood of believers, as well as our belonging to the human
community we are legitimately designated to serve as a pastoral minister to another individual or group of individuals. Often a family
member, relative, friend, or neighbor can fulfill this role better than
someone with more extensive training, a set of official credentials, or
a specific pastoral designation. Yet, while our natural human emotions
and intuitions can be invaluable in responding sensitively to another
in their need, there are certain approaches that are more helpful and
others that are less helpful. These eight questions are meant to guide
us to both utilize more effectively some of these pastoral helps while
avoiding or minimizing certain hazards that might lessen or even destroy our desired pastoral sensitivity and effectiveness.

While one doesn't have to answer or explicitly address each and
every one of these questions in a programmatic fashion, I do think they
are helpful in formulating a response that is both concrete and pastorally helpful. After listing the eight questions I will elaborate on them
briefly in turn, and then apply them to a couple of sample moral cases.

The Eight Starting Questions: ·

1) What is my *pastoral role* in this case and what am I being *asked* to do?
2) What are the *morally relevant features* of this case?

3) What are the *presuppositions* I and the other(s) bring to this case?
4) What further *information* is needed in order to respond to this case?
5) What are the *moral principles* operative in this case?
6) What kind of pastoral *response* should I make in this case?
7) What kind of pastoral *strategies* would I use in my response?
8) Who and/or what is *most in need of reconciliation* in this situation?

A Sample Case to Test Our Questions

You are a member of the chaplaincy team at a hospital. John and Mary Smith, a couple in their late 30s, come to you in great distress as the woman has just given birth to a Downs Syndrome baby who also has a closed esophagus. Though the closed esophagus can be corrected fairly easily the doctor suggests that perhaps, in view of the Downs Syndrome, it would be better to try to keep the baby as comfortable as possible but not perform the operation. The baby would then die within a matter of days. The couple has one other healthy two-year old. The couple asks you to help them in coming to a decision in this case.

1) What is my *pastoral* role in this case and what am I being *asked* to do?

Keeping in mind the role that one plays when asked to engage another in a pastoral encounter can give the first set of important insights as to how we might proceed. If you are being asked for your help as a friend, then respond as a friend, but if someone has come to you because they recognize you for exercising some specific role in the community then it is important to bear that role in mind in fashioning your response. In dealing for many years with those preparing for regular ministry in the Church, whether it be as an ordained, lay, or religious person, I have noticed that there is a certain innate tendency on the part of these people to fall into the role of being a sort of quasi-spokesperson or answer guide for Church teachings. While it is true that on occasion people might wish to consult us in a professional capacity as a teacher or interpreter of various Church moral positions, the vast majority of the time we are really called not to answer technical questions as much as to be a companion and support to another person as they seek to discern what it might be that God is asking of them in this particular crisis moment in their life.

If we are serving in some official capacity, whether it be as a chaplain, parish worker, high school counselor, or lay volunteer, we do have to keep in mind that it is not just our personal opinion on an issue that counts, but what the Church teaches as well. As we have seen by now, "what the Church teaches" in many cases has a varied history of positions and applications, as well as a broad range of possible interpretations and debates in the present. This past and present are part of "what the Church teaches" on a specific issue and, depending on the particular set of circumstances, it may be important to indicate the unsettledness of a certain issue if this is the case.

In other circumstances such an exposition would probably be counter-productive. For example, a hospital chaplain is confronted by a family grieving over their son who was severely injured in a motorcycle accident and is now in a persistent vegetative state (PVS). In dealing with that family and their decision on what level of treatment to authorize, the chaplain might have to explain that this is an area in which the best theologians in the Church are still engaged in considerable debate. There is no nice and neat definitive answer, and the family might need to acquaint themselves about some of the various aspects of the discussion so they can make the best informed decision.

A different pastoral scenario though might require a quite different approach. For example, if a chaplain were called to the bedside of an elderly man who is in the last hours of his life and is surrounded by close family members, this would *not* be the time to launch into a complicated discourse on ordinary and extraordinary means, the principle of the double effect, and /or the standards for palliative care given in "The Gospel of Life" (*Evangelium vitae*); it would be enough to remain with the family in compassion and prayerful support. If a doubt should arise as to whether the Church would sanction administering pain killers to a dying person in order to reduce his suffering, then the chaplain might simply respond "Yes, the Church supports this type of treatment since it is only to relieve pain and its aim is not to kill the man."

One aspect of responding appropriately in a given pastoral role is to look carefully at what you are being asked to do, both explicitly *and* implicitly. On rare occasions people might be asking you to do something inappropriate, such as make the decision for them ("Just tell me what to do, Father"). If that happens I gently remind them that this decision cannot be mine to make, but that I will do the best I can to enable them to come to a good decision themselves. Once I say that, people are usually ready to enter into that process and take an active role in the decision-making. But when I say it is important to look at what people are asking of you both explicitly and implicitly, I am simply highlighting a certain facet of human nature, namely, that often it is difficult for us to express exactly what it is that we are seeking.

I've found that the first question people bring to me is frequently not the question that is really uppermost in their minds and hearts, but they feel that such a question is "proper" to put before me, while if they were simply to express their deeper anguish or confusion, this emotional messiness might not be as appropriate to have me tackle. Yet, as I stress with my students, we cannot expect people to make good informed, conscience-based decisions if they are overwhelmed by strong human emotions or confusion.

We need often to minister to these needs first before we can move on to any of the other issues that are related to our moral discernment. In our sample case with John and Mary Smith, while it is clear that my role is a hospital chaplain, and that they have come with a clearly stated need, i.e., to come to a decision regarding their newborn child. *Before* we can hope to process that decision, it will be important to acknowledge and deal with the whole range of emotions they are likely experiencing at the moment: grief, disappointment, anguish, fear, guilt, and so on. If the chaplain simply moved to a clinical discussion of the case or were to give them a quick "here's what the Church says," then I would argue that from a pastoral perspective the couple has not really been heard, much less responded to with the kind of pastoral sensitivity that Jesus himself modeled.

The case of John and Mary Smith recalls for me a wise priest I know who has spent his life in pastoral counseling in the Philippines and tries to practice what he calls "empathetic listening." In order to respond well to people we have to understand them as fully as possible, and if we are really going to understand where people are coming from, we have to seek to understand the whole person and not just this or that dilemma with which they're faced. This deep-level understanding, he says, is best achieved if we first listen rather than talk, and the goal of our listening is to enter into a real communion with them. As my own way of trying to facilitate this empathetic listening I have developed the rest of my pastoral questions.

2) What are the morally relevant features of this case?

If we want to understand both the person and the circumstances in which they find themselves, then we need to do as broad a look as possible at all the factors, facets, and aspects that go into the mix. As we saw in chapter 1, the particular moral paradigm we use will have a lot to do with what we consider to be genuinely "morally relevant" features of a case. By now it should be clear that in general I believe the personalist paradigm is better suited than the physicalist paradigm for uncovering more of the morally relevant features of most concrete situations. In the case of John and Mary Smith, a physicalist paradigm approach might focus simply on whether the intended surgery to repair the esophagus was ordinary or extraordinary means. If it were judged to be ordinary then the surgery would be morally obligatory and the decision would have to be to authorize this medical procedure. From an abstract perspective I would agree with this analysis. But from a pastoral perspective I don't think that this narrow act-centered analysis is the best approach to respond to all of John and Mary's issues. A personalist paradigm can often arrive at the same decision, but I would argue that the journey is a fuller one which will go much further in helping people both discern, decide, and then act on their moral analysis.

So from a personalist perspective, what would be some of the major morally relevant features in the case of John and Mary Smith? I once asked precisely this question in a college honors class and my students began to answer with some of the obvious features: the child needs the operation to survive; the child has Downs Syndrome; the operation is fairly routine, and so on. However, I pushed my students to look a bit further to see if they might be overlooking something. I asked if the age of the couple could be morally relevant, and if the fact that they had a two-year old at home could be considered morally relevant. Was it morally relevant that the doctor had suggested that surgery might be foregone? At this point one of my students threw up her hands in exasperation and said, "Well, if *those* things are morally relevant, then *everything* in this case is morally relevant!" She thought the case was pretty simple from a moral standpoint and that we should just quickly acknowledge that the child had a right not only to life but to the surgery as well. Say that and be done with it! While at the end of the whole process I would come out most likely at the same place, I underscored a key difference between morally relevant features and morally determinative principles.

A morally relevant feature simply means that this is an aspect of the case that we should bear in mind, since it likely will figure in some way in our pastoral response, if not directly in the decision-making process. My student in fact had hit on the right answer without realizing it: just about everything in this case really is morally relevant in the sense that we have to keep it in mind as we move forward. Therefore, I hope that as John and Mary Smith work through this difficult moment in their lives they do not lose sight of their two-year old at home, nor that they forget their age, and so on. It certainly *is* morally relevant that they have seemingly received this troubling medical suggestion to let their newborn child die. All of these features are morally relevant, but none of them is morally determinative. This means that we need to keep these pieces of the case in mind—somewhat like pieces of a mosaic that we are trying to assemble. If we throw any of them out, then our resulting picture will be incomplete and have telltale holes in it.

3) What are the presuppositions I and the other(s) bring to this case?

I have suggested above that we try to use the approach of empathetic listening when we engage in pastoral discernment and counseling. However, there is a danger that, instead of toiling to put ourselves with the other person, we come to a judgment of the situation much too quickly and then try to get the other person to see the situation as we see it. I might call this a "telepathic" approach, i.e., we are so convinced that we see the moral case in its completeness that we can almost read the mind of the other, much as a person with extraordinary psychic powers could. We are on very shaky ground indeed when we feel that we are able to look accurately into another's heart and judge them as we believe God would judge them. If we catch ourselves doing this, I would recall a key point in the tradition of moral theology: it is God alone who can fully and accurately read the human heart, and not even the individual himself or herself knows their own selves as they stand in God's eyes. *Coram Deo* ("before God") was the traditional axiom that expressed this notion, which was contrasted with how the situation might appear to finite human beings *(coram hominibus)*. If this is true for reading the human heart, it is also true for reading the complexity of the whole situation that the moral tradition termed the "circumstances" of an action. This, along with the act in itself and the individual's own intentions, had to be considered together before one could arrive at an accurate assessment of the moral meaning of the action. Only God has the power to do this reading completely and accurately, but we can make good faith efforts to judge as best we can.

As one check or balance on our moral judgment, I think it is helpful to attend explicitly to the presuppositions I bring to a consideration of a situation, as well as the presuppositions the others involved might bring. We are not aiming at some sort of *tabula rasa* type of neutrality, but simply a deeper awareness of how we in fact reason and discern—in short, our religious ethical world view and value system. In order to highlight how this system operates in our moral analysis, I suggest that the question regarding presuppositions might be formulated in this way: What are some of the beliefs that I or others hold, which, if they were different, might lead to a different analysis and/or conclusion? This question does not ask us necessarily to change these beliefs, e.g., to stop believing that life is sacred, but asking it might open the possibility that there could be another legitimate way of interpreting the various morally relevant features and/or of weighing the moral principles involved. For example, while I might believe that life is sacred, do I tend to hold as a moral presupposition that life may never be ended or sacrificed for any reason whatsoever? If this were so, then my presupposition might unduly color my analysis of a medical situation in which the doctors say there is virtually no hope of recovery and that further treatment would be useless.

In the case of John and Mary Smith, I confess to having some strong presuppositions. I believe that a Downs Syndrome child is fully a human being and therefore precious in God's eyes and that his or her life ought to be safeguarded. I would also presume that the surgery to repair the closed esophagus in this instance would be relatively routine, would carry little risk, would have significant benefits to the child, and therefore would clearly qualify as ordinary means that would be morally obligatory from the perspective of bioethical principles. While I would not likely change my presuppositions in this regard, simply by attending to them explicitly does help me to remember that my pastoral role here is not that of a classroom teacher elucidating the ordinary/extraordinary means principle, but rather a chaplain who has to minister to John and Mary Smith in their distress. It is this concrete couple before me who has the responsibility to make the final decision regarding their child.

My awareness of all of my presuppositions, including the presuppositions I have just highlighted regarding my pastoral role, helps me bring them back into balance so that I can better respond pastorally to this couple in their need. In short, my presuppositions should tell me that life indeed is sacred, but that my role in this case is to minister to the couple's needs so they can make the very best decision of which they are capable. No one makes the best possible decision in a complex case if they are operating under great pressure, fear, distress, and so on. Therefore, as a pastoral companion I have to help them with these emotions before we can move to a consideration of the other issue of what is best for their child in these circumstances.

4) What further information is needed in order to respond to this case?

This question aims at completing the preceding questions, especially in regards to resolving any doubts the reflection on presuppositions might have raised, as well as uncovering any morally relevant features that might have heretofore escaped our attention. If we have looked at the preceding questions carefully, then we may well discover that in order to refine our presuppositions or amplify our reading of the morally relevant features, we simply need to have some critical information we lacked at the beginning. I highlight the word "critical" here: we can never know everything involved in a certain situation, and if we aim at that kind of knowledge, we will simply paralyze ourselves. But on the other hand, if we give pastoral advice or counseling based on seriously incomplete information, then we may well end up doing more harm than good. The pastoral response is the goal we keep in mind as we ask for further information. In other words, what do I absolutely need to know before I can respond more effectively in a pastoral manner to these persons in their need? The goal of the additional information question is not to put myself in a better position to judge morally the individuals involved; that is God's role, not mine!

What further information might be helpful in the case of John and Mary Smith? In answering this question I look to the pastoral challenges that confront us. John and Mary are in extreme distress. Why? Certainly one reason is because the child which has just been born to them has an array of life-threatening and life-diminishing medical complications. But I suspect (and here one of my presuppositions is probably at work) that the medical complications themselves are not the sole cause of their current anguish but that this comes from some other source. I see two possible sources which I would like to clarify quickly before proceeding further with them. It could be that they were caught totally unawares that their child would be born with Downs Syndrome. Mary is in her late thirties and while amniocentesis, which among other things would help determine whether the fetus was Downs Syndrome, would be a fairly standard exam she might have had in the course of her pre-natal care, it could be that Mary chose not to have this test. She might have made this choice because she knew that a woman of her age ran a higher risk for delivering a Downs

Syndrome baby and that this certain knowledge would have caused her greater distress in her pregnancy. If in fact John and Mary did not know their child would be born with Downs Syndrome, I would not therefore presume that they would choose to let the child die—if anything I would presume the opposite, since unfortunately the amniocentesis test is being used in increasing numbers of cases in which a fetus who is diagnosed with Downs Syndrome is then aborted. If John and Mary elected not to have the amniocentesis, I would presume (and this presupposition would need to be checked) that they stood ready to accept even a Downs Syndrome child into their family.

So the source of their distress might come from some other avenues. It is likely they did not know their child would be born with a closed esophagus, as this would be harder to detect in pre-natal screening, and it could be that this added malady is overwhelming them. If this is the case, this would be important to address in our pastoral response.

However, I suspect that the real cause of their distress might come from the counsel the doctor gave them. If this is in fact the primary source of their current anxiety, then it would be very crucial to know this so a proper response could be made. As a way of both verifying this hunch and filling out the critical information needed, I would seek to find out just what the doctor said to them. While this would not be my opening question to them (for reasons I will explain below in the pastoral strategy section), it is a question I would want to address, since a doctor's advice would normally carry great weight with people, and this would pose a challenge of its own. On the other hand, it could well be that the couple has not "heard" the doctor accurately, and that she or he did not mean to suggest that the child be left to die. The doctor may have just listed this as a possible choice, since the doctor would put before the couple all of their medical options. The couple may have misinterpreted what the doctor in fact said or what the doctor intended to communicate.

5) What are the moral principles operative in this case?

Moral principles are obviously crucial to every case, but I intentionally put this question near the end of our consideration rather than at the beginning. In the concrete world the application of moral principles is not a simple matter of mathematical deduction. Casuistry with a human face requires discovering that human dimension before we can call anyone to fulfill a moral obligation. If we recall our discussion on the natural law and moral norms, we remember that Thomas Aquinas did not render the first, universal precept of the natural law as "Do good and avoid evil" as if this were a mathematical formula for correct moral living. Rather, Thomas suggested that the first principle is "the good is to be done and fostered and evil is to be avoided" (*ST I-II*, q. 94, a. 2). This means that putting our moral principles into action is a matter of discernment followed by decision and then moving to application, which in turn is followed by reflection and (if necessary) reform. Yet, we do not make up morality as we go along, and in this discernment–decision–action–reflection process the moral principles we utilize are critically important.

As we saw in chapter 2, moral norms and principles are not independent entities that exist outside of human life like the laws of physics or the properties of the chemical elements. Nor do we find moral principles stored in some ethical pantry, ready to be pulled off the shelf when the case seems to call for their inclusion. Rather, the moral principles are already present within the situation. We recall Thomas Aquinas' famous expression that the moral law is first and foremost inscribed in the human heart *(lex indita non scripta)*; it is *not* "out there" somewhere waiting for us to bring it out of the cupboard and mix it in like yeast into the dough of moral response. We respond to God's prompting in our heart, which is accomplished not through an iron law of instinct, laws of nature, or deterministic compulsion, but through the dispositions given by God in graced freedom (cf. *ST I-II*, q. 106, a. 1).

Thus first and foremost in most every moral case is the dignity of conscience that must be respected and nurtured. Certainly this is done through proper formation and information, but our conscience is not like a slate on which the right (or wrong) answers are written and then read back to us. Rather, our conscience is our privileged means of discovering what God is asking of us and the force which holds us accountable to those demands we discover in the depths of our heart. In our sample case we see that John and Mary Smith have to make a serious decision and this must be done in accord with a conscience that is free, formed, and informed. This basic principle will help guide the articulation of our pastoral goals and identification of effective strategies to realize these goals, which we will discuss in the next two questions. So while conscience is always a key moral principle, there are usually others that come into play that help guide us in cases both difficult and easy.

When we ask what moral principles are operative in a given situation, it may be that we will find several, and it may seem that at times some of these do not mesh perfectly with one another. For example, in many situations at the end of one's life the principle of sanctity of life seems to clash with the principles of autonomy and/or death with dignity. All of these principles are valid, but it is very rare indeed that one principle alone could determine just what should be done in this or that situation. Therefore, it is important that we carry over the discernment process begun with the above questions into the evaluation of our relevant moral principles as well.

So in our sample case, besides the dignity, freedom, and responsibility of John and Mary's conscience for the final decision, what other principles might we find in our discernment? Sanctity of life certainly would be one, yet this is not an absolute stand-alone principle in the sense of vitalism, which could consider it wrong to end any form of life regardless of reasons or burdens (cf. *Evangelium vitae* #47 for a denunciation of vitalism). This principle of the sanctity of life is interpreted and qualified by other principles that point to other values, including the quality of life. In medical ethics often these considerations are included in the principle of ordinary and extraordinary means by which we try to determine what sorts of treatments, therapies, surgeries, etc., are morally obligatory and what are not.

6) What kind of pastoral response should I make in this case?

This question could also be formulated as "What are my pastoral goals in responding to this situation?" It is important to keep in mind that our primary goal is always person-oriented, i.e., we are called upon to minister pastorally to people, and not to abstract principles or disembodied moral decisions. This person-oriented response is an indispensable feature of a casuistry with a human face. While this may seem obvious to us, my own experience over the years is that often people have a strong tendency to focus on the decision aspect of the case and neglect the people who have to make that decision (and live with it), as well as the process that would lead to a good decision made with as much freedom and information as possible. Morally speaking, a person is much more than the sum total of his or her individual moral decisions. Therefore our accent in pastoral care should fall on helping people develop and deepen their moral character, rather than simply trying to get them to make what we believe to be a correct choice. We see this point most clearly in our understanding of Christian conscience, which tells us that our lives are not merely making right choices, but responding in creative fidelity to what we believe God is asking of us, and which at the same time God's grace is enabling us to be and do.

7) What kind of pastoral strategies would I use in my response?

"Strategies" may initially sound like crass manipulation, but that is hardly what we are aiming at here. Rather, strategies are simply the effective steps we take to realize the goals we have uncovered through the process of the preceding six steps. If human morality is indeed primarily a matter of character formation and discernment, then our pastoral strategies should be aimed at helping people get in deeper contact with this character, which in turn will provide the moral core and reference point for their concrete decisions and actions.

We can see this dynamic clearly in the case of John and Mary Smith. They presumably are a caring, generous, and committed couple. If this were not the case, they very likely would not have chosen parenthood in the first place, nor would they have sought to bring a second child into the world. It is the unfortunate coincidence of events, coupled with the misleading advice from a medical professional that have conspired to knock them off balance. Perhaps our principal strategy then would aim at helping them regain their moral balance.

How might this be done? Obviously there is more than one "correct" or possible approach, but I would start with inviting them to join me in a brief prayer if they seemed open to this. Beginning with prayer is a good strategy since it helps all parties involved realize that the particular issue or problem involves not just the individuals themselves, but also God—who wishes to be very much involved. However, while beginning with prayer is a good general strategy, it may not be appropriate in every instance. For example, if John or Mary were to come in saying, "How could God have allowed this to happen to us!?" then I might judge that they would be too distraught to turn directly to prayer at this point.

Clearly John and Mary are deeply troubled, and our pastoral strategy should include bringing them to a state of some greater peace. Very few people make their best decisions, moral or otherwise, when they are in great distress. If we want to aid them in coming to good decisions, we have to help create the space and climate in which this is possible. This is an important point to keep in mind in a case like this since I have heard many of my students over the years indicate that their most urgent concern is that John and Mary decide as quickly as possible to agree to the corrective surgery for their child. It is almost as if the whole encounter loses sight of all the parties involved and collapses into just a single decision, with the resulting conclusion being that the only really important concern is that the morally right decision be made. I certainly believe that this sort of case has a "morally right" decision, but my role with John and Mary is not to be the decision-maker, nor decision-educator, but rather their pastoral companion along the way.

While this particular case is clearly a life-or-death issue with definite urgency, it is not a decision that must be made in the first thirty minutes. Therefore, I would like to give John and Mary time to come to terms with all of their conflicted feelings and emotions. To this end I would ask them first to tell me their whole story in their own words. This strategy gives them implicit permission to open up a bit more and helps them recall the larger perspective in which this current decision is found. I would not try to talk too much or interrupt them, but I might have to prod them gently with some questions such as "tell me a bit about the plans and preparations you'd made for this baby" and "what name(s) had you picked out for the child?" The point of these questions would be in part to humanize their child for them. Perhaps a couple might be able to say it's better to terminate a medical "case," but if that medical case happens to be their newborn child whom they had planned to christen as "Kathy," and who was conceived in part to be a companion for their two-year old son Mike, then we have casuistry with a human face.

Fear (especially of the unknown), shame, guilt, anger, loss of control, and despair are all powerful enemies of sound moral judgment, and so my strategies would have to detoxify their effects on John and Mary before I would ask them to come to a decision about their child. What do John and Mary know about Downs Syndrome? Have they family members, relatives, or close friends who have children with Downs Syndrome? This may be the place in the conversation I might share my memories of my own Uncle John, my mother's second youngest brother, who also had Downs Syndrome. As I was growing up we used to visit him when we made our annual trek to South Dakota to see my grandfather and my mother's other brothers. While we could not have long or deep conversations with Uncle John, he was always cheerful and easy to be with. He always knew my mom, he knew we lived in Milwaukee, and he knew that he liked going for a car ride as it would take him by one of his favorite places—the local ice cream parlor. My uncle lived at home until he was around thirty years old and only when my long-widowed and aging grandfather was simply unable to care for him adequately did he reluctantly agree to send John to the state home. While this institution wouldn't be my first choice for a domicile, it was, as far as I could tell, a happy place for the residents and they were well cared for. My uncle had his own routine, including a small job, and he had his friends and hobbies. Visits from the family were always welcomed, but it was also clear that he was happy to get back to his familiar environment after our outings.

The point of telling this story to John and Mary would be to help mitigate the fear of the unknown and help them see that Downs Syndrome in itself is not a sentence to painful suffering or a pointless existence. Their child Kathy will undoubtedly bring them much joy and quickly become a key member of their family. Certainly Kathy will have limitations, and probably will not win a Nobel Prize in nuclear physics, but there is no question that she will win their hearts and the hearts of all those who come to know her, just as my uncle won the hearts of all the people in the tiny town of Tyndall where he lived.

Shame and guilt can also be strong players in this sort of a case and it is important to keep in mind that these are emotions first. While neither John nor Mary caused their child to be born with Downs Syndrome or the closed esophagus, they may nevertheless feel that somehow they are to blame. "If only we hadn't waited so long to have children—if only we had taken it easier during the pregnancy—if only we had prayed more—if only, if only!" These and many other self-accusatory thoughts might be running through their minds as they grapple with despair.

What kind of pastoral strategy might help them navigate these troubling emotional shoals? Here I would counsel a bit of patience. Our first response might be a quick and emphatic, "Of course you're not to blame!" but I would suggest it might be better to have John and Mary come to this realization themselves rather than to hear it too quickly (and too facilely they might feel) from the chaplain (after all, aren't chaplains supposed to be nice?). Instead, I might ask them to tell me a little bit more about their feelings and help me see how they might be to blame. Of course, I wouldn't believe that they were to blame, but as they start to tell me more, they might begin to see how their self-condemnation just doesn't really hold up as an adequate or accurate judgment of the situation.

Anger and loss of control often go hand in hand in many situations and in a case like John and Mary's it may be exacerbated by the feeling that something they might have done, or not done, has caused this state of affairs. "God must be punishing me" is a mournful line I've heard countless times in my priestly ministry. When I was younger I used to respond quickly with a strong negative: "No, of course not— God is not like that; God is loving, kind, merciful, and compassionate!" Yet, over time I have come to realize that the truth of this statement is not always completely self-evident to people in great distress. So the strategy I usually adopt now is to ask the person to tell me a bit more why they believe God is punishing them, and then I follow up asking them to tell me a bit more of who they believe God to be. In answering the last part of my question people often give me an insight into how to help them to see that their own views of God are contradictory.

Usually people will describe God as all good and loving, and at this point I might break in and ask, "Would you punish your child so harshly for a mistake or failing?" The answer is always "no," and so I then say, "Well, if you wouldn't act this way to your child (and I wouldn't either), then let's trust that God is at least as good as we are." While this simple line does not always result in a quick and complete change of a belief system about God and the explanation for evil in the world, it usually does open up a little space for reconsideration of the earlier conclusion that this tragedy is God's just punishment. In other words, a bit of hope might find its way into their reflections.

Confusion probably is another important aspect of John and Mary's current state of mind that the chaplain should be aware of and try to lessen. If I were responding to a couple who had told me that the doctor suggested that maybe the best thing would be to let the baby die, my immediate reaction might be to say, "The doctor said what?!" But I don't know if this would be the best strategy to adopt since its effect might be to place John and Mary in between two "experts"—one medical and the other ecclesial. Instead of trying to establish my authority over that of the doctor, I think a better approach would be to ask John and Mary to tell me as best as they can remember just exactly what the doctor actually said to them. Perhaps their initial statement was in fact an accurate summary of the doctor's advice, but it could be that in their distress they might have condensed a bit of all that the doctor had said into a misunderstanding of what was said. In any event, allowing them to recount what the doctor said will give some further insights into what are all the critical issues as John and Mary see them. It might also furnish some clues as to the best way to proceed with them.

If we were to give John and Mary the time, space, and support to regain their bearings, to work through some of their feelings, and to let them talk the issues out, they would probably come to the conclusion that they should go ahead with the surgery and take little Kathy home. But coming to this decision is a process and this process may take some time. The chaplain has to give John and Mary this time and support them in the process. If the chaplain were to engage as a sort of high-pressure lobbyist for John and Mary to vote to have the surgery, then the necessary stages in the decision-making process may well get short-circuited.

However, for the sake of argument, let's take an extreme scenario in which at the end of the whole process John and Mary still are either undecided as to what to do or feel inclined to take the doctor's advice and let the child die. What then? Here is where a return to the relevant moral principles may be of some help. From the medical moral perspective the surgery in question is clearly what we would call "ordinary means," i.e., the kind of medical procedure that we would judge to be morally obligatory. From an objective perspective the surgery is neither experimental, unduly burdensome, nor especially risky. The benefits are clear and considerable: a healthy life for the child, albeit still with Downs Syndrome. Of course, from a subjective perspective the couple might believe this procedure to be burdensome, and if this seemed to be the case it would certainly have to be discussed with them at some length. However, for the purposes of role-playing just one scenario, let us presume that the couple agrees that this procedure would have clear benefits. Even though knowledge of this moral principle may be helpful to the chaplain, I would not necessarily use this vocabulary of ordinary and extraordinary means with John and Mary. Instead I might pose the moral question in this way: "If Kathy had been born otherwise normal and healthy, but with a closed esophagus, would you not elect to have the surgery?" Presumably John and Mary would tell me that certainly they would have the surgery in that case. Then I would ask them that if Kathy were otherwise healthy but had been born with Downs Syndrome, would they abandon her? Again I am presuming that they would answer in the negative. Then, and only in this extreme scenario, would I suggest to them that the simple coincidence of these two maladies doesn't seem to be morally determinative. In other words, if an otherwise healthy baby has a closed esophagus, we would agree to have the surgery, and if a Downs Syndrome child is otherwise healthy we wouldn't abandon the child, then what is it about these two symptoms coming together which would so dramatically change our response to the situation if only one or the other of them had occurred?

I repeat that this would be the last thing I would say, and *not* my lead-off response. This would be my last card, so to speak, and I would play it as a strategy only if and when the other attempts to help John and Mary come to a decision had seemed to fail. It still is my operating hypothesis that most people honestly do try to make good decisions in their lives, but sometimes the very complexities of the inter-mingled issues make the truly best decision difficult to discern. However, if we take time with the process and try to keep before us all. the morally relevant features, then I believe we will come to sound judgments.

8) Who and/or what is most in need of reconciliation in this situation?

This brings us to my last question. At first it may seem odd: if there is no "sin" in a particular case, then why should we talk about the need for reconciliation? Obviously I am suggesting that the term reconciliation has a broader meaning in the sense of helping people come to terms with the concrete aspects of their life situation which have been troubling them. Focusing on the issue of reconciliation in this broader perspective may help to pull together many aspects uncovered in the first seven questions. It also is a helpful reminder to all involved that the proper response to a given moral or pastoral issue is usually *not* judgment about an abstract ethical right or wrong decision, but rather a proper focus on the people involved.

To illustrate this point let me return to the possible feelings of anger against God or fate that John and Mary may have. How could the pastoral minister help them deal with these feelings? This can be very difficult to handle since our belief system tells us that God is all good and completely just, and so if something bad has happened to us there must be a reason for it. I have heard it said that sometimes parents of a newborn child with Downs Syndrome are told, "God must have chosen you to be parents of this baby since he knew that this baby would need very special parents." I think such a remark, even though well-intentioned, is dreadfully off the mark. First, it makes God look to be either a bit of a monster who chooses to send handicapped babies into the world, or else a second-rate deity evocative of Tennyson's oft-quoted lines from his *Idylls of the King:* "For why is all around us here As if some lesser god had made the world, But had not force to shape it as he would." I think that neither image of God is accurate, and so I would not use this tactic with John and Mary.

When anger, hurt, and despair are bound up in events beyond our control, I think it is important to turn to God, but not to engage in some sort of bargaining or pleading to get God to wave a magic wand and put things back the way they were. Instead I think it useful to help John and Mary let all of their negative feelings out, and if this means expressing anger at God I think that God can take it. The summer before I began my theology studies, a high school boy I had taught drowned in a tragic accident. He was the youngest son of a widow and was her only child still living at home. Though Betty was a strong woman of faith, this blow seemed almost too much to bear, and she confided in her pastor that she was very, very angry with God. The pastor, a man of great wisdom, simply said, "Well Betty, let God have it!" This advice gave Betty the necessary permission to let all of her feelings out, and therefore to let the healing begin. In the healing God will be playing a key part. In this case, after telling Betty to express her anger, the pastor suggested that she might also turn to the Blessed Mother, who also lost a child. Betty was able to do that and though the process took time, real reconciliation did occur. But if Betty, or John and Mary, or anyone else were to feel that they simply could not legitimately "have" certain feelings, then the resulting repression of those emotions will make them all the harder to heal and resolve.

Further Points to Ponder

These eight questions are not a precise mathematical formula or recipe for pastoral or moral correctness, but hopefully they may help open up the situation by uncovering more of what is actually involved and allowing for greater creative grace-filled and effective responses. I would like to conclude this section by offering a few practical pastoral points that I've drawn from my own experience, in the hope that they may be of some assistance to others.

Take an appropriate amount of time and avoid trying to rush a session. People need time to tell their stories, and it's probably best to let them do so in their own way, in their own words, and at their own speed. Yet, this is not an absolute "rule"—some people will need help in bringing the session to both a close and closure. Don't feel that everything must be either addressed or solved in one session. Don't be afraid to set up one or more follow-up sessions.

Track your questioning carefully and please be judicious in your use of questions. Why are you asking this or that question? Certainly ask a question for clarification if there is some item which seems crucial to your understanding of the person's story, but isn't clear to you (yet) in their telling of the story. However, I'd avoid asking questions just in order to have the "full picture" or "all the facts," since the purpose of the session is healing and not some after-the-fact adjudication of responsibility or criminality. I think this last point is particularly important in dealing with situations involving a long-past event that continues to haunt someone, such as abortion. Rather than go into great detail about just how the pregnancy came about and the circumstances that led to the abortion decision, it probably would be more helpful to stay with the person where she or he is here and now. What do they feel "now"? Why? How can we bring God more tangibly into this person's life and self-awareness here and now?

Try to focus not merely on the "intellectual" but also on the emotional and affective dimensions. The heart, more than the head, is probably crucial in our moral living. Questions like, "Do you believe God can forgive you?" may elicit an intellectual "yes" (a notional assent), which has not reached the depths of the person's heart which is still crying out "No! God can't forgive me!" Effective pastoral counseling will have to try to convince and change the heart more than the head. Keep this in mind in devising your pastoral strategies.

Take their problem seriously, but watch the problem-solving tendency. This guideline calls for a definite balancing act. The person must feel that she or he is being taken seriously and that you really do understand their issue (even if it is not or would not be a troubling issue for you). Be careful not to homilize or too easily present a solution based on generalities like "God will hear and answer your prayers." On the other hand, try not to get sidetracked into a discussion of how to resolve the issue in a social service mode. This is a natural tendency for those in the helping professions—to try to resolve the pastoral issue by "solving" the problem that brings the person to you. Stick with the pastoral issue itself, and bring the person into a deeper relation with God, which usually should be the focus of the encounter. Remember, too, that some problems just cannot (or will not) be solved this side of heaven. Entrusting the person and his or her problem to God's loving

Providence may be the only (and/or best) thing that can be done at this point in time.

Avoid the tendency to adjudicate questions of moral guilt and relative culpability. In most cases your pastoral role does not call for you to determine the person's subjective guilt and/or relative moral culpability that may have existed when he, she, or others did whatever it is that seems to be part of the case. Stay with the person(s) you have in front of you and help them resolve guilt issues by turning to God's forgiveness and reconciliation. Help move them forward into the future, and backwards to replay the past. This does not mean paying no attention to the past; clearly this must be done. But the relevant pastoral role and issue rarely legitimately center on trying to judge the past in great detail to determine relative subjective guilt and responsibility.

Keep God in the picture. Even if God has to remain in the background for the person you're talking to (if that person would not be "ready" for a more explicit referencing of the discussion to God and God's loving presence), you should keep in mind that God is very much present and working with and through you.

Stay in the present tense. Many pastoral issues obviously will have their roots in the past, but we cannot go back in time and change whatever action, decision, event, etc., that had a part to play in bringing the person to you. However, you can deal with the person in the present and move them to the future. God forgives the past; God does not "erase" it so that we can then "re-record" our lives in a different way. Forgiving the past allows us to move ahead (not back) into our present and future.

Be careful of using technical jargon or abstract principles. While it is important that you do know these things, it probably is not useful to bring them into your pastoral conversation, except in rare circumstances when you might want to clarify a key point with the person you're speaking with.

Be careful of suggesting an action-plan if you don't know the person's situation adequately. One size doesn't fit all in pastoral counseling, and total honesty may not always be the best policy. For example, in dealing with a woman who underwent an abortion some years before she married her present spouse, it may not always be the best thing for her to tell her husband. Much would depend on this woman, her relationship with her husband, and a host of other issues. A related principle would be to keep a number of possible options or various pastoral strategies open so that if one line or approach doesn't seem to be working, you can fall back on Plan B or Plan C, and so on.

Track your own feelings and reactions. This is always important, but is absolutely crucial when dealing with someone whose problem, character, politic leanings, etc., rub you the wrong way. Remember that your pastoral role rarely (if ever!) would call for you to "judge" the person or get them to ascribe to your political leanings. This also applies even in cases where you know that you're "right" and/or in complete agreement with what the Church clearly teaches on a certain matter. Pastorally the key is to facilitate God's working in this person, and God often convinces in subtle and slow ways, so it is important to keep the person open to God's Spirit. Remember that true conversion takes time and may involve a number of detours.

Don't feel you have to go it alone. You can make referrals and you can ask others for advice. A trusted mentor that you check in with periodically can also be helpful as you reflect on your pastoral experiences and approaches. Nevertheless, remember that the person did come to *you*, and if you make a referral too quickly or too easily they may feel either rejected or that their problem is so great or their sin is so terrible they cannot easily find help or forgiveness. Yet, do not try to handle a situation or a question you realize is clearly beyond your competence. You can say, "Let me pray about this a bit and let's meet again," or "Part of your issue involves a technical question (e.g., a point in canon law) that I am not sure of, and I'll need to clarify this point with someone better versed" (assuring them that this will be done in both an anonymous and confidential manner!). Don't be afraid to ask one of your old teachers or someone in the parish or diocesan office for help in these sorts of cases.

Keep the person(s) in your prayers. Not everyone will be comfortable enough to actually pray with you, or to be prayed over, but I think with most people you can let them know that you will continue to keep them in your prayers, which means that you are telling them that God continues to keep them (and you!) in his provident care, concern, and love. Please remember that as God's minister you are also in his special care as well!

7

Sin and Failure
in a Morally Complex World

We come now to our last chapter and I am aware that sometimes moral theology books read a little bit like computer or car manuals: they seem to suggest that if you just follow all of the directions and perform no "illegal operations," you will be assured of a relatively happy life free of serious glitches or major breakdowns. In other words, often moral theologians pay insufficient attention to the darker side of the human moral life, namely, the world of sin and failure. To a large extent this book admittedly suffers also from this same short-coming, since the whole topic would require at least another tome of its own in order to probe carefully this most perplexing reality.[1] After all is said and done, perhaps the best description of sin is to call it a dreadful, tragic mystery. St. Paul saw this dark mystery at work in his own life when he uttered his heartfelt lament, "I do not understand

---

[1] Sin is obviously a topic with a substantial bibliography, and while none of the following titles is fully sufficient in itself, they do provide helpful assistance for further study of this area. See Hugh Connolly, *Sin* (New York and London: Continuum, 2002) and for some Protestant perspectives see L. Gregory Jones, *Embodying Forgiveness: A Theological Analysis* (Grand Rapids, Mich.: Eerdmans, 1995); and Cornelius Plantinga, Jr., *Not the Way It's Supposed to be: A Breviary of Sin* (Grand Rapids, Mich.: Eerdmans, 1995). Also very helpful are the following two chapters from Bernard Häring, C.SS.R., "Sin and Conversion," ch. 8 in *Free and Faithful in Christ: Moral Theology for Priests and Laity* (Middlegreen, Slough, United Kingdom: St. Paul Publications, 1978) 378–470; and his "Sin in Post-Vatican II Theology," in *Personalist Morals: Essays in Honor of Professor Louis Janssens*, ed. Joseph A. Selling (Louvain: University Leuven Press, 1988) 87–107. This last article traces briefly the manualistic heritage, the development of the theology of sin in Vatican II (especially in *Gaudium et spes*), the theology of fundamental option, new developments and challenges posed to a theology of sin (e.g., from Marxism and liberation theology); then Häring examines the 1983 Bishops' Synod on sin and the subsequent Apostolic Exhortation, *Reconcilatio et Paenitentia*, before concluding with a brief overview of shortcomings that need to be overcome in a renovated theology of sin.

my own actions. For I do not do what I want, but I do the very thing I hate" (Rom 7:15, but see 7:15-25 for the full passage). If this is true of one of the greatest of Jesus' apostles, how much more will it apply to those of us who would rank lower on the scale? Yet we must keep in mind St. Paul's other great insight regarding sin, namely, that no matter where sin is, and how strong its hold on us and our world, God's grace is there all the more, and all the more strongly (cf. Rom 5:20-21). While we cannot unravel this troubling mystery in great detail, nevertheless no book that hopes to deal with the complexity of the moral world can neglect this theme entirely. Let us take a brief look then at sin and moral failure as we complete our outline of living in a morally complex world.

Scriptural Insights on Sin and Moral Failure

The Bible clearly does address sin and moral failure in both the Old and New Testaments and those of us who accept the claim this sacred text has need to pay careful attention to the key insights Scripture offers us. However, as we noted in chapter 3, we also need to remember that no biblical passages should be taken out of their contexts and that no single verse stands alone as the last word on the subject. Moreover, since God's definitive revelation of God's self is not found in its fullness in any particular biblical passage, but rather only in Jesus Christ, that means we need to submit our own discernment of a proper understanding of, and response to, sin and moral failure to Jesus' own attitudes and responses. Recalling William Spohn's approach to Scripture and ethics touched upon in chapter 3, it is this gospel portrait of Jesus Christ that is the concrete universal that should guide our moral imagination. This New Testament Good News tells us that Jesus Christ did not come to condemn sinners and punish their sins, but rather to forgive and reconcile them: first to themselves, to one another, and to God. Therefore I repeat that I must respectively disagree with Cardinal Siri and Father McDermott and anyone else who would concur in their judgment that a great evil such as the dreadful disease of AIDS is somehow God's just punishment on malefactors for their misdeeds. While logic may tell us that we indeed do deserve punishment for our misdeeds, our faith tells us that God is a God of immense love, care, compassion, mercy, forgiveness, and reconciliation. Revenge and retribution do not seem to fit well in God's deepest revelation of God's self found in Jesus Christ.

In order to avoid a selective or decontextualized reading of Scripture in speaking of sin, I believe it is helpful to do a *lectio continua,* or ongoing reading, of the various Scripture passages in order that our reflections will be truly Christian in the sense of being both biblically grounded and scripturally nourished. If I were to ask people what is the central moral teaching of the Bible, I imagine that many would reply by naming the Ten Commandments. While I might largely agree with this answer, I believe we must look carefully at the context of these commandments if we are to judge their moral message correctly. The Ten Commandments were given on Mount Sinai *not* primarily as a way for God to reign in the moral excesses of the Israelites, but rather as a gift of the Covenant which expressed the vision of how the Israelites were to live in harmony and justice with both God and themselves. In fact, the Jewish tradition refers to this gift as the Decalogue, namely, the Ten Words (which is what Decalogue means in Greek). In a double sense we can call the Decalogue a Holiness Code—a codification of moral laws to be sure, but also a special gift—a sort of secret code that set the Israelite community apart from other nations, since God chose to reveal this special holiness code to them at that point in salvation history, and not to others.

How did God deal with the moral failings and sins of the Chosen People when they fell short of living up to the vision expressed in the Decalogue and the other commandments contained in the Torah? There are obviously many verses which could help answer this question, but I think the following passage taken from the prophet Hosea captures well the image of how God loves us even in the midst of our own sinfulness and moral failures:

> When Israel was a child, I loved him, and out of Egypt I called my son. The more I called them, the more they went from me; they kept sacrificing to the Baals, and offering incense to idols. Yet it was I who taught Ephraim to walk, I took them up in my arms; but they did not know that I healed them. I led them with cords of human kindness, with bands of love. I was to them like those who lift infants to their cheeks. I bent down to them and fed them. They shall return to the land of Egypt, and Assyria shall be their king, because they have refused to return to me. The sword rages in their cities, it consumes their oracle-priests, and devours because of their schemes. My people are bent on turning away from me. To the Most High they call, but he does not raise them up at all. How can I give you up, Ephraim? How can I hand you over, O Israel? How can I make you like Admah? How can I treat you like Zeboiim? My heart recoils within me; my compassion grows warm and tender. I will not execute my

fierce anger; I will not again destroy Ephraim; for I am God and no mortal, the Holy One in your midst, and I will not come in wrath. They shall go after the LORD, who roars like a lion; when he roars, his children shall come trembling from the west. They shall come trembling like birds from Egypt, and like doves from the land of Assyria; and I will return them to their homes, says the LORD (Hosea 11:1-11).

In this passage God is portrayed as struggling to let compassion and not anger rule God's heart, and we have to admit that sometimes certain passages from the Old Testament do seem to suggest a picture of God as a harsh, exacting, and punishing deity. Yet, if we read the whole of the Old Testament and step back to reconsider the faith history presented, we can see that the overall picture is indeed a God who loves, forgives, and does *not* ultimately hold our sins and failings against us. In the Old Testament sin was usually painted not so much as a personal short-coming or individual transgression, but more as the whole Israelite community's corporate rebellion against the Covenant established with God. Though there certainly was a personal dimension to sin, the emphasis was on the collective accountability the people had for their actions. The Old Testament prophets like Hosea called the people back to this original Covenant vision of justice and harmony through a process of conversion. Sin often was portrayed as having elements of power, a state of being, and even to some degree a mystery.

The primary ritual response of the Jewish people to the reality of sin in their lives was to celebrate Yom Kippur, the annual Day of Atonement, with a pair of goats. All the sins of the community were symbolically loaded onto one goat selected by lot, and then this goat was driven off into the desert, carrying with it the people's sins. This practice gives us the term "scapegoat." The other goat was then killed and sacrificed as a peace offering to God, and the whole community celebrated the restoration of their relationship to God. Besides sin, the Old Testament also recognized a variety of failures, including tragedies and misfortunes that might drive some of the community into debt. Thus, every fifty years a special Jubilee Year was to be celebrated in which all debts would be canceled and the original status of harmony and justice would be restored to the whole Covenant community.[2]

---

[2] For a fuller discussion of this Jubilee theme, see the section on "Ethics in the Hebrew Scriptures" in my *Bibliography on Scripture and Christian Ethics* (Lewiston, N.Y.: Edwin Mellen Press, 1997) 55–103. One particularly helpful work is Sharon H. Ringe's *Jesus, Liberation, and the Biblical Jubilee: Images for Ethics and Christology*, Overtures to Biblical Theology, 19 (Philadelphia: Fortress Press, 1985).

While it seems that historically this Jubilee Year was not actually put into concrete practice by the Israelite nation, it nevertheless remained as an important vision of how God wanted the people to live together and Jesus quoted Isaiah 61:1-2 to lay out this theme as his central platform for his public ministry: "'The Spirit of the Lord is upon me, because he has anointed me to bring good news to the poor. He has sent me to proclaim release to the captives and recovery of sight to the blind, to let the oppressed go free, to proclaim the year of the Lord's favor'" (Luke 4:18-19). The jubilee also furnishes part of the basis of our own Catholic tradition of the Holy Year, celebrated every twenty-five years, in which special indulgences are given to the faithful who participate. These indulgences and the whole theology of grace show us that God is always ready to forgive and that all God really wants of us is our acceptance of this free gift.

Isn't there a place though where no sin or moral failure exists? Certainly. That place is called Ὑτοπια (*Utopia*), which is literally the Greek for "no place." Every other location this side of the coming of the fullness of God's Kingdom we have to leave with moral complexity, ambiguity, sin, failure, and ongoing trials and temptation. The Bible does give us some important insights to help us recognize that temptations are not equated with sin and that there are also various levels of failure when we do not successfully resist temptation. As we noted in chapter 3, translation from the biblical languages into English often results in missing some of the breadth and nuance of meaning found in the original biblical language. In this case the Greek word for "temptation" (πε ιρασμοσ *peirasmos*) happens to also be the same word for "test."[3] Probably most of us could recognize that to "tempt someone" is quite different than to "test someone," yet often times we miss this second meaning and fixate just on the first. In the Old Testament both individuals and whole communities are tested and tempted (cf. the "testing" of Abraham with the sacrifice of Isaac in Gen 22:1-19). Individuals as well as communities also "tempt" or "test" God, such as the Israelites did on numerous occasions during their forty-year procession in the desert. Even God's chosen leaders, such as Gideon, are allowed to test God in order to prove to themselves that God is indeed with them (cf. Judg 6: 26-40).

[3] See Heinrich Seesman's article on *Peira* in the *Theological Dictionary of the New Testament*, vol. 6, ed. Gerhard Freidrich, trans. Geoffrey W. Bromiley (Grand Rapids, Mich.: Eerdmans, 1968) 23–26.

A related aspect to this notion of testing is to admit that sometimes testing and its subsequent failure on our part do not represent sin at all. Rather they point out that we have not yet individually and/or collectively reached the wholeness which comprises the holiness of God's Kingdom. Jesus himself was tempted, or tested, as the devil tried to deflect him from obedience to God and trust in the Father. It was only after passing that period of trial that Jesus could begin his public ministry in service to God's Kingdom. We need to pay attention to the paradigm of his response, which is a corrective or counter-example to Israel's failed response to its own testings in the desert. We also need to remember that Jesus has truly come and while that Kingdom is already partially arrived, its fullness will not be realized in this world, but rather in the next. Therefore this world has a provisional character and is something like a staging ground to prepare us for entry into the fullness of God's Kingdom. This entry requires of us a changed heart and Jesus' initial proclamation in his public ministry was a call to *metanoia*, namely, a call to conversion, because God's Kingdom was near (cf. Matt 4:17; Mark 1:15).

Often the Greek word με τανοια *(metanoia)* is translated as "repent," and while this captures part of what is involved in the process of conversion, it is not the whole picture. Too often our understanding of "repentance" focuses on regret, or even a wish that we could somehow undo what has been done by rewinding the video tape of our life to the point just before we had committed a misdeed, and then re-record that section by doing things differently. We can never erase the past in this way, and true *metanoia* calls us to go forward with a new heart and a renewed spirit. It is precisely this proclamation to *metanoia* that is also addressed to us, and just like his first disciples, we too need to respond by following Jesus' model and teachings in the midst of our own trials and temptations. The gospel proclamation is a message of hope and not condemnation, so therefore we must be heartened in realizing that Jesus did *not* appear on the scene to announce the doom of an impending harsh Last Judgment.

In confronting sin and moral failure we need to look at how Jesus Christ dealt with these same realities. It is helpful to recall the various encounters Jesus had with sin, sinners, and the (self-)righteous. As St. Paul reminds us in this regard we not only "should" but *must* make our attitude the same as that of Christ (cf. Phil 2:5), and therefore a passage like the following encounter with the woman caught in adultery in John's Gospel can be a helpful reminder of how Jesus dealt with both the sinner and those who were ready to condemn another of a particular sin of which they themselves might not have been guilty:

> The scribes and the Pharisees brought a woman who had been caught in adultery; and making her stand before all of them, they said to him, "Teacher, this woman was caught in the very act of committing adultery. Now in the law Moses commanded us to stone such women. Now what do you say?" They said this to test him, so that they might have some charge to bring against him. Jesus bent down and wrote with his finger on the ground. When they kept on questioning him, he straightened up and said to them, "Let anyone among you who is without sin be the first to throw a stone at her." And once again he bent down and wrote on the ground. When they heard it, they went away, one by one, beginning with the elders; and Jesus was left alone with the woman standing before him. Jesus straightened up and said to her, "Woman, where are they? Has no one condemned you?" She said, "No one, sir." And Jesus said, "Neither do I condemn you. Go your way, and from now on do not sin again" (John 8:3-11).

With whom do we most identify in this passage? To be honest I have to say that I more often find myself secretly harboring the sentiments of the Pharisees who stood in condemnatory judgment of the woman. Jesus did not say to the woman that what she did was of no importance, but the truly important words he spoke were, "neither do I condemn you; go and sin no more." If we take these words to heart, doesn't this discourage us when we find ourselves like St. Paul committing sin, and often the same sin, over and over again?

While Paul's writings have often played a crucial role in the Church's theological reflections on sin, I would like to turn our attention to the treatment found in 1 John. Sometimes I fear that we read this epistle a bit too quickly or center just on its famous verses on abiding in God and love. However, sin is taken seriously in this epistle precisely because the author recognizes that forgiveness of sin is the central mission of Jesus Christ. A sharp dichotomy is drawn between abiding in sin or abiding in God. In this understanding of sin the author calls sin "lawlessness," and anyone who commits sin a "child of the devil" (1 John 3:4; 8). In this context we read a verse which might initially make us lose hope, or strike us as terribly naive and/or romantic: "No one who abides in him [Jesus] sins; no one who sins has either seen him or known him" (1 John 3:5). Yet the same epistle tells us emphatically that Jesus came to save us from our sins, and so we have to accept God's salvific will realized in Jesus Christ, or in other words, that we called are first and foremost to be released from the bondage of sin, and not that we are called to be free of all imperfections (cf. also 1 John 1:8–2:6; and 3:7-10). Taking sin seriously means taking it as God does, something that is both real and horrible, but which bonds for humanity in general have been already broken by Jesus. That part of our human "vocation," is to accept this calling to receive this gift.

The Scriptures give us then an important starting point and ground for our moral theology of sin: namely, God's revelation of God's love, forgiveness, and call to conversion and reconciliation. It is this biblical message that lays a sacred claim to our moral discernment, rather than starting with an ethics of failure, retribution, and punishment. As we go on in our moral deliberations and reflections, it is important to keep our consideration of sin theological, that is, focused on the Word of God and words about God which correspond to the definitive revelation of God in Jesus Christ. Revenge and retribution do not seem to qualify as sound theological words about God. If we fail to do this we run the risk of speaking of sin in terms that will ultimately distort its meaning in the context of the Christian gospel understanding of salvation. If we think of sin primarily as "failure" or "imperfection" or "lack of personal fulfillment," and/or negative individual integration, this runs the danger of turning ourselves in on ourselves and away from God's compassionate mercy, love, forgiveness, and reconciliation.

The Tradition of Dealing with Sin and Moral Failure

It would be marvelous if we could look to the history of the Church in general and moral theology in particular and conclude that this is just how the Christian community has in fact always dealt with sin and sinners. Regrettably this has not always been the case, yet the best sense of the Church's Tradition does contain many positive and helpful threads that are part of the fabric woven into the tapestry of God's reconciling love. Probably the most important part of this Tradition is the establishment and subsequent development of the sacrament of reconciliation. Originally this was a "non-repeatable" sacrament, like baptism, which could be used just once in a person's lifetime. As a rule it was employed only for serious sin, with a long public penance, sometimes lasting several years.[4] Often during this time the penitent

---

[4] Still the best book on the history and theology of the sacrament of reconciliation is James Dallen's *The Reconciling Community: The Rite of Penance* (New York: Pueblo Publishing, 1986; Collegeville: The Liturgical Press, 1990).

sat outside during the eucharistic gathering of the community. When at last the period of penance was completed, the whole community brought the penitent back into the church, and they together celebrated the Eucharist—a true thanksgiving of God's mercy ("eucharist" means "thanksgiving" in Greek). In fact the term "confession" referred first and foremost to praise of God for God's mercy and for bringing the penitent into graced contact with God. It was this grace that made conversion possible. Only later and secondarily did the word "confession" come to be identified primarily with the admission of our human sins and failings. It is crucial to restore this ancient connection. In the sacrament we celebrate God's constant love that is poured out in the forgiveness of our sins and the grace to help us continue with the process of conversion and reconciliation.

As the sacrament of penance developed in the Middle Ages the focus turned more to a concern with individual sinful actions for which the penitent had to enumerate according to degree of gravity and number of times committed. Sin was viewed as a penal crime against the law. If sin was a crime, then sinners were criminals and the proper response was to punish the sinners and exact some sort of repayment from them. This led to an understanding of the sacrament of penance as a sort of tariff system, with the priest serving as a sort of judge, weighing the penitent's relative guilt and assigning an appropriate penance, which was the tariff penalty for the crime committed.[5]

Sin was also divided into the major categories of mortal, which put to death the relationship with God, and venial, which meant that while it was still an offense, it was less grievous and left the fundamental relationship between God and the human person intact. It was always part of the traditional theoretical distinction between mortal and venial sins that mere commission of a sufficiently grave action did not in itself constitute mortal sin (cf. *Catechism of the Catholic Church*, #1854–64). In addition to this so-called objective aspect termed "grave matter," there were two other subjective criteria, called "full knowledge" and "full consent." In other words, for genuine mortal sin to exist one had to not only commit this very serious action, one had also at the same time to

---

[5] For a fuller discussion of this point, see Patrick McCormick's article, "Human Sinfulness: Models for a Developing Moral Theology," *Studia Moralia* 26 (1988) 61–100; or the first chapter of his *Sin as Addiction* (New York: Paulist Press, 1989). For a theological and historical analysis of the tariff tradition in the sacrament of penance, see Hugh Connolly's *The Irish Penitentials and Their Significance for the Sacrament of Penance Today* (Blackrock, Co., Dublin: Four Courts Press, 1995).

realize the awfulness of the action. This is what is meant by the term "full knowledge." It is *not* getting the right answer to a true/false question on whether the Church holds this or that action to be considered mortally sinful; the knowledge we are speaking of here is moral knowledge, not academic knowledge. In other words, one has to realize the true maliciousness of the action, and then even with that full knowledge one still has to want to commit this action. Here again, full consent does not mean simply absence of external force, but a real desire to commit this truly awful deed. One practical problem with examining these three criteria is that two of them are buried deep in the individual's heart and not particularly accessible to outside analysis. Because of this in practice mortal sin often became acquainted with the objective aspect, the "grave matter" alone, and so many people believed that if one committed any such action, in the absence of strong external coercion, then one had in fact sinned mortally.

At the same time a whole casuistry grew up around the deciphering of a person's relative culpability for the sinful actions committed. Relative gravity of the sinful act, whether the person avoided the occasion or temptation to sin, whether this occasion could be said to be proximate or remote, levels of awareness and degrees of consent, mitigating factors such as the passions or sobriety, and so on, were all part of the vocabulary of sin that dominated in this period. The overall result this focus had for moral theology as a whole led, according to John Mahoney, to three serious negative emphases: "a preoccupation with sin; a concentration on the individual; and an obsession with law."[6]

Unfortunately, some of this tradition remains with us today and uneasily coexists with a more biblically nourished vision of sin, forgiveness, and reconciliation. While some still express a desire to return to this pre-Vatican II understanding of sin, it has so very many weaknesses and inconsistencies with the basic gospel message that Jesus preached and entrusted to the Church to carry on. This tension raises the recurring question of whether or not the notion of the biblical voice found in the scriptural section functions indeed as the *norma normans,* the norming norm, of our moral theological vision. The major problem with the theology of sin during this long period of the Church's history is that it became preoccupied with sin seen as individual acts. It neglected sufficient emphasis on the development of a

---

[6] John Mahoney, s.j., *The Making of Moral Theology: A Study of the Roman Catholic Tradition* (Oxford: Clarendon Press, 1987) 27.

person's moral character and the whole dynamic of conversion as a life-long process of continually turning away from sin and a simultaneous turning back to God. Thus, this pre-Vatican II view of sin also to some extent skewed our understanding of who God really is—not a harsh taskmaster, but much more the loving and forgiving Father who longs to welcome back his prodigal sons and daughters (cf. the parable of the Prodigal Son and the Forgiving Father in Luke 15: 11-32).

A Contemporary Theology of Sin and Forgiveness

With the reform of the sacrament after Vatican II, there was a re-turn, at least in theory, to a greater focus on the ongoing process of healing and conversion, both of the individual and the community. The communal dimension is seen more clearly in the Second and Third Rite of the sacrament, in which the confession of sins and the celebration of God's forgiveness is done by the community as a whole. Perhaps one of the most important insights that we have realized in this post-Vatican II period is that no sin is ever private and individual but always has a social effect—even if it is committed by a person in the privacy of his or her heart. Therefore the liturgical and sacramen-tal response to sin should also have a communal dimension.[7]

Certainly one of the major developments in our understanding of sin in recent years is to recognize that it goes beyond just individual persons and can infect our communities, our cultures, and especially our social and economic structures and institutions. Even though the paradigm of individual sin probably still is pre-eminent in most people's minds, sin and moral failure are much more complex than can be accounted for by any collection of individuals alone.[8] Those

[7] Regrettably there is still a considerable unease in certain circles and especially in the Vatican with the communal celebration of the sacrament of reconciliation. This tension is another example of competing paradigms and the difficulty involved in shifting from one model to another. Some helpful works which grapple with some of these difficulties are found in a series of articles published in an issue of *Chicago Studies* (August 1995) dedicated to this theme. Of these see especially Ladislas Orsy's "The Revival of the Sacrament of Penance: A Proposal," 136–44; Kenan Osborne's "The Ambiguity of Communal Penance," 123–35; and Thomas Ventura's "Old Wine in New Wineskins," 111–22.

[8] For some helpful theological reflections on social sin, see Margaret Ellen Burke, "So-cial Sin and Social Grace," *The Way Supplement* 85 (January 1996) 40–54; Josef Fuchs, S.J., "The 'Sin of the World' and Normative Morality," ch. 8 of his *Personal Responsibility and Christian Morality* (Washington, D.C.: Georgetown University Press, and Dublin: Gill and Macmillan, 1983) 153–75; Josef Fuchs, S.J., "Structures of Sin," ch. 4 in his *Moral Demands and Personal Obligations* (Washington, D.C.: Georgetown University Press, 1993) 62–73; Mark O'Keefe, O.S.B., *What Are They Saying About Social Sin?* (New York: Paulist Press,

who do theology in contexts marked by structures of oppression and/or marginalization, such as those doing liberation or feminist theology, see the reality of social sin perhaps more clearly than do those others of us who enjoy positions of authority and power, whether this privileged status be conferred academically, socially, politically, economically, culturally, or clerically. Returning to an insight from chapter 5, our moral discourse often has a narrative dimension, and like any story that people use to talk about the world as they see it, there can be a dark side to our narratives as well. Certainly we have seen stark and tragic examples of these dark stories in the narratives that have supported slavery, racism, apartheid, ethnic cleansing, and the Holocaust.[9] But all of us have our own cover stories which tend to mask from us and others the true aspect of reality as God sees it. Here is where continued engagement with God's story as found in Scripture and critically applied to our own lives can be a real source of grace in dealing with our own sins and failings, the sins and failings of others, and the sinful and imperfect social structures and institutions in which we have no choice but to live. Utopia is not paradise; it simply doesn't exist.

Even though the vocabulary of social sin and structural evil is relatively new, there are certain resonances with these basic insights we can find in the earlier tradition of the Church. Probably the clearest example of this is the whole theology of original sin. This doctrine recognizes that there is real moral evil in the world in which we are born and which none of us, save the Blessed Virgin Mary, has escaped. Even Mary was touched by original sin in the sense that she certainly experienced evil in her life, especially as she had to witness the capital punishment of her only child. Earlier theologians, such as Augustine,

---

1990); and Marciano Vidal, C.SS.R., "Structural Sin: A New Category in Moral Theology?" in *Conscience: Studies in Honour of Seán O'Riordan, C.SS.R.* ed. Raphael Gallagher, C.SS.R., and Brendan McConvery, C.SS.R. (Dublin: Gill and Macmillan, 1989) 181–99.

 [9] In probing this aspect of how our cultural narratives can hide the darker side of our communal lives from ourselves, I have found particularly helpful the work of Roger G. Betsworth, *Social Ethics: An Examination of American Moral Traditions* (Louisville: Westminster, John Knox Press, 1990). Stanley M. Hauerwas is another ethician who has written extensively on telling the Christian story truthfully. In his *A Community of Character: Toward a Constructive Christian Social Ethic* (Notre Dame, Ind. and London: University of Notre Dame Press, 1981) see especially Part One: The Narrative Character of Christian Social Ethics, chs. 1–4, ch. 5, "The Church in a Divided World: The Interpretative Power of the Christian Story," and ch. 7, "Character, Narrative, and Growth in the Christian Life." Also helpful is the anthology Hauerwas co-edited with L. Gregory Jones, *Why Narrative? Readings in Narrative Theology* (Grand Rapids, Mich.: Eerdmans, 1989).

puzzled over how this original sin came to be passed on throughout the history of humanity, and while this particular question has not occupied contemporary theologians in the same way, I believe it is important to take all sin seriously if we hope to navigate safely in this morally complex world.[10]

Besides original sin, there was yet another important set of moral principles in the manualist tradition that we might say implicitly recognized social sin and structural evil. The moral manualists actually were very adept at recognizing the complexity and ambiguity of the real world, and they knew that oftentimes it is simply beyond our power to avoid all evil absolutely. Several principles in particular were developed to help people deal responsibly in concrete situations in which it is simply impossible to do the right thing and have only good effects result. The first of these is the principle of the double effect, in which one action has two foreseen effects, one of which is good and intended, and the other is evil, but tolerated. Amputating a diseased limb to save a life is a classic example of the principle of the double effect.

However, there were other principles which go beyond the tough calls in medical situations. Three of these are closely related, the principle of tolerance, the principle of compromise, and the norms for possible material cooperation with evil. Can you ever tolerate evil or compromise what you feel should ideally be done in a certain situation, or even in some circumstances in which you find yourself cooperating in some way with the evil being done? The short answer is yes—a qualified yes to be sure, but a yes all the same. The principles of tolerance, compromise, and material cooperation with evil are not recent inventions to rationalize or sanitize our sinful tendencies, nor are they used as a sort of moral shortcut. Rather, these principles are quite well established in the moral tradition and by looking carefully at them we can be helped in confronting failure of a non-moral variety, as well as safeguarded from falling into a sort of moral dogmatism and/or false dichotomization of the world into "good" and "bad" spheres or populations. These principles take cognizance of our finiteness and limitedness—what is sometimes called our

[10] For some current theological reflection on the moral aspects of original sin, see James Alison, *The Joy of Being Wrong: Original Sin through Easter Eyes* (New York: Crossroad, 1998); Marjorie Hewitt Suchocki, *The Fall to Violence: Original Sin in Relational Theology* (New York: Continuum, 1994); Mary McClintock Fulkerson, "Sexism as Original Sin: Developing a Theacentric Discourse," *Journal of the American Academy of Religion* 39 (1991) 653–75; James Wetzel, "Moral Personality, Perversity, and Original Sin," *Journal of Religious Ethics* 23 (Spring 1995) 3–25; and Siegfried Wiedenhofer, "The Main Forms of Contemporary Theology of Original Sin," *Communio* 18 (1991) 514–29.

facticity. We live in a sinful world and none of us is morally omnipotent. Therefore, we will all have to cooperate and/or tolerate evil situations at some time or another. This is easy enough to say, but my experience both as a teacher and confessor has taught me that people are nevertheless still reluctant to accept for themselves, or others, that tolerating an evil situation or even substituting what one would *like* to do with what one *can* do could ever be honest, morally correct, and even the best option at times.

Compromise in a moral matter is not in itself something necessarily dangerous or a betrayal of moral good. Compromise is better seen as an honest attempt to realize the best *possible* particular good in a concrete situation. Compromise involves the moral act of making the "possible" become reality. Such practical possibilities are often limited, and these limitations are not a defect due to compromise itself. The end of compromise is not to reduce the good, but rather to seek its maximum possible realization in the concrete situation at hand. Pope John Paul II reaffirmed the traditional moral principles of compromise and cooperation with evil in his encyclical on the "Gospel of Life" *Evangelium vitae* when he stated that it would be moral for politicians to support a particular piece of legislation that allows for abortion, as long as this intended legislation was the best that could be achieved at this particular point in time and would hold the prospect of somehow reducing the perceived necessity of recourse to abortion (cf. *EV* #73–74).

Conclusion: A Spirituality for Living in a Morally Complex World

Treating these principles and their related corollaries would take at least another book, but my purpose in bringing them up here is simply to reaffirm the reality of our morally complex world. It is almost never an all black or white, good or bad, right or wrong set of choices which confronts us. Sometimes the very best we can achieve in trying to do and foster the good is rather just to try to minimize the evil. In those sorts of circumstances minimizing the evil is not doing the second best thing; it is truly doing the very best thing! Doing the very best that we can in any and every concrete situation will always be moral. There is an old theological axiom to this effect: *Deus impossibilia non iubet,* "God does not command the impossible." If something is really not possible, then it simply cannot be desired for us by God.

When we speak of "impossibility" here we do not just mean physically impossible in the sense of violating a physical law such as the law of gravity, but rather that which would seriously harm someone or cause them great suffering. God cannot be the author of any such command, and this is a good reality check to bear in mind as we seek to navigate our way in the morally complex world. In much the same vein the oft-quoted Serenity Prayer is worth reflecting on here: "God, grant me the courage to change the things I can; the serenity to accept the things I cannot change; and the wisdom to know the difference." Courage, serenity, and wisdom are all foundational virtues for living responsibly as Christians in the here and now, while still maintaining a firm faith and a dynamic hope for the fullness of God's Kingdom yet to come.

Living that prayer requires a certain sort of spirituality and this will have to be the last word in this book. One of the traditional axioms for the real nature of the Church was to call it the *ecclesia semper reformanda,* the "Church always being reformed." This was not a sort of false humility. Like any human structure, even recognizing its divine institution, the Church is made up of fallible and sinful individuals at every level, and the Church as a whole—as well as its individual members—always needs to be engaged in the same process of *metanoia* or conversion. While we always ought to aim to do our very best, we should not be discouraged by the realization that at times we fall short of the mark. In fact, this falling short of the mark was one of the vocabulary terms for sin in Hellenistic culture of the New Testament world. The Greek word is ʿαμαρτια *(hamartia)* and was originally an archery term for "missing the mark," for not hitting the intended bull's eye of one's actions. In fact, the technical term for the theology of sin is hamartology, the study of missing the mark. This ʿαμαρτια *(hamartia)* is certainly part of St. Paul's anguished cry in Romans 7:15: "For I do not do what I want, but I do the very thing I hate."

There was another Greek word which expressed another aspect of sin, namely, ὑβρις *(hubris)* which is usually translated as pride. However, for the Greeks this ὑβρις *(hubris)* did *not* mean being conceited, but rather forgetting that one was a human and not a god. At the oracle of Delphi, where the Greeks went to consult the gods, there was the famous inscription "Know thyself." Again, this was not an injunction to do an introspective assessment of one's strengths and weaknesses, but rather a caution to remember that you as a human were approaching the holy ground where the gods dwell. Of course, we do not believe in the Greek gods, but for us one aspect of the Christian theological equivalence of hubris might be to believe that we are responsible for our own salvation and that it will be these righteous lives and good works that merit us salvation. While there is a certain attractive logic in this proposition, it has nevertheless been condemned by the Church as the heresy of Pelagianism, which a wise spiritual director of mine once called a particularly American heresy.

As we noted above in our brief discussion of the First Letter of John, the epistle tells us emphatically that Jesus came to save us from our sins, and so we have to accept God's salvific will realized in Jesus Christ. In other words we are called first and foremost to be released from the bondage of sin, and not that we are called to be free of all imperfections. Taking sin seriously means taking it as God does, something that is both real and horrible. Taking sin seriously also demands that we remember that the bonds of sin have been already broken by Jesus and that part of our human "vocation" is to accept this calling to receive this gift. This was the central insight of Martin Luther, which he expressed in his axiom that human beings are *simul iustus et peccator*, namely, we are all sinners, but we are also justified by Jesus Christ. It is not our own actions that justify us, but rather God's grace poured out through Jesus Christ, what Luther meant by the expressions *sola gratia*, "grace alone," and *solus Christus*, "Christ alone."[11]

I suspect that what we really need is a recovery of sin—not in the sense that we further its practice, but that we regain the awareness that sin is something that struggles to exert its sovereignty over us. As British Church historian Norman Tanner puts it, a weakness of our contemporary society, "fueled by the media and consumer advertising, is that people are cajoled into believing that they can, and therefore to some extent should, do everything. [This] . . . has led to a too great emphasis on attaining perfection by personal striving; people all too easily give up completely if they cannot achieve everything—an all or nothing mentality that especially in recent years has had a sad consequence upon Catholics lapsing unnecessarily from the practice of their religion."[12] One side effect of this effort to avoid confronting real sin and failure in our lives is to look at the world in such a way as to divide it into two classes of good and bad. Of course, we locate our-

---

[11] Catholics would do well to read a bit more Lutheran theology here! I would recommend along these lines the insightful chapter, "Christian Life—Brave Sinning" by Eric W. Gritsch and Robert W. Jenson, ch. 10 in their *Lutheranism: The Theological Movement and Its Confessional Writings* (Philadelphia: Fortress Press, 1976) 137–52.

[12] Norman Tanner, S.J., "Sin in the Middle Ages," *The Month* 254 (September/October 1993) 373.

selves firmly in the former, while placing in the latter all those with whom we have difficulty. "The neo-Nazis, the racists, the anti-feminists, the polluters of the environment, they are all the unworthies. We are O.K. because we are not like them (at least not like the particular group that happens to be centre-stage at the time) and would never dream of having such base instincts."[13]

While Tanner suggests as a remedy a return to a medieval conception of sin, I think we need to go back even earlier—right to the time of Jesus and Paul, who remind us that "God saved us and called us with a holy calling, not according to our works but according to his own purpose and grace. This grace was given to us in Christ Jesus before the ages began" (2 Tim 1:9). If we can really believe this message, then we will be in a better position to recover the true relation of sin and grace, and find true liberation from sin. We will achieve this not by somehow re-making ourselves into clones of the Immaculate Conception, but by accepting the freely given offer of true life which we must live out in the process of the original meaning of confession, namely, first an awareness and then praise of God's love and mercy, which then gives us the strength to admit our sins and failings. This admission though is never the last word, just the next word. After this confession we are energized by this grace to take up the lifelong process of conversion.

In Vatican II there was a protracted debate over how to talk about the Church. The preparatory schema drawn up by the Roman curia preferred to repeat what it considered to be the tried and true ecclesiology of the Council of Trent which pictured the Church as essentially a hierarchical "perfect society." But when the Council Fathers finally approved "The Dogmatic Constitution on the Church" (*Lumen gentium*), the foundational mark of the Church that emerged front and center was not the hierarchical aspect, but common inclusive dimension of the People of God (*LG* ch. 2).

By our baptism we all share in the royal priesthood of all believers and therefore our spirituality has to reflect this changed perception that there can be no longer any first, second, or third class citizens in God's Church. *Lumen gentium* (ch. 5) also states emphatically that *all* those in the Church are called to holiness. "Holiness" therefore cannot be seen as the special calling of the professional religious class in the Church, but is the vocation of all believers. The venues in which we believers live out our vocation will, of course, differ, but there is one

---

[13] Ibid.

common element, namely, that this vocation will have to be lived out in *this* world. This real world in which we live is complex to be sure, but its complexity offers a Christian challenge to live in creative fidelity and freedom to the vision and values of God's Kingdom that Jesus Christ has not only announced but also inaugurated.

While we no longer look for him to walk our earth in the flesh, we believe Jesus' promise that he has gifted us with the Holy Spirit and that indeed he himself remains with us until the end of not only our own individual time on earth, but until the end of the world itself (Matt 28: 18-20). The gift of the Spirit is a gift to the *whole* Church and not just this or that subset within the Church. Just as Jesus' promise to remain is given to all of us, in the same way his commission to go and teach all peoples is addressed to *all* of us disciples. We do this together as a Pilgrim People in an *ecclesia semper reformanda*, a "Church always being reformed." A pilgrimage suggests a holy goal, but it also points out that while we are on the way, we have not yet arrived—we are still on the journey. As pilgrims, if we are to believe in Jesus' promise, to fulfill his commission, and to do all this in this imperfect Church that is found in a messy world, we need a spirituality of this world—a spirituality for the long haul and a spirituality which takes the world as it is, in all of its complexity, ambiguity, messiness, failure, and even sin and sinfulness. However, hopefully this spirituality does not simply take the world as it is and leave it at that, but engages the world forthrightly with courage, hope, prudence, and love—the basic virtues to living faithfully in a morally complex world.

Works Cited

Alison, James. *The Joy of Being Wrong: Original Sin through Easter Eyes*. Foreword by Sebastian Moore. New York: Crossroad, 1998.

Allsopp, Michael E., and John J. O'Keefe, eds. *Veritatis Splendor: American Responses*. Kansas City: Sheed & Ward, 1995.

Baccani, Teodoro, D.D. *The Church and Birth Control*. 2nd rev. ed. np. 1991, 1993.

Barth, Karl. *Church Dogmatics*. Edinburgh: T & T Clark, 1955–1961.

_____. *Ethics*. Geoffrey W. Bromiley, trans. Dietrich Braun, ed. New York: Seabury Press, 1981.

Betsworth, Roger. *Social Ethics: An Examination of American Moral Traditions*. Louisville: Westminster, John Knox Press, 1990.

Billy, Dennis J., C.SS.R., and James Keating. *Conscience and Prayer: The Spirit of Catholic Moral Theology*. Preface by Mark O'Keefe. Collegeville: The Liturgical Press, 2001.

Böckle, Franz. "Nature as the Basis of Morality." In *Readings in Moral Theology, No. 7: Natural Law and Theology*, 392–412. Charles E. Curran and Richard A. McCormick, S.J., eds. Mahwah, N.J.: Paulist Press, 1991. Originally appeared in *Personalist Morals: Essays in Honor of Professor Louis Janssens*, 45–60. Joseph A. Selling, ed. Louvain: University Leuven Press, 1988.

Braaten, Carl E. "Protestants and the Natural Law." *First Things* (January 1992) 20–26.

Bretzke, James T., S.J. *Bibliography on Scripture and Christian Ethics*. Studies in Religion and Society, 39. Lewiston N.Y.: Edwin Mellen Press, 1997.

_____. "The Common Good in a Cross-Cultural Perspective: Insights from the Confucian Moral Community." In *Religion, Ethics & the Common Good*, 83–105. Annual Publication of the College Theology Society, 41. James Donahue and Theresa Moser, eds. Mystic, Conn.: Twenty-Third Publications, 1996.

_____. *Consecrated Phrases: A Latin Dictionary of Theological Terms*. 2nd ed. Collegeville: The Liturgical Press, 1998, 2003.

_____. "Cultural Particularity and the Globalization of Ethics in the Light of Inculturation." *Pacifica* 9 (1996) 69–86.

_____. "Life Matters: 6 'C's' of Moral Discourse." *New Theology Review* 15 (May 2002) 48–59.

_____. "A New Pentecost for Moral Theology: The Challenge of Inculturation of Ethics." *Josephinum* 10 (2003).

_____. "Scripture and Ethics: Core, Context, and Coherence." In *Moral Theology: Fundamental Issues and New Directions. Festschrift for James Hanigan.* James Keating, ed. New York: Paulist Press, 2003.

_____. "Through Thick and Thin: Teaching Ethics in a Cross-cultural Perspective," *Horizons* 27 (Spring 2000) 63–80.

Bretzke, James T., S.J., and Monika Rodman. "After the Choice." *America* 181 (6 November 1999) 14–19.

Burke, Margaret Ellen. "Social Sin and Social Grace." *The Way Supplement* 85 (January 1996) 40–54.

Cahill, Lisa Sowle. "Catholic Sexual Ethics and the Dignity of the Person: A Double Message." *Theological Studies* 50 (1989) 120–50.

_____. "Current Teaching on Sexual Ethics." In *Readings in Moral Theology No. 8: Dialogue About Catholic Sexual Teaching,* 525–35. Charles E. Curran and Richard A. McCormick, S.J., eds. New York: Paulist Press, 1993.

_____. *Sex, Gender and Christian Ethics.* New Studies in Christian Ethics. New York: Cambridge University Press, 1996.

Callahan, Daniel. "An Ethical Challenge to Prochoice Advocates: Abortion and the Pluralistic Proposition." In *Bioethics,* 21–35. Thomas A. Shannon, ed. 4th ed. New York: Paulist Press, 1993.

Callahan, Sydney. "Abortion and the Sexual Agenda: A Case for Prolife Feminism." In *Readings in Moral Theology No. 9: Feminist Ethics and the Catholic Moral Tradition,* 422–33. Charles E. Curran, Margaret A. Farley, R.S.M., and Richard A. McCormick, S.J., eds. New York: Paulist Press, 1996.

_____. *In Good Conscience: Reason and Emotion in Moral Decision-making.* San Francisco: Harper & Row, 1991.

Catechism of the Catholic Church. "Part Three: Life in Christ." Garden City: Doubleday Image, 1995.

Congregation for the Doctrine of the Faith. "Doctrinal Note on Some Questions Regarding the Participation of Catholics in Political Life." 2003. Http://www.vatican.va/roman_curia/congregations/cfaith/documents/rc_c on_cfaith_doc_20021124_politica_en.html.

_____. *Questio de abortu* (Declaration on Procured Abortion) 18 November 1974. Found in *Vatican Council II. More Post-Conciliar Documents,* 441–53. Austin Flannery, O.P, ed. Collegeville: The Liturgical Press, 1982.

Conn, Walter E. *Christian Conversion: A Development Interpretation of Autonomy and Surrender.* New York: Paulist Press, 1986.

Connolly, Hugh. *The Irish Penitentials and Their Significance for the Sacrament of Penance Today.* Blackrock, Co. Dublin: Four Courts Press, 1995.

_____. *Sin.* New Century Theology. New York and London: Continuum, 2002.

Croatto, J. Severino. *Biblical Hermeneutics: Toward a Theory of Reading as the Production of Meaning.* Robert R. Barr, trans. Maryknoll, N.Y.: Orbis Books, 1987.

Curran, Charles E. *The Catholic Moral Tradition Today: A Synthesis.* Moral Traditions and Moral Arguments Series. Washington, D.C.: Georgetown University Press, 1999.

Dallen, James. *The Reconciling Community: The Rite of Penance.* Studies in the Reformed Rites of the Church. New York: Pueblo Publishing, 1986; Collegeville: The Liturgical Press, 1990.

Donahue, James A. "The Use of Virtue and Character in Applied Ethics." *Horizons* 17 (1990) 228–43.

Donahue, John, S.J. *The Gospel in Parable: Metaphor, Narrative, and Theology in the Synoptic Gospel.* Philadelphia: Fortress Press, 1988.

Douglas, Mary. "Morality and Culture." *Ethics* 93 (1983).

Dulles, Avery, S.J. *Models of the Church.* Garden City: Doubleday, 1974; Image Books, 1978. Dublin: Gill and Macmillan, 1976.

Fiedler, Maureen, and Linda Rabben, eds. *Rome Has Spoken: A Guide to Forgotten Papal Statements and How They Have Changed through the Centuries.* New York: Crossroad, 1998.

Flanagan, Owen, and Amélie Oksenberg Rorty, eds. *Identity, Character, and Morality: Essays in Moral Psychology.* London: MIT Press, 1990.

Flannery, Austin P., O.P., trans. and ed. *The Documents of Vatican II.* New York: Pillar Books, 1975.

Fowl, Stephen E., and L. Gregory Jones. *Reading in Communion: Scripture and Ethics in Christian Life.* Grand Rapids, Mich.: Eerdmans, 1991.

Fuchs, Josef, S.J. *Christian Morality: The Word Became Flesh.* Brian McNeil, trans. Washington, D.C.: Georgetown University Press; Dublin: Gill and Macmillan, 1987.

_____. "The 'Sin of the World' and Normative Morality." *Gregorianum* 61 (1980) 51–76. Also found as ch. 8 of *Personal Responsibility and Christian Morality,* 153–75. William Cleves, et. al., trans. Washington, D.C.: Georgetown University Press; Dublin: Gill and Macmillan, 1983.

_____. "Structures of Sin." Ch. 4. *Moral Demands and Personal Obligations,* 62–73. Washington, D.C.: Georgetown University Press, 1993.

Fulkerson, Mary McClintock. "Sexism as Original Sin: Developing a Theacentric Discourse." *Journal of the American Academy of Religion* 39 (1991) 653–75.

Furnish, Victor Paul. *The Moral Teaching of Paul: Selected Issues.* 2nd ed. Nashville: Abingdon, 1985.

Gaffney, James. "On Paranesis and Fundamental Moral Theology." *The Journal of Religious Ethics* 11 (1983) 24–34. Also found as ch. 10 in Gaffney's *Matters of Faith and Morals,* 134–51. Kansas City: Sheed and Ward, 1987.

Gallagher, Raphael, C.SS.R., and Brendan McConvery, C.SS.R., eds. *Conscience: Studies in Honour of Seán O'Riordan, C.SS.R.* Dublin: Gill and Macmillan, 1989.

Gilléman, Gerard, S.J. *The Primacy of Charity in Moral Theology.* Trans. William F. Ryan, S.J., and André Vachon, S.J., from the 2nd French ed. Westminster, Md.: Newman Press, 1959.

Gilligan, Carol. *In a Different Voice: Psychological Theory and Women's Development.* Cambridge, Mass., and London: Harvard University Press, 1982.

Gorney, Cynthia. *Articles of Faith: A Frontline History of the Abortion Wars.* New York: Simon and Schuster, 1998.

Graneris, Giuseppe. "Conscience." In *Dictionary of Moral Theology.* Compiled and edited by Francesco Cardinal Roberti and Pietro Palazzini. Trans. from the 2nd Italian ed. under the direction of Henry J. Yannone. London: Burns & Oates, 1962.

Grisez, Germain. *The Way of the Lord Jesus. Volume One: Christian Moral Principles.* Chicago: Franciscan Herald Press, 1983.

Gritsch, Eric W., and Robert W. Jenson "Christian Life—Brave Sinning." Ch. 10 in *Lutheranism: The Theological Movement and Its Confessional Writings,* 137–52. Philadelphia: Fortress Press, 1976.

Gula, Richard M., s.s. "Conscience." In *Christian Ethics: An Introduction,* 110–22. Bernard Hoose, ed. Collegeville: The Liturgical Press, 1998.

_____. *Moral Discernment.* New York: Paulist Press, 1997.

_____. *What Are They Saying About Moral Norms?* New York: Paulist Press, 1982.

Gustafson, James M. *Ethics and Theology.* Chicago: University of Chicago Press, 1984.

_____. *Protestant and Roman Catholic Ethics.* Chicago and London: University of Chicago Press, 1978.

_____. *Varieties of Moral Discourse: Prophetic, Narrative, Ethical, and Policy.* Grand Rapids, Mich.: Calvin College and Seminary, 1988.

Hall, Pamela M. *Narrative and the Natural Law: An Interpretation of Thomistic Ethics.* Notre Dame, Ind.: University of Notre Dame Press, 1994.

Häring, Bernard, c.ss.r. *Free and Faithful in Christ: Moral Theology for Priests and Laity: Volume 1, General Moral Theology.* Slough, United Kingdom: St. Paul Publications, 1978.

_____. *The Law of Christ: Volume 1, General Moral Theology.* Westminster, Md.: Newman Press, 1963.

_____. "Sin in Post-Vatican II Theology." In *Personalist Morals: Mélanges Louis Janssens,* 87–107. Joseph A. Selling, ed. Louvain, 1988.

_____. "A Theological Evaluation." In *The Morality of Abortion: Legal and Historical Perspectives,* 123–45. John T. Noonan, Jr., ed. Cambridge: Harvard University Press, 1970.

Harrison, Beverly Wildung. "The Morality of Procreative Choice." Ch. 2 in *Our Right to Choose: Toward a New Ethic of Abortion,* 32–56. Boston: Beacon Press, 1983.

_____. *Making the Connections: Essays in Feminist Social Ethics.* Carols S. Robb, ed. Boston: Beacon Press, 1985.

Hauerwas, Stanley M. "Abortion: Why the Arguments Fail." Ch. 12 in *A Community of Character: Toward a Constructive Christian Social Ethic,* 212–19. Notre Dame, Ind. and London: University of Notre Dame Press, 1981.

_____. *A Community of Character: Toward a Constructive Christian Social Ethic.* Notre Dame, Ind. and London: University of Notre Dame Press, 1981.

_____. "Natural Law, Tragedy and Theological Ethics." *American Journal of Jurisprudence* 20 (1975).

_____. "Nature, Reason, and the Task of Theological Ethics." In *Readings in Moral Theology, No. 7: Natural Law and Theology,* 43–71. Charles E. Curran and Richard A. McCormick, S.J., eds. Mahwah, N.J.: Paulist Press, 1991. Originally appeared as ch. 4 in Hauerwas' *The Peaceable Kingdom: A Primer in Christian Ethics,* 50–71. Notre Dame, Ind. and London: University of Notre Dame Press, 1983.

_____. *With the Grain of the Universe: The Church's Witness and Natural Theology.* Ada, Mich.: Brazos Press, 2001.

Hauerwas, Stanley M., and L. Gregory Jones, eds. *Why Narrative? Readings in Narrative Theology.* Grand Rapids, Mich.: Eerdmans, 1989.

Hauerwas, Stanley M., and William H. Willimon. *Resident Aliens: Life in the Christian Colony: a Provocative Christian Assessment of Culture and Ministry for People Who Know That Something Is Wrong.* Nashville: Abingdon Press, 1989.

Henry, Carl F. H. "Natural Law and a Nihilistic Culture." *First Things* 49 (January 1995) 54–60.

Hogan, Linda. *Confronting the Truth: Conscience in the Catholic Tradition.* New York: Paulist, 2001.

Hoose, Bernard. *Proportionalism: The American Debate and its European Roots.* Washington, D.C.: Georgetown University Press, 1987.

_____. "Proportionalists, Deontologists and the Human Good." *The Heythrop Journal* 33 (1992).

Horst, Carl H. "The Death Penalty and Church Teaching." *Homiletic and Pastoral Review* (June 2000) 63–65.

Ignatius of Loyola. *The Spiritual Exercises of St. Ignatius: A Literal Translation and a Contemporary Reading.* Adapted by David L. Fleming, S.J. St. Louis: Institute of Jesuit Sources, 1978.

Janssens, Louis. "Artificial Insemination: Ethical Considerations." *Louvain Studies* 5 (1980) 3–29.

_____. "Personalism in Moral Theology." In *Moral Theology: Challenges for the Future. Essays in Honor of Richard A. McCormick, S.J.,* 94–107. Charles E. Curran, ed. New York: Paulist Press, 1990.

John Paul II, Pope. *Evangelium vitae* ("On the Value and Inviolability of Human Life") 1995. www.vatican.va.

_____. *Veritatis splendor* ("On Fundamental Moral Theology") 1993. www.vatican.va.

Jonas, Hans. *The Imperative of Responsibility: In Search of an Ethic for the Technological Age.* Hans Jonas and David Herr, trans. Chicago: University of Chicago Press, 1985.

Jones, L. Gregory. *Embodying Forgiveness: A Theological Analysis.* Grand Rapids, Mich.: Eerdmans, 1995.

Jonsen, Albert, and Stephen Toulmin. *The Abuse of Casuistry: A History of Moral Reasoning.* Berkeley: University of California Press, 1988.

Jung, Patricia Beattie, with Joseph Andrew Coray, eds. *Sexual Diversity and Catholicism: Toward the Development of Moral Theology.* Collegeville: The Liturgical Press, 2001.

Keenan, James, S.J. "Can a Wrong Action Be Good? The Development of Theological Opinion on Erroneous Conscience." *Eglise et théologie* 24 (1993) 205–19.

_____. *Goodness and Rightness in Thomas Aquinas' Summa Theologiae.* Washington, D.C.: Georgetown University Press, 1992.

_____. "The Return of Casuistry." *Theological Studies* 57 (1996) 123–39.

Keenan, James F., S.J., and Thomas A. Shannon, eds. *The Context of Casuistry. Washington.* D.C.: Georgetown University Press, 1995.

Kelly, James R. "Pro-life, Anti-Death Penalty?" *America* 182 (1 April 2000) 6–8.

Kelly, Kevin. *New Directions in Sexual Ethics: Moral Theology and the Challenge to AIDS.* London: Geoffrey Chapman, 1998.

Kennedy, Terence, C.SS.R. "Casuistry and the Problem of Pragmatism." *Australasian Catholic Record* 69 (1992) 67–77.

Kohlberg, Lawrence. *Essays on Moral Development.* 2 vols. San Francisco: Harper and Row, 1981 and 1984.

Lonergan, Bernard, S.J. "The Transition from a Classicist World-View to Historical-Mindedness." In *Law for Liberty: The Role of Law in the Church Today,* 126–33. James E. Biechler, ed. Baltimore: Helicon Press, 1967.

MacNamara, Vincent. *Faith and Ethics.* Dublin: Gill and Macmillan; and Washington, D.C.: Georgetown University Press, 1985.

Macquarrie, John. "Rethinking Natural Law." In *Three Issues in Ethics,* 82–110. New York: Harper and Row, 1970. Also found in *Readings in Moral Theology, No. 2,* 121–45. Charles E. Curran and Richard A. McCormick, S.J., eds. New York: Paulist Press, 1980; as well as in Curran and McCormick's *Readings in Moral Theology, No. 7: Natural Law and Theology,* 221–46. Mahwah, N.J.: Paulist Press, 1991.

Mahoney, John, S.J. *The Making of Moral Theology: A Study of the Roman Catholic Tradition.* The Martin D'Arcy Memorial Lectures, 1981–1982. Oxford: Clarendon Press, 1987.

Mannion, Michael T. *Abortion & Healing: A Cry to Be Whole.* 2nd ed. Kansas City: Sheed & Ward, 1986.

Mathewes-Green, Frederica. *Real Choices: Listening to Women, Looking for Alternatives to Abortion.* Ben Lomond, Calif.: Conciliar Press, 1997.

McCormick, Patrick. "Human Sinfulness: Models for a Developing Moral Theology." *Studia Moralia* 26 (1988) 61–100.

_____. *Sin as Addiction.* New York: Paulist Press, 1989.

McCormick, Richard A., S.J. *Corrective Vision: Explorations in Moral Theology.* Kansas City: Sheed & Ward, 1994.

_____. "Value Variables in the Health-Care Reform Debate." *America* 168 (29 May 1993). Also found in McCormick's *Corrective Vision.*

McDermott, John Michael, s.j. "Is AIDS God's Punishment?" *Homiletic and Pastoral Review* 7 (1991) 32, 50–58.

Meier, John P. "The Bible as a Source for Theology." *Proceedings of the Forty-Third Annual Convention.* Catholic Theological Society of America, 43 (1988) 1–14.

Miller, Richard B. *Casuistry and Modern Ethics: A Poetics of Practical Reasoning.* Chicago: University of Chicago Press, 1996.

Niebuhr, H. Richard. *The Meaning of Revelation.* New York: Macmillan, 1941 and 1960.

_____. *The Responsible Self: An Essay in Christian Moral Philosophy.* With an introduction by James M. Gustafson. New York: Harper & Row, 1963.

_____. "War as the Judgment of God." *Christian Century* 59 (1942) 630–33; "Is God in the War?" (with Virgil C. Aldrich). *Christian Century* 59 (1942) 953–55; "War as Crucifixion." *Christian Century* 60 (1943) 513–15.

Noonan, John T., Jr. "An Almost Absolute Value in History." In *The Morality of Abortion: Legal and Historical Perspectives*, 1–59. John T. Noonan, Jr., ed. Cambridge: Harvard University Press, 1970.

_____. *Contraception: A History of Its Treatment by the Catholic Theologians and Canonists.* Enlarged ed. Cambridge: Harvard University Press, 1965, 1986.

_____. "Development in Moral Doctrine." *Theological Studies* 54 (1993) 662–77.

_____. "On the Development of Doctrine." *America* 180 (3 April 1999) 6–8.

_____. *Power to Dissolve; Lawyers and Marriages in the Courts of the Roman Curia.* Cambridge: Belknap Press of Harvard University Press, 1972.

_____. *The Scholastic Analysis of Usury.* Cambridge: Harvard University Press, 1957.

O'Connell, Timothy E. *Principles for a Catholic Morality.* Minneapolis: Seabury Press, 1976, 1978. Rev. ed., San Francisco: Harper and Row, 1990.

O'Keefe, Mark, o.s.b. *What Are They Saying About Social Sin?* New York: Paulist Press, 1990.

Orsy, Ladislas, s.j. "The Revival of the Sacrament of Penance: A Proposal." *Chicago Studies* 34 (August 1995) 136–44.

Osborne, Kenan B., o.f.m. "The Ambiguity of Communal Penance." *Chicago Studies* 34 (August 1995) 123–35.

Patrick, Anne. *Liberating Conscience: Feminist Explorations in Catholic Moral Theology.* New York: Continuum, 1996.

Plantinga, Cornelius, Jr. *Not the Way It's Supposed to Be: A Breviary of Sin.* Grand Rapids, Mich.: Eerdmans, 1995.

Porter, Jean. *Natural and Divine Law: Reclaiming the Tradition for Christian Ethics.* Grand Rapids, Mich.: Eerdmans, 1999.

Quay, Paul M., s.j. "Contraception and Conjugal Love." *Theological Studies* 22 (1961) 18–40.

Rahner, Karl, s.j. "The Problem of Genetic Manipulation." In *Theological Investigations. Vol. 9: Writings of 1965–76, I*, 225–52. Graham Harrison, trans. London: Darton, Longman & Todd, 1972.

Ratzinger, Joseph Cardinal. "Magisterium of the Church, Faith, Morality." In *Readings in Moral Theology, No. 2* 174–89. Charles E. Curran and Richard A. McCormick, s.j., eds. New York: Paulist Press, 1980.

Rhoads, David. "Losing Life for Others: Mark's Standards of Judgement." *Interpretation* 47 (1993) 358–69.

Ringe, Sharon H. *Jesus, Liberation, and the Biblical Jubilee: Images for Ethics and Christology.* Overtures to Biblical Theology 19. Philadelphia: Fortress Press, 1985.

Schneiders, Sandra. *The Revelatory Text: Interpreting the New Testament as Sacred Scripture.* San Francisco: HarperSanFrancisco, 1991; Collegeville: The Liturgical Press, 1999.

Schüller, Bruno, S.J. "A Contribution to the Theological Discussion of Natural Law." In *Readings in Moral Theology, No. 7: Natural Law and Theology,* 72–98. Charles E. Curran and Richard A. McCormick, S.J., eds. Mahwah, N.J.: Paulist Press, 1991.

_____. "The Debate on the Specific Character of a Christian Ethics: Some Remarks." Ch. 1 of *Wholly Human: Essays on the Theory and Language of Morality,* 15–42. Peter Heinegg, trans. Dublin: Gill and Macmillan; Washington, D.C.: Georgetown University Press, 1986. Also found in Charles E. Curran and Richard A. McCormick, S.J., eds., *Readings in Moral Theology, No. 2: The Distinctiveness of Christian Ethics,* 207–33. New York: Paulist Press, 1980.

Seesman, Heinrich. *"Peira."* In the *Theological Dictionary of the New Testament.* Vol. 6, 23–26. Gerhard Freidrich, ed. Geoffrey W. Bromiley, trans. Grand Rapids, Mich.: Eerdmans, 1968.

Selling, Joseph, and Jan Jans Kok, eds. *The Splendour of Accuracy: An Examination of the Assertions Made by Veritatis Splendor.* Grand Rapids, Mich.: William B. Eerdmans; Campen, The Netherlands: Pharos, 1994.

Seow, Choon-Leong, ed. *Homosexuality and Christian Community.* Louisville: Westminister/John Knox Press, 1996.

Shelton, Charles, S.J. *Morality of the Heart: A Psychology for the Christian Moral Life.* New York: Crossroads, 1990.

Siker, Jeffrey. "How to Decide? Homosexual Christians, the Bible, and Gentile Inclusion." *Theology Today* 51 (1995) 219–34. This same article is also found as "Homosexual Christians, the Bible, and Gentile Inclusion: Confessions of a Repenting Heterosexist." In *Homosexuality in the Church: Both Sides of the Debate,* 179–94. Jeffrey S. Siker, ed. Louisville: Westminster/John Knox Press, 1994.

Spohn, William C. *Go and Do Likewise: Jesus and Ethics.* New York: Continuum, 1999.

_____. "Passions and Principles." *Theological Studies* 52 (1991) 69–87.

_____. "The Reasoning Heart: An American Approach to Christian Discernment." *Theological Studies* 44 (1983) 30–52. Also found in *The Reasoning Heart: Toward a North American Theology,* Frank M. Oppenheim, S.J., ed. Washington, D.C.: Georgetown University Press (1986) 51–72.

_____. *What Are They Saying About Scripture and Ethics?* 2nd ed. New York: Paulist Press, 1984, 1995.

Steichen, Donna. *Ungodly Rage: The Hidden Face of Catholic Feminism.* San Francisco: Ignatius Press, 1991.

Suchocki, Marjorie Hewitt. *The Fall to Violence: Original Sin in Relational Theology*. New York: Continuum, 1994.

Tanner, Norman S.J. "Sin in the Middle Ages." *The Month* 254 (September/October 1993) 372–75.

Taylor, Charles. *Sources of the Self: The Making of Modern Identity*. Cambridge: Harvard University Press, 1989.

Thomas Aquinas. *Summa Theologiae*. Fathers of the English Dominican Province, trans. Benzinger Brothers Inc., Hypertext Version 1995, 1996. New Advent Inc. http://www.newadvent.org/summa/.

Ventura, Thomas. "Old Wine in New Wineskins." *Chicago Studies* 34 (August 1995) 111–22.

Vidal, Marciano, C.SS.R. "Structural Sin: A New Category in Moral Theology?" In *Conscience: Studies in Honour of Seán O'Riordan, C.SS.R.*, 181–99. Raphael Gallagher, C.SS.R., and Brendan McConvery, C.SS.R., eds. Dublin: Gill and Macmillan, 1989.

Waddell, Paul. *The Primacy of Love: An Introduction to the Ethics of Thomas Aquinas*. New York: Paulist Press, 1992.

Wetzel, James. "Moral Personality, Perversity, and Original Sin." *Journal of Religious Ethics* 23 (Spring 1995) 3–25.

Wicks, Jared, S.J. "Teologia manualistica." In *Dizionario di Teologia Fondamentale*, 165–1269. René Latourelle with Rino Fisichella, eds. Assisi: Cittadella, 1990.

Wiedenhofer, Siegfried. "The Main Forms of Contemporary Theology of Original Sin." *Communio* 18 (1991) 514–29.

Wilkins, John, et al., ed. *Understanding "Veritatis splendor." The Encyclical Letter of Pope John Paul II and the Church's Moral Teaching*. London: SPCK, 1994. It is also published as *Considering Veritatis Splendor*. Cleveland: Pilgrim Press, 1994.

Yoder, John Howard. "Exodus and Exile: The Two Faces of Liberation." In *Readings in Moral Theology No. 4: The Use of Scripture in Moral Theology*, 337–53. Charles E. Curran and Richard A. McCormick, S.J., eds. New York and Ramsey: Paulist Press, 1984.

_____. *The Politics of Jesus*. 2nd ed. Grand Rapids: Eerdmans, 1972, 1994.

Zecha, Gerhard, and Paul Weingartner, eds. *Conscience: An Interdisciplinary View: Salzburg Colloquium on Ethics in the Sciences and Humanities*. Theology and Decision Library. Dordrecht: D. Reidel, 1987.

Glossary

Actus hominis/actus humanus

Latin pair of terms which traditionally are translated into English as "act of man" and "human act." The *actus hominis* refers to an action performed by a human person, but which may in itself have no *moral* significance. While certain involuntary actions could fit into this category (e.g., sneezing), it is more helpful to consider this term as referring to actions which due to some combination of lack of intention, freedom, or mitigating circumstances combined to render the act devoid of moral meaning. For example, if the brakes fail on my Hertz® rental car (through no fault of my own, since I have sought to rent a car from a reputable agency!) and my car hits a pedestrian, I am *not morally guilty* of a crime, as this would be an *actus hominis* and *not* an *actus humanus*. Similarly, other actions, even if they involve freedom and intention might not have what is normally seen as a moral end (i.e., something which aims at the doing or fostering of the good, or the avoidance or minimizing of evil). Putting on my black wing-tips instead of my black penny-loafers would not usually be considered a moral act (unless one took "fashion" VERY seriously indeed!).

The moral manuals describe an *actus humanus* as an act that proceeded from the free will with a knowledge of the end of the act itself. The end of the act is understood as a moral end (cf. *finis operis*). Not every action or activity of a person would normally be understood as a moral act. For example, choosing which shirt to put on might involve freedom and intention, but as a general rule we would not understand this action to be a moral action. Instead, we might call this an *actus hominis*. Thus, distinguished from *actus hominis* the *actus humanus* refers to the moral dimension, responsibility, etc., for one's actions. Thus, an *actus humanus* is a "moral" act, and this distinction was made by St. Thomas Aquinas in the *Summa Theologiae* I-II, q. 1, a.3.

Autonomy

In moral theology the term autonomy is used usually in one of two ways. In the area of health care ethics, autonomy refers to the presumptive right of patients (or designated delegate) to have the ability to make health care decisions regarding their own care. However, in this book autonomy refers to a foundational aspect of the human person, which means that she or he has a basic freedom to discover in conscience the moral law and then to follow it. Autonomy does *not* mean that the individual "invents" the moral law for her/himself. The roots of the word autonomy come from two Greek words, *nomos* νομος ("law") and *autos* αὐτος ("self"). In moral theology autonomy is sometimes contrasted with heteronomy, which means that the moral law and its required obedience come from some outside authority, which is then imposed on the individual which means that the individual first discerns and then applies the law to her/himself. The teaching on conscience as found in *Gaudium et spes* #16 and the *Catechism of the Catholic Church* recognizes the importance of both freedom and autonomy for genuine moral personhood and action.

Bonum est faciendum et prosequendum et malum vitandum

Latin for "The good is to be done and fostered, and evil avoided," which Thomas Aquinas states as the first, foundational, and universal precept of the natural law. Aquinas defines the nature of the "good" as that which all things seek after, and states that this principle would be self-evident to all reasonable persons upon rational examination, and need not (nor cannot) be further proved (cf. St. Thomas Aquinas' *Summa Theologiae* I-II, 94:2). This principle grounds all other moral norms, and much of the contemporary discussion on contested moral issues hinges upon how this first principle is interpreted and applied. See also *Moral Norms, Levels of.*

Canon

This word comes from the Greek *kanon* (κανων) and means a standard or rule of judgment. When used in the theological context the term usually refers to the books of the Bible which have been accepted as divinely inspired and therefore contain the written form of God's revelation to humankind. The notion of canon underscores the sacred claim that the Scriptures have on the Christian community. See also *Sola scriptura.*

Casti connubii

Latin title coming from the first two words, "Of chaste wedlock," of Pius XI's encyclical on Christian Marriage, in which he banned any use of artificial birth control (1930). This encyclical was written in response to the Anglican Church's Lambeth Conference of the same year, in which the practice of artificial contraception was allowed if deemed necessary by the married couple in order to exercise responsible parenthood. *Casti connubii* became an important part of the heritage of sexual ethics that was essentially confirmed in Pope Paul VI's 1968 encyclical *Humanae vitae.*

Casuistry

Casuistry is the tradition of applied moral reasoning that looks at the morally relevant features of a concrete situation and evaluates the intended moral action or response in light of the relevant moral principles. The term "casuistry" comes from the Latin *casus,* which means "case." In the manualist moral tradition such cases of conscience were often employed to teach seminarians and priests how best to help people in the confessional forum sort through some of the complex situations in their lives. While casuistry has often been criticized for its approach in the past, which overemphasized rather abstruse logical nuances and distinctions, casuistry continues to play a very important role in helping people discern what is really going on in complex situations so that the best possible response can be made. Casuistry in the Catholic tradition has helped develop a heritage of moral principles such as the principles of the double effect, euthanasia, tolerance, and so on.

Classicist worldview/Historical worldview

This expression comes from the work of Bernard Lonergan, s.j., who described two worldviews that play an important role in shaping how one views human nature and morality. The classicist worldview looks at human nature as a "given," and both it and the larger world are described in terms of relatively static, unchanging essences that in turn can aid in a deductive approach to formulate universal, immutable, and unchanging moral norms. The physicalist paradigm was often employed in this deductive analysis. The historical (or historicist) worldview by contrast points to the developing and fluid nature of both the world and human history. In this worldview a static, deductive analysis is less conducive to discovering the world as it actually exists in all of its concrete particularities, and so those who find the historical worldview more congenial tend to employ an inductive approach that emphasizes discovery of norms and values, and which stresses the concrete and particular, the individual and the personal, the contingent, as culturally and/or historically conditioned. In the historical worldview the personalist paradigm is often employed as the preferred method to get at both moral norms and their application in the concrete.

Conscience

Conscience is obviously a very complex and rich concept, and is treated in depth in chapter 4. As *Gaudium et spes* states, conscience is that sanctuary where the individual meets God in a very privileged way and seeks to respond to God's call to live morally. Conscience also refers to the process and ability to make moral judgments and discern with the use of right reason what is morally correct or incorrect. Conscience can err in these judgments, but the constant tradition of the Church is that an individual should always follow his or her conscience, even if it should be in error. This moral imperative to always follow one's conscience is called the primacy of conscience. See also *Erroneous conscience* and *Faculty.*

Contingency

This word has a special meaning in the theology of Thomas Aquinas which is rather different from its usage in contemporary English. For Thomas contingency refers to the aspect of our concrete world that is changeable and which must be taken into account in trying to give the best moral response in a particular situation. Because of contingency certain concrete material moral norms might be quite appropriate for a given point in time or in a particular set of circumstances, but in a different context a different sort of response might be more appropriate. In

Thomas' understanding of the term, contingency does *not* refer to a fall-back plan but simply the changeability of the real world. See also *Ut in pluribus* and *Moral norms, Levels of.*

Contra naturam

Latin for "against nature," this term is associated with teleological moral reason, and used especially in scholastic moral theology to denote any action that went against the perceived "natural order," understood as related to the human being's true moral nature. Such an action, since it countered or obstructed true human moral nature was *ipso facto* against the natural law as well, and therefore intrinsically evil. A difficulty with the term is that in traditional practice it was often identified with activities not thought to exist among other animals, and therefore bestiality and homosexual actions were two examples often cited as being *contra naturam.* The contemporary magisterium tends to use the expression "disordered" to refer to behaviors which in the past had been labeled *contra naturam.*

Cooperation with Evil *(Cooperatio in malum)*

Traditional term that is divided into two major categories, formal and material cooperation, plus a number of further specifications and distinctions. One can never cooperate "formally" in the sense of sharing the same evil intent of another, but in the actual world we all at some time or another find ourselves in situations of "material" cooperation, in which *de facto* our actions abet the commission of a morally bad action by another. Thus, a hostage might be forced to drive a get-away car in a bank robbery. This would be an example of "material" cooperation, but not "formal" cooperation. However, a member of the same gang of robbers who helps plan the heist is guilty of "formal" cooperation as well as "material" cooperation. "Formal" cooperation is always morally culpable. "Material" cooperation may or may not be morally culpable, and to a greater or lesser degree, depending on a wide variety of circumstances, motives, and other factors.

Coram Deo/coram homnibus

The first term, *coram Deo,* means "before God," and refers to how we stand in relationship to God, before God's face, which posture should indicate a certain stance of humility. This expression also relates to the notion of the sanctuary of conscience, in which the human person seeks to follow God's voice. *Coram homnibus* translates as "before men and women" and refers to what will appear or be evident before or by other people. Since no human can fully and accurately read another's heart, the key for the moral life is not how we appear before our fellow humans, but how we present ourselves before God. In this regard, see also *Conscience* and *Solus cum solo*.

Dei verbum

The Latin title of Vatican II's "Dogmatic Constitution on Divine Revelation" (1965) means "Word of God" and comes from the first two words in the document. This document stresses that Scripture is the *norma normans* (norming norm) of theology and needs to be continually meditated upon and interpreted so as to go ever deeper into God's revelation. See also *Heremeneutics, Sensus plenior,* and *Sola Scriptura*.

Deontology

Deontology comes from the Greek word δε ον *(deon)*, which means "duty." This moral theory emphasizes the do's and don'ts of moral norms which establish parameters of what should not be done (proscriptions) and other things that should always be done (prescriptions). In this view, to be moral means to do one's true duty and to live within the boundaries of human morality. The moral philosophy of the German Enlightenment philosopher Immanuel Kant would be a good example of a strong deontological approach. While deontology is very important in many areas of morality, it is insufficient for all of moral reflection and in the Catholic tradition is usually complemented by the moral theory of teleology which stresses more the goal orientation and character aspects of moral development.

Deus impossibilia non iubet

Latin for "God does not command the impossible." Thus, no command of God, whether in divine or natural law, would be impossible for humans to fulfill, since God's grace is always available. This principle has been used often in ethics, especially sexual ethics, to answer the charge that the teaching of the Church might be impossible to fulfill (e.g., as used by Pius XI in *Casti Connubii*, his 1930 encyclical on artificial contraception). The point to bear in mind though is that if something is really morally or humanly impossible to fulfill without great harm and suffering to the individual(s), this action cannot have been commanded by God.

Deus semper maior

Latin phrase for "God is always greater" than our human attempt and ability to understand God totally. This expression also refers to the inexhaustible mystery of God's presence, which can never be completely and fully grasped by humans whose knowledge will always be partial and limited. In terms of moral theology this principle should provide a certain caution or epistemological humility at our human attempts to state with absolute certitude just what particular concrete moral norm is actually the full will of God.

Dignitatis humanae

Vatican II's Declaration on Religious Liberty (1965), the Latin title means "dignity of humans," and this document stresses the sanctity of conscience and the right of all individuals to freely choose their own religion since this is the way in which they seek to follow God.

Donum vitae

Title taken from the first two Latin words ("Gift of life") of the Congregation for the Doctrine of the Faith's 1987 Instruction on Respect for Human Life in Its Origin and on the Dignity of Procreation, which judged as morally illicit all artificial insemination, even with a husband's sperm, and all forms of in-vitro fertilization techniques. This document would be another good example of how the physicalist paradigm is employed in moral analysis.

Double Effect, Principle of

Moral principle developed to discern the best thing to do in complex cases, often in medical, self-defense, and Just War situations, in which one action has two foreseen effects. This principle has a very long tradition in moral casuistry and is founded in the teaching of Thomas Aquinas on the legitimacy of self-defense (cf. *Summa Theologiae* II-II, q. 64, n. 7). One of these foreseen effects was intended and was good (e.g., to save a life through the amputation of a gangrenous limb), while the other foreseen effect was bad, but tolerated (e.g., the loss of the limb itself). If one had proportionate reason for causing the bad effect, then the action was seen as morally permissible. This whole principle of the double effect has been the locus of considerable debate among moral theologians in the last thirty years, especially with what is often called the theory of proportionalism.

Ecclesia semper reformanda

Latin for "the Church must always be reformed," this traditional maxim underscores the necessity of the ongoing reform and conversion of the Church. Whatever in the Church distorts or does not correspond fully and completely to Christ and his will must be reformed. Inasmuch as the Church is sinful due to her human members and institutions, it is also part of the Church's essential nature to be engaged in a continual process of self-reformation.

Ectopic pregnancy

This is a pregnancy in which the developing embryo implants itself in the fallopian tube rather than in the uterine wall. In roughly 50 percent of such cases the fetus will spontaneously abort, but in the other 50 percent of the cases there must be some intervention to prevent the ultimate rupture of the fallopian tube that will result not only in the death of the fetus but also in great harm and possible death to the mother. In an ectopic pregnancy the fetus is not ultimately viable (i.e., no matter what is done or not done the fetus will not live to full term). The ectopic pregnancy scenario is a classic example of the use of the principle of the double effect, which allows for the removal of the fetus in order to save the mother's life. In this sort of case, the death of the fetus is not willed, but only tolerated, and there is proportionate reason to allow for the removal of the fetus, since the fetus will not survive in any case, and if left untreated the mother may die as well.

Epikeia

A Greek word meaning "fitting," "suitable," or "reasonable" and used by Aristotle in his *Nichomachean Ethics* (5.10) as a principle to correct a defective law in terms of universal legal justice. Such a correction was envisioned in terms of interpreting the intent or mind of the law-giver as it would be applied to this anomalous situation which was either not foreseen and/or covered by the actual law. In other words, one used *epikeia* to apply a law to a particular situation using as a principle that if the lawmakers could have foreseen this particular set of circumstances they would have reformulated the law to allow for the exception created by the circumstances (e.g., allowing for an exception to the night-time highway speed limit if one were transporting a heart attack victim to the hospital). Thus, when *epikeia* was applied to human-made law it allowed for a morally legitimate dispensation from the law in a particular instance. Two other exempting or dispensing conditions used in the traditional understanding of *epikeia* were if the law were considered to be either impossible (e.g., if a teacher were to ask his students to memorize John's Gospel in Greek within the space of a day), or if the law were considered to be inhuman (e.g., if a teacher were to assign her students to do a thirty-page research paper giving them only three days' notice). While some moralists such as the late Medieval Jesuit philosopher Francisco Suarez (died 1617) looked on *epikeia* primarily in terms of just a dispensation from the law in a rather narrowly circumscribed set of circumstances, Thomas Aquinas considered *epikeia* to be a positive virtue and an exercise of reason that should be practiced, since it aimed at perfecting the law itself, and not just at legitimating isolated dispensations from the law.

Erroneous conscience/Vincible and Invincible Ignorance

In the traditional approach to conscience, if one were to choose the morally incorrect thing to do in a given situation, this could be due to some sort of moral ignorance on the part of the person. If this ignorance could have been relatively easily corrected it was termed "vincible ignorance," and the person would be morally culpable for his or her bad choice. For example, if a hunter who shot a person in the field because he thought he saw a deer, but had not really taken the time or effort to make sure that it was not in fact a person, this would be vincible ignorance. If, on the other hand, the moral blindness was due to circumstances that largely could not be corrected by the individual, then the person would not be morally responsible for the resulting evil action, since the ignorance could be termed "invincible," that is, not easily overcome. For example, those who persecuted people and denied them their free choice of religion several hundred years ago were very likely acting in good faith and out of a religious cultural blindness that did not recognize freedom of religion as a basic human right, and so while the persecution would be morally wrong, since the cause was invincible ignorance the individuals who did this persecution probably were not morally culpable.

Exitus et reditus

Latin phrase that means "exit and return." This refers to the notion that since everything in creation comes from God and returns to God, we ought to consider ourselves and all of creation in this relation to God. In other words, union with God is our final end or goal, and thus our moral life and the natural law should live in accordance with this basic orientation and goal of our lives. Cf. St. Thomas Aquinas' *Summa Theologiae* I-II, q. 94.

Extra ecclesia nulla salus

Latin phrase that translates as "outside of the Church there is no salvation." This traditional theological maxim, dating from Cyprian (*Epistles* 73, 21), holds that the Church is the place of salvation for all. However, over the centuries this term was much debated as to its precise meaning, and one position held that some sort of "membership" in the Church is required of all people if they are to be saved. The understanding of what "membership" and "Church" mean have been major issues in ecclesiology and ecumenism over the centuries. Thomas Aquinas held that one should always follow one's conscience, even if this would result in being excommunicated from the Church which, when read against this understanding of *extra ecclesia nulla salus,* shows the fundamental primacy of always following one's conscience no matter what.

Faculty

In manualist moral theology, a "faculty" referred to some aspect of a human person that should be oriented to a proper end in order to be morally correct. For example, the faculty of speech was described as the ability to communicate the truth, and therefore any failure in speech to tell the truth would be seen to be an improper use of this faculty and therefore not ordered to the faculty's proper end or goal, i.e., it would be contrary to the proper nature of the faculty (*contra naturam*). Similarly, the faculty of sex was seen as being ordered to procreation, and therefore any other use of the sexual faculty that was not aimed at procreation would be judged to be *contra naturam* and immoral. This moral reading of faculties is strengthened by the classicist world view and the physicalist paradigm. See also *Classicist worldview; Contra naturam; Locutio contra mentem;* and *Physicalist paradigm.*

Finis operis/finis operantis

Latin pair of terms that translate respectively as the "end (goal) of the action performed" and the "end (goal or intention) of the moral agent performing the action." *Finis operantis* focuses on the moral agent's own motive for doing a particular action, and *finis operis* looks at the goal or "end" of the action performed. Thus, a person who gives a large sum of money to the poor merely to receive praise of others performs an action that in itself is good (i.e., the *finis operis* is good), but whose motive (the *finis operantis*) is bad (seeking vainglory). For the moral agent this is a morally bad action. There remains an ongoing debate among moralists about the precise understanding of what constitutes the actual moral distinction between *finis operis* and *finis operantis* in certain actions that have both good and bad effects, such as those which might involve the principle of the double effect or cooperation with evil.

Fontes moralitatis

Latin expression that translates as "sources (fonts) of morality" and refers to the three factors which taken together constitute the traditional understanding of the objective content of a moral action: (1) the end of the action itself (the "object" of the action); (2) the circumstances surrounding the agent in the commission of the action; and (3) the intention, purpose, or motive of the agent in committing said action. If one fails to consider adequately one or more of these three fonts, then no adequate moral evaluation of the corresponding action can be achieved.

Freedom

Human freedom is the absolutely indispensable criterion for human morality and is essential for genuine human dignity (see *Veritatis splendor* #34 and #86). Morally speaking there are two important aspects of freedom, namely, liberty and authenticity. Liberty refers to freedom from conditions that make genuine human action and/or human flourishing very difficult or impossible. Authenticity refers to the freedom we use to commit ourselves to our human flourishing and moral living. It is the ability humans have to become ever more truly human. Moral freedom demands that we can exercise moral autonomy, especially in following our conscience. See also *Actus hominis/humanus; Autonomy;* and *Conscience.*

Gaudium et spes

Vatican II's "Pastoral Constitution on the Church in the Modern World" (1965). The Latin title comes from the initial words in the document, *gaudium et spes,* which translate as "joy and hope." *Gaudium et spes* contains a very important section on human conscience, calling it the deepest core and sanctuary where the individual meets God (cf. #16).

Hermeneutics

This term refers to the discipline of textual interpretation, including biblical interpretation. A basic axiom of hermeneutics is that no written text is self-interpreting, and so each and every text needs careful study of its various literary forms and overall dynamics in order to arrive at an interpretation that will be faithful to the text. Hermeneutics is a somewhat inexact science since one can never arrive at a once-and-for-all interpretation of text in the way that one might interpret a mathematical or chemical formula. Much of interpretation depends not only on the context of the original text, but also on the context of the contemporary readers. See also *Dei verbum; Sensus plenior;* and *Sola Scriptura.*

Heteronomy

Heteronomy is contrasted with moral autonomy and refers to the imposition of the moral law from some outside source (*hetero* means "other" or "different" in Greek). Heteronomy is *not* the accepted Roman Catholic position on conscience and the moral law since conscience is where we meet God and honestly seek to respond to God's voice (see *Gaudium et spes* #16). Therefore whatever authority one believes is absolute is in effect the voice of God for that person, and if we allow any outside authority—no matter how respected—to supplant the person's individual conscience, then we are in effect making this heteronomous moral authority into God for that person.

Humanae vitae

Pope Paul VI's 1968 encyclical on the Regulation of Births. The title comes from the first two words of the Latin text which translate as "human life." This encyclical emphasized the notion of responsible parenthood and allowed for the practice of natural family planning to limit the number of children but held that any artificial means of contraception was an *intrinsece inhonestum*, i.e., an "intrinsically dishonest" action not in harmony with human dignity. Ignorance, vincible and invincible: See *Erroneous conscience*

Imago Dei

Latin for "image of God," this phrase expresses the basic Judeo-Christian tenet of theological anthropology. We are made in the image of God, and thus in our being and action we are called to image God's own holiness and because of this image we have an inherent dignity which grounds the Christian understanding of respect for the human person, the sanctity of life, and the very notion of human rights.

Intrinsic evil. See *Intrinsece malum in se*

Intrinsece malum in se

Latin expression for "intrinsically evil in itself." This is probably one of the most contested and difficult terms to understand in contemporary moral theology. *Intrinsice malum* means "intrinsically evil," but it is crucial to retain the whole expression for a proper understanding of the term. *In se* refers to the essential or inherent quality of something. In moral matters an act that is *intrinsece malum in se* is inherently evil "in itself," i.e., of its very nature (and irrespective of further extenuating circumstances and/or motives). The *in se* (in itself) includes an implicit consideration of the three traditional fonts of morality, the so-called *fontes moralitatis*, and thus to call anything "intrinsically evil," has to include some analysis of intention and circumstances. For example, not all killing or homicide is intrinsically evil, but all murder is. What is the difference between a simple killing of a human person and murder?

Intention and circumstances, or the *in se* aspect of the *intrinsice malum*. The notion of intrinsic evil has been strongly reaffirmed by Pope John Paul II and Cardinal Ratzinger, but its applications in some complicated individual concrete situations are still very difficult to discern, e.g., whether or not laprascopic surgery to remove an ectopic pregnancy would constitute the intrinsically evil act of a direct abortion. Because of this great confusion many moralists prefer not to use the term "intrinsically evil" at all, since it can so easily be misunderstood to refer just to the physical aspect of the action itself without taking into proper consideration the accompanying intention and circumstances. Yet, since the term is so deeply entrenched in the moral tradition it would seem difficult simply to abandon it altogether.

Ipsissima verba

Latin term for "the very words of Jesus," which would seem to suggest a very high normative claim when applied to morality. However, as we have seen in chapter 3, it is both difficult to ascertain with sufficient precision just which words are actually those spoken by Jesus, and even if we can determine this with reasonable assurance, there still remains the challenge of how to interpret these words. A proper consideration of the *ipsissima verba* should include good exegesis and a hermeneutical interpretation of the biblical text, and should *not* be employed in a simplistic, fundamentalist manner.

Iudicium de actu ponendo

Latin for "judgment (of conscience) concerning the act to be undertaken." In the manualist tradition of moral theology, there was a distinction drawn between two kinds of judgment made in conscience. The first judgment refers primarily to the "objective" nature—the rightness or wrongness of the moral act in itself and was referred to as *iudicium de actu ponendo*. However, the individual moral agent could be in "error" about his or her judgment of this act. This error in turn could be totally non-culpable (i.e., invincibly ignorant), or more or less culpable (thus, vincibly ignorant—i.e., able to have been overcome). This basic distinction is key to the Church's traditional teaching on sanctity of conscience, the necessity for good formation of conscience, and the notion of an erroneous conscience and vincible and invincible ignorance.

Iudicium de positione actus

Latin for "judgment (of conscience) about the position of the act." This term, coupled with the notion of *iudicium de actu ponendo* discussed above, was the second type of moral judgment made in conscience by a moral agent. This second judgment is related more closely to the subjective judgment of the moral agent that an act will be "right" and therefore "good" (i.e., the "position" of the contemplated moral act in relation to one's life and the good as one sees it). In traditional moral theology this distinction about the two types of judgment allowed for the possibility that one could "err" about the objective moral nature of an act and yet still be acting in good faith (or sometimes called good conscience). The "error" would be an error of judgment *de actu ponendo*. In acting in good faith one could not "err" in the second sort of judgment though *de positione actus*. In summary we could say that the person believes that doing "X" is morally good: this is the *iudicium de positione actus*. If the person believed that "X" was not morally good, but did it anyway, this would be malicious. However, this "judgment" so far only has taken into account the "subjective" judgment of the moral agent about the action. The action itself could in fact be morally (or "objectively") wrong. This "objective" moral judgment is the *iudicium de actu ponendo* (judgment concerning the act to be undertaken). Thus, for a person acting in good faith, his or her *iudicium de actu ponendo* (judgment concerning the act to be undertaken) can be "erroneous" while the *iudicium de positione actus* (judgment about the position of the act) could not in principle be erroneous—i.e., a person who is acting in good faith will always try to do what she or he judges be right.

Lectio continua

Latin phrase for "continuous reading" refers to the ongoing reading of a text, and usually refers to the sequential reading of the Bible. Thus, the Sunday Lectionary is a *lectio continua* over a three-year period of most of the Scripture. As a theological principle, *lectio continua* refers to the need to be in continual contact with the *whole* of Scripture in some systematic fashion in order to hear the entire biblical message of Revelation, and to act against the natural tendency to create a "canon-within-the-canon" of elements of Scripture which one holds central to one's faith life, and yet which may tend to neglect or ignore other scriptural elements that may modify or call into question some of those scriptural assumptions. See also *Canon* and *Sola Scriptura*.

Lex indita non scripta

Latin phrase that refers to the moral "law inscribed and not written down." This moral law is written on the human heart, and in the scholastic tradition of Thomas Aquinas the *lex indita* is a basic affirmation of the nature of the natural law, i.e., innate moral knowledge that each person has and can come to understand in a given situation through the exercise of right reason *(recta ratio)*. The *lex indita non scripta* is found in human conscience as the voice of God that the individual seeks to listen to and follow.

Lex orandi, lex credendi

Classic theological axiom which translates as "the law of praying is the law of believing." This expression goes back to St. Prosper of Aquitane (ca. 390—ca. 463), which affirms that liturgy is the norm of faith, i.e., how the Church prays witnesses to what the Church believes. The fuller form of the axiom is *legem credendi lex statuat supplicandi* ("let the law of prayer establish the law of belief").

Locus classicus

Latin for "classic location (place)," which in theology refers to a proof-text or authoritative reference for a certain doctrine, or the usual textual reference given to demonstrate a certain point. E.g., the *locus classicus* for the New Testament expression of the natural law is Romans 2:12-15.

Locutio contra mentem

Latin for "speech against what one is in fact thinking." In traditional manualistic moral theology this was the definition, and condemnation, of lying, based on a reading of the "faculty" of speech. Any violation of the "nature" of such a "faculty" would be in itself (intrinsically) immoral, and could never be justified due to extenuating circumstances and/or otherwise good intentions. However, as we have discussed in chapter 2, mere factual accuracy or inaccuracy in speech may not always correspond to moral goodness. See also *Contra naturam* and *Faculty*.

Lumen gentium

"Light to the nations," the title of Vatican II's "Dogmatic Constitution on the Church" (1964). This document used People of God and Pilgrim People as the principal models of the Church and stressed that all those on this pilgrimage are called to holiness, and not just those who are in religious life or the clerical state.

Magisterium

The Latin word refers to "authority of the master or teacher," and while in its general form this concept refers to the authority granted to one by his or her "mastery" of a position, art, trade, or discipline, in reference to the Church Thomas Aquinas spoke of a twin magisterium *(magisteria)*: the pastoral magisterium of the bishops and the professional magisterium of theologians. In more recent centuries the term is usually reserved to the authoritative teaching role of the hierarchy (bishops and pope). In moral theology the magisterium is a special source of moral wisdom individuals should take cognizance of in forming their consciences.

Manualist tradition

This refers to the long period of the establishment of theological textbooks, especially in moral theology, which aimed at giving a comprehensive synthesis of the whole discipline. The manuals usually treated as major themes law, human acts, conscience, and sin, and often were structured according either to the Ten Commandments or the cardinal and theological virtues. The moral manuals recognized three principal sources or fonts for moral theology: Scripture, Tradition, and the (current teaching of the) magisterium. For a particular position on a given issue, the manuals usually started with the current teaching of the magisterium at that particular time and then worked back to Scripture and Tradition to demonstrate how this teaching was harmonious and constant through the ages. The manuals often employed a rather detailed casuistry and reached their apex of development in the seventeenth century, though they continued to be widely used until the time of Vatican II.

Material cooperation. See **Cooperation with evil**

Material Norms. See **Moral Norms, Levels of**

Middle Axioms. See **Moral Norms, Levels of**

Moral Norms, Levels of

In this book I have tried to follow Thomas Aquinas' thought by expressing a differentiation of three levels of moral norms: *universal precepts*, which are expressed in abstract terms and that will always and everywhere be true; *middle axioms*, which are concrete norms of a more general nature and that are usually, though not always, true; and *concrete material norms*, which are very specific and the most open to both revision and error. The universal precepts come from conclusions discovered through the use of speculative reason that will be always and everywhere true. In the *Summa Theologiae* I-II, q. 94 on the natural law Thomas Aquinas gives his definition of the nature of the good as the first example of the universal precept which grounds all other moral judgments, namely *bonum est faciendum et prosequendum et malum vitandum* (the good is that which is to be done and fostered and evil is that which is to be avoided). "Drive safely" might be another example of a universal precept. While this sort of universal precept is always true, its concrete application will be made using practical reason and those concrete judgments are open both to change and to error, e.g., just what it means to "drive safely" here and now. The next level of moral norms is middle axioms, which are concrete in their formulation and are usually without too many exceptions. These are said to bind *ut in pluribus*, i.e., in most cases, and the occasional exception does not necessarily change the overall validity of the middle axiom. "Drive according to the posted speed limit" might be an example of a middle axiom. The last level of moral norms is a very concrete material norm since it tries to spell out in detail what should be done in a particular given situation. "Drive 15 m.p.h. in a school zone" is an example of a concrete material norm. However, Thomas Aquinas observes that as we descend more into matters of detail our moral norms will become more changeable since their formulation depends on varying situations (what he calls "contingency") and on the prudential judgments made in practical reason of individuals who will have varying degrees of relevant experience, wisdom, and virtue.

Natural Law

In Thomistic theology the natural law refers to the human participation in God's eternal law. Chapter 2 is largely devoted to a discussion of natural law, but for the purposes of a short definition we could call the natural law that which humans are called to follow if they hope to live truly moral lives which in turn will promote genuine human flourishing. The natural law involves a recognition of the objective nature of the moral order, grounded in God's providence, and which is accessible to human understanding and obedience through the use of reason. See also *Casuistry; Contingency; Moral Norms, Levels of; Practical Reason; Right Reason; Speculative Reason;* and *Ut in pluribus.*

Neo-scholasticism/Scholasticism

These terms refer to the moral tradition that grew out of the work of Thomas Aquinas, and sometimes is used interchangeably with Thomism. While the theology of Thomas Aquinas is of immense significance in the history of the Church, it also has a very important value for contemporary moral theology. However, certain neo-scholastic approaches are legitimately criticized as being overly intellectualistic and insufficiently engaged with many of the cultural and historical particularities that constitute human personhood. Neo-scholasticism was also tied in with a classicist worldview and a narrow physicalist approach to the natural law. Thomism was mandated as virtually the official philosophy and theology of the Church by Pope Leo XIII in his 1879 encyclical *Aeterni patris.*

Norma normans non normata

Latin expression for "norming norm not normed by something else," this concept refers to a principle that grounds a discussion, since it establishes itself and does not depend on anything else for its basic legitimacy or authority. Whatever we hold to be a *norma normans non normata* in our moral discernment would be the decisive content or principle to which we ought to conform ourselves or our actions.

Odium theologicum

Latin for "theological hatred," this term refers to the oft-found controversy among theologians concerning their opponents' doctrinal or moral positions. Regrettably such "hatred" rarely advances theo-logical knowledge in a constructive manner.

Optatam totius

Vatican II's decree on the Training of Priests (1965), which decreed that Scripture was to be foundational (literally the "soul") of the study of all of theology. The initial Latin words in the document, *optatam totius*, translate as "desired by all." This document was very important in giving an impetus to move from a manualist approach to moral the-ology to a more biblically grounded and scripturally nourished under-standing of this sacred science.

Ordinary and Extraordinary Means

This is an important moral principle in the arena of health care ethics. Ordinary means are all medicines, treatments, and operations that offer a reasonably good chance of benefit to a patient's life and health, and are not considered to be experimental or cause undue bur-den, either physically, psychologically, economically, ecologically, etc. Ordinary means are considered to be morally obligatory to preserve both life and health whereas extraordinary means are not morally obligatory. Extraordinary means would be those medicines, treat-ments, operations which either offer a lesser chance of real benefit to the patient, or which involve excessive burden on the patient or those charged with the patient's care. See also *Palliative care* and *Vitalism*.

Palliative care

Palliative care refers to the medical treatment of pain and suffering. Since such pain is an evil it can not be a good in itself, though for suf-ficient reasons it can be tolerated for proportionate reason since this type of evil is non-moral (sometimes also called physical, pre-moral, or ontic evil). The traditional position of the Catholic Church is that palliative care or treatment of pain is always allowed, even if it is fore-seen that such treatment might have the effect of hastening an indi-vidual's death. In this instance the aim is not to cause death (which is what is meant by euthanasia), but the intended end of the action is the alleviation of physical suffering. The principle of the double effect, as well as the distinction between ordinary and extraordinary means both would allow for such treatment. In his encyclical on the Gospel of Life, *Evangelium vitae*, Pope John Paul II explicitly confirms this traditional teaching (see *EV* #65). See also *Vitalism*.

Pars propter totum. See **Totality, Principle of**

Personalist Paradigm

The Personalist Paradigm grew out of the renewal of moral theology after Vatican II that emphasized more the individual relation of the person with God, and also of a dissatisfaction with the manualist tradition's tendency to evaluate morality in terms of individual acts through the perspective of the physicalist paradigm. The Personalist Paradigm places the accent on the individual human person and stresses attention not only to the biological faculties connected with individual acts, but a broader understanding of human flourishing in terms of the fundamental dimensions of the human person that include not only the physical aspects, but also the inter-relational, psychological, and spiritual aspects of the human person. The Personalist Paradigm emphasizes the moral source of individual human experience and tends to favor a historical worldview over the classicist worldview. Since every human person is to some extent unique it is more difficult in the Personalist Paradigm to come to clear and concrete moral norms which will apply to each and every person, precisely because each and every person is in many important ways significantly different from other persons in both makeup and concrete material situation. See also *Classicist Worldview* and *Personalist paradigm*.

Physicalist Paradigm

The Physicalist Paradigm is an act-centered approach to morality that seeks to come to a moral knowledge of God's will by looking primarily at the physical and biological aspects of creation, often seen in terms of a classicist worldview. Corresponding moral norms are formulated in terms of obligations derived from a view of an understanding of the structures of acts related to certain faculties of the human person. To be morally correct the act has to be done in a natural way that respects the end or finality of the given faculty. For example, in the physicalist paradigm the finality of the human sexual faculty is procreation, and therefore any act that would block or frustrate this procreative end (such as masturbation, contraception, homogenital acts, etc.) would be considered *contra naturam*, and *ipso facto* immoral. See also *Classicist Worldview; Contra naturam; Faculty;* and *Personalist paradigm.*

Practical Reason

Term used by Thomas Aquinas for right reason *(recta ratio)* as it was applied to concrete situations. It refers to reason put into practice. Thomas distinguished practical reason from speculative reason. The former deals with concrete matters, while the latter deals with abstract truth. Practical reason does *not* mean "practical" in the sense of being handy with tools, or pragmatic in one's approach to life. Since practical reason deals with prudential judgments and applications to concrete situations, it will sometimes be in error, or people may find themselves in disagreement as to the best way to proceed in a given situation. Thomas Aquinas recognized this necessary aspect of practical reason and stated that these differences would occur both because of concrete differences in various situations (what he termed "contingency") as well as different abilities of individuals to see the wisest course of action to follow.

Q.E.D.

Latin abbreviation for *quod erat demonstrandum*, "that which was to be demonstrated (proven)." Usually appended to mathematical or logical proofs to indicate successful conclusion of the proof of the initial hypothesis, this expression indicates any logical "proof" of any argument or hypothesis.

Recta ratio

Latin for "right reason"; see the entry for "Right reason" below.

Right reason

The basic moral faculty of discernment. Each human person, through a process of rational reflection, can come to a correct moral understanding of the rightness and wrongness of moral actions, etc. See also *Lex indita non scripta; Practical Reason;* and *Speculative Reason.*

Scholasticism. See Neo-scholasticism

Sensus plenior

Latin for "fuller sense," this term refers to the hermeneutical affirmation that a classic text (here traditionally understood as the Scriptures) contains meanings that go beyond the literal sense or meaning explicitly intended by the original human author for the specific cultural-historical audience of the period in which the text was written. Thus, the Scriptures can always yield new and deeper meanings which may come up in new and different situations, or which are realized through ongoing study and/or reflection and meditation.

Sola fide

Latin for "Faith alone," and along with *sola gratia* and *sola scriptura,* one of the three basic principles which Martin Luther used to ground his theology, in contrast to what he considered to be the false reliance of Roman Catholicism upon Tradition, as well as a justification based on works or merit, which he believed was another principal heresy of Roman Catholicism.

Sola gratia

Latin for "Grace alone," *Sola gratia* held that God's gratuitous gift of grace was totally unmerited, and also could never be "earned" through good works or pious exercises. Therefore, the human person was called to acceptance of this grace through faith alone.

Sola scriptura

Latin for "Scripture alone," *Sola scriptura* referred to the primacy of God's Revelation in the Sacred Scriptures as the touchstone for all theology and ethics. Thus, Luther rejected moral casuistry based on the natural law, and also appeals to Tradition rather than Scripture alone for validation of any theological position. See also *Dei verbum; Hermeneutics;* and *Sensus plenior.*

Solus Christus

Latin for "Christ alone," this term was often employed with the three traditional Reformation *"solas"* (*sola fide, sola gratia,* and *sola scriptura*). The expression emphasized that it is Christ alone, and no one else, and not even our own good deeds which save us.

Solus cum solo

Latin for "alone with the alone," this traditional theological term refers to the fundamental stance of each person who ultimately must stand alone before God, who alone is the absolute. In this regard see also *Conscience* and *Coram Deo*.

Speculative Reason

Thomas Aquinas used this term to describe reason of a more abstract nature. Speculative refers to those things one can come to know to be necessarily true with the aid of reason. For example, once the terms have been properly defined we can come to know that in Euclidian geometry a triangle necessarily will be a three-sided polygon, the sum of whose interior angles will equal 180. Universal precepts, such as good is to be done and fostered and evil is to be avoided, are also necessarily true and discovered by speculative reason. In Thomistic usage the term "speculative" does *not* refer to something that is either imaginary or about which we really cannot come to a firm conclusion due to limitations of our ability to gather relevant data, such as whether there is any other intelligent life in the universe. Speculative reason for Thomas is contrasted with practical reason, but practical reason builds on speculative reason and tries to put it into concrete application. So, we move from knowledge of the universal precept about good and evil, which we gain through the use of speculative reason, and then we try to apply this principle using practical reason in our concrete decisions about what we should do morally.

Summa Theologiae

While the Latin translates this as the "summary of theology," and can refer to any number of manualist texts on theology, e.g., the *Summa Theologiae* of St. Antoninus of Florence (1389–1459), in general one can presume that, unless otherwise clearly noted, *Summa Theologiae* refers to St. Thomas Aquinas' masterpiece, intended by him to be a summary and introduction of the main points of the study of theology. Thomas' work is divided into three major sections, called *Pars* in Latin. References are usually given in a standard set of abbreviations which begin with *ST,* followed by the particular major section, question, and article. Thus, *ST* I-II, q. 94, a. 1 would signify Article 1 of Question 94 of the Prima secundae (Second part of Part One) of the *Summa Theologiae*.

Teleology

One of two major traditional approaches (the other being deontology) to moral reasoning which begins with a consideration of the true "nature" of the person, or aspect of the person (often called a faculty), and then evaluates a given moral action in terms of fostering or obstructing the end or goal (its *telos*) of that nature or faculty. In this sense teleology considers the ends/consequences of an action in order to discover the moral rightness or wrongness of the given action. Teleology is not understood as a simple consequentialism, but always looks at the consequences in respect to the proper nature or the human person, and/or the authentic goal of a given human faculty. Thus, the goal of speech is communication of the truth and anything that would intentionally obstruct or counter this goal would be morally wrong (i.e., *contra naturam*).

Totality, Principle of

This moral principle comes from the Latin axiom *pars propter totum*, which can be translated as "the part [sacrificed] on account of the whole." For example, in a therapeutic operation on a diseased organ or bodily function it was considered permissible to sacrifice that organ or function when no other possibility existed to secure the well-being of the total organism, for example, to amputate a gangrenous limb that if left untended would cause death of the whole person. Originally this principle was interpreted strictly in regards to an individual's own body (according to a physicalist paradigm). Thus, if an operation would aid the body of an individual it could be done (e.g., the amputation of a diseased limb), but if it did not directly aid the body of this person, it could not be done (thus ruling out organ donations to aid another party). However, as time went on this principle came to have a personalist application as well, such that one could morally donate a healthy organ to aid another person. The Pontifical Commission on the Regulation of Births (1959–1965) used this personalist interpretation of the principle of totality to argue for the moral acceptability of the possibility of artificial contraception (looking at the whole of the marriage, rather than just isolated individual conjugal acts), but this approach was specifically denied in Pope Paul VI's 1968 encyclical *Humanae vitae*.

Universal Precepts. See **Moral Norms, Levels of**

Ut in pluribus

Shorthand for the Latin axiom, *lex valet ut in pluribus,* which translates as "the law is valid in most [but not all] cases." This is a most important distinction in the understanding and application of concrete moral norms. A concrete norm or law that holds *ut in pluribus* serves as a generally useful principle, but, as Thomas Aquinas noted, these should not be treated as if they bound absolutely in every case. See also *Moral Norms, Levels of.*

Veritatis splendor

Pope John Paul II's 1993 encyclical on Fundamental Moral Theology. *Veritatis splendor* are the first two Latin words in the encyclical, which translate as "Splendor of the Truth." A key point of this encyclical is the stress on an objective moral order that binds all human persons and the reaffirmation of the traditional moral concept of intrinsically evil actions. The encyclical lists a number of such actions as intrinsically evil, including abortion and any use of artificial contraception.

Vitalism

This is an approach which puts an exaggeratedly high value on the maintenance of physical life. It holds that one should do virtually everything one can in order to maintain the biological life of the human person, even when it is clear that the person is in the process of dying, or has reached a point where only basic physical functions can be maintained (e.g., in cases of brain death in which the person is kept on life-support). Vitalism is *not* endorsed either in traditional Catholic moral theology nor by the magisterium of the Church. In his encyclical on the Gospel of Life, *Evangelium vitae,* Pope John Paul II explicitly counters this concept that physical life must be maintained at all costs. Nevertheless, some people mistakenly believe that the official teaching of the Church holds that anything that might either hasten or end life is *ipso facto* immoral. See also *Palliative Care* and *Ordinary and Extraordinary Means.*

Index